READERS' REVIEWS

Once I started reading this book I couldn't stop! It kept my interest and was easy reading. The story picked up where the first book left off, and Cora's writing style made it a seamless transition.

Karen Clevenstine
Tacoma, WA

Mary Alice Gypsy no more is a beautiful sequel to Mary Alice Gypsy nurse. This story spans twenty-seven years; from 1907 to 1933. I was inspired by way the main character deals with struggles and joys and looks to God in good times and bad. She was a role model for everyone who knew her.

The author does a wonderful job depicting life in her great-grandmother's time. I felt like I was right there with them!

Lori Quick
Yelm, WA

I have been waiting patiently for the second book in the Mary Alice series. The author does not disappoint. She writes her family's history with the aplomb of the well-known romance novellas.

As with the first book, I had to keep reminding myself that the main characters were real people, not just figments of the author's imagination!

Linda Ingersoll
Kent, WA

Having read Mary Alice, Gypsy Nurse, I have been eagerly awaiting the sequel. I read the first novel in one day! The stories are so interesting; as you follow the different families you are taken back to a different place and time. You root for their victories and feel the depth of their pain when tragedy occurs.

I grew to admire every character in the book for their commitment to family and their resilience in bad times.

I have read part of the 2nd. book and I am very much looking forward to getting my copy!

If you love a good story of family values and taking a peek at the history of the Pacific Northwest, you will fall in love with this book and all the characters in it.

I was disappointed when I finished reading the first book, I wanted to know more about this family, and now I can!

It's a fun, fascinating trip back in time that is so well written it keeps you captivated from beginning to end.

Nancy Phelps
Covington, WA

MARY ALICE

Gypsy No More
(The Sequel to Mary Alice, Gypsy Nurse)

Cora Brantner

authorHOUSE®

AuthorHouse™
1663 Liberty Drive
Bloomington, IN 47403
www.authorhouse.com
Phone: 1 (800) 839-8640

Artist Name: Scott Bovard

Published by AuthorHouse 09/22/2016

ISBN: 978-1-5246-3841-2 (sc)
ISBN: 978-1-5246-3840-5 (e)

Library of Congress Control Number: 2016914671

Print information available on the last page.

Any people depicted in stock imagery provided by Thinkstock are models,
and such images are being used for illustrative purposes only.
Certain stock imagery © Thinkstock.

This book is printed on acid-free paper.

Foreword

from the author's husband

I witnessed my wife's journey; from finding her mother's manuscript of MARY ALICE, GYPSY NURSE, finishing and adapting it and getting it published.

When her friends' urging prompted her to write this sequel, I was equally supportive of this new venture. I had enjoyed reading the first book as much as they had and had experienced Cora's spiritual and intellectual growth as she studied, researched and struggled throughout those seven years.

As I read through this new book, which is a completion of the work her mother started, I found that my wife's writing talents now equal her mother's.

I am certain that her fans won't be disappointed. I'm looking forward to reading it myself, not as a critic, but for the pure enjoyment of it!

Acknowledgments

from the author

I want to thank:

My mother, who started this journey by writing about her grandmother.

My father, who saved Mom's writings after she had to quit writing.

My daughter Carissa and her husband Leland for their tech support.

My readers, for encouraging me to pursue this path and to keep going.

My husband Dan for financing this project, helping me with manuscript inspections and feedback, for never complaining, and for being my rock.

My new friend Breanne Ciccone for taking the photo on the back cover.

To my friend Vicki Kobberod for helping me with the editing.

To Jesus my savior, who gives me strength and spiritual wisdom; for being "the Lamp for my feet and the Light on my path".

Prologue

from the author

When I finished and published the first novel, which my mother had written years before, and I had found in my garage, I hadn't planned on writing another book. But once my friends and relatives read it, they immediately started clamoring for a sequel. They said they loved it and wanted more! The first half of my great-grandmother's life story wasn't sufficient for them. They wanted to read the rest of the story.

After resting up from the stress of dealing with computers, publishers and such, I started to work on the sequel, little by little, as the ideas came to me and the Spirit led. I had to learn a lot of things, such as Twitter, Facebook, blogging; which I'm still struggling with; new programs, better and easier ways of doing things...

Fast forward nearly four years, and it's finally done! I plan to take some time-off and relax for a while. Of course, I'll have to continue with the promotions and social media, but now I should have the time and available brain cells to increase my outreach even more. If I write any more books, it will be through a traditional publisher, or as a ghost writer. I'm getting too old for this type of stress! I'm not saying that I haven't enjoyed this journey, but it's also been hard work.

Because I wrote this book by myself, not tweaking and editing someone else's work, I was able to make it a true Christian-themed novel from beginning to end. I hope God is pleased with the results, and that my readers enjoy this book as much as its predecessor, which I recommend reading before this one.

Timeline

1906: Carson is 20, Ilda is 18 1/2, Grace is 17, Tucker is 15 1/2, Frank Jr is 8 1/2, Lafe is 6 1/2 & Delores is 4 ½, Ilda marries Albert Newman

1907: Frank Senior dies

Ilda's children: Faye; born 1907, Frank (Buddy), born 1910, Elsie May, born 1914, Cleo, born 1917, (adopted in 1918: Nina, born 1913, Joseph (Jojo), born 1915)

1914: Grace marries Guy Rowley

Grace's step children: Gerald (Jerry), born 1907, Guy Jr. (Chip), born 1909, Ronald (Ronny), born 1911, non-step Children: Ercyline Rose, born 1916, Virginia and Alice, born 1918, Merle, born 1920, Leon, born 1922, Ernest (Ernie), born 1925

1917: Carson marries Gretchen

1918/19: Gretchen and Ercyline Rose died from flu

1918: Frank marries Mary

Frank's children: Dolores, born 1921, Frank Jr (J.R.), born 1925

1918: Cleora (Doley) marries John Bauer

Doley's children: Ilda, born 1919, Carson (Bud), born 1921, John Jr (Johnny), born 1924

1923: Lafe marries Nettie Dawson

Lafe's children: Ernest, born 1929, Marion, born 1931

1933: Carsie marries Rebecca, Alice dies

Recurring Characters

Alice Walden: Title character
Carsie: Alice's oldest son
Ilda (I'll-dah): Alice's oldest daughter
Grace: Alice's second daughter
Tucker: Alice's second son
Frank II: Alice's third son
Lafe: Alice's youngest son
Doley: Alice's youngest daughter
Ercyline (Ursaline) Beebe: Alice's Mother
Ernest Beebe: Alice's father
Frank Walden Sr: Alice's husband
Rachael: Alice's friend and co-worker
Mattie: Waif rescued from junkyard
Ka-teen-ha: Alice's Indian friend
John Harney: Frank Sr's former boss
Stephen Thatcher: Waldens' former preacher
Bettina Thatcher: Stephen's wife

New Characters

Albert Newman: Ilda's husband

Charles Brown: Mattie's husband

Harold and Clara Brown: Charles' parents

Faye Newman: Ilda's first daughter

Dr. Alexander: New Bridal Veil Dr.

Mr. & Mrs. Caufield: Store owners/Tucker's employers

Teresa Bailey: Alice's relative & Portland hospital's head nurse

Alice Marie: Mattie's daughter

Frank (Buddy): Ilda's 1st son

Pete and Elsie Bauer Dressler: Ilda's Neighbors

John Bauer: Elsie's brother & Doley's beau/husband

Daniel and Rose Bauer Koch: John's sister and brother-in-law

Henry and Caroline Bauer Krausse: John's sister and brother-in-law

Carl and Lena Bauer: John's brother and sister-in-law

Guy Rowley: Grace's beau/husband

Gerald (Jerry): Guy's oldest son

Guy Jr. (Chip): Guy's 2nd son

Ronald (Ronny): Guy's 3rd son

Ercyline Rose: Grace's 1st daughter

Elsie May: Ilda's 2nd daughter

Harry Brown (Little Harry): Mattie's son

Gretchen: Carson's 1st wife

Cleo Newman: Ilda's 2nd son

Virginia (Ginny) & Alice (Ginger) Rowley; Grace's twin girls

Nina (Nini): Newmans' adopted daughter

Joseph (Jojo): Newmans' adopted son

Dolores Walden: Frank & Mary's daughter

Ilda (Audie) Bauer: Doley and John's daughter

Merle Rowley: Grace's 1st natural son

Anja Schmidt: German immigrant & ex-prisoner's wife

Nettie Dawson: Lafe's sweetheart/wife

Carson (Bud) Bauer: Doley's 1st son

Leon Rowley: Grace's 2nd son
John Bauer Jr: Doley's youngest son
Keith: Ka-teen-ha's husband
Rebecca: Keith's daughter & Carsie's sweetheart/wife
Ernest Rowley: Grace's 3rd son
Frank Walden III (J.R.): Frank II's son
Ernest (Ernie) Walden: Lafe's and Nettie's son
Marion: Lafe and Nettie's daughter

Chapter One

WELCOME BACK

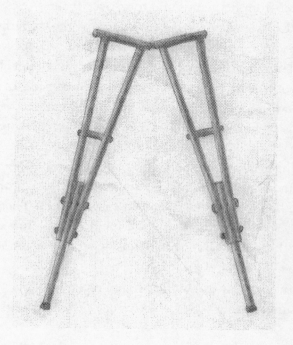

On the morning of October 11th, 1907, a telegram arrived at the Walden home just after the children had left for school. Alice was at the hotel cooking breakfast. Doley was staying with her grandma, and Grace was home alone.

Grace read the telegram, thanked the delivery boy and immediately removed her apron and grabbed an umbrella. She rushed to the hotel as fast as her legs would carry her. She burst through the back door of the hotel kitchen just as Alice was emerging from the pantry with a bag of potatoes.

"Grace, you know you're not supposed to be here while I'm working! Oh my goodness, did you run all the way from home? What's wrong?"

Grace paused a moment to catch her breath as she took the telegram out of her pocket and held it out. "It's Carsie; he's been hurt."

Alice took the telegram and read it carefully, while Rachael dried the dishwater from her hands and took over at the stove. Alice didn't need to ask her friend. She and Rachael had worked together for many years in the logging camp before Rachael's husband, Jim, was hurt on the job, and now again at the hotel for the last three years. Jim was still unable to work, as his brain had been injured too badly in the logging accident that had almost claimed his life. But he had recovered enough to stay home by himself, while Rachael worked at the hotel. They had no children.

Alice finished reading, and stood thinking for a moment. "Well, there's not much we can do about it right now. I'll stop at the telegraph office when I'm done here and send an answer back." Then she turned to Rachael. "Could you take over for me here for a few days while I go to be with Carsie? Grace can probably spare a few hours a day to help out, too."

"We'll manage somehow," her friend replied.

"Of course, Mama," Grace spoke up, "We'll all help as much as we can."

The next afternoon, the telephone rang at the hotel office. A few moments later, the manager came into the kitchen. "Mrs. Walden, there's a call for you from The Dalles hospital."

Rachael took the whisk from Alice's hand and took over beating the eggs, as her friend followed Mr. Brothers into his office. Daniel pulled out a chair for Alice and left, closing the door behind him.

"Hello? Yes, this is she."

"Mrs. Walden, my name is George Clavor. I'm the head surgeon here at The Dalles hospital. Your son Carson was transferred to our care an hour or so ago. We have examined him and determined that his condition is serious, but not critical. He has some minor internal bleeding and a compound leg fracture that will require surgery. He'll have to stay here for a few days for treatment and observation, then he'll be able to go home. I talked to a Mr. Harney at the logging company's main office, and he assured me that you are a nurse, and quite capable of handling your son's post-surgical care. Do you have any questions at this time?"

"No, thank you. I'll make arrangements to come there tomorrow. I'll talk with you again after I see my son. Good day, Dr. Clavor. Thank you for calling."

The hospital was quiet the next day as the nurse led Alice down the hallway and into the room Carsie was sharing with two other men. "He just came out of surgery half an hour ago and should be waking up any minute now," she told Alice. "Call me if you need anything."

Carsie's left leg, from hip to ankle, was in a splint, rigged to a cable, strung to a bar over the foot of the bed. Alice peeked under the blanket and gave Carsie a cursory examination. Satisfied that the staff was taking good care of him, she pulled a chair up to his bedside and sat holding his hand, waiting for him to awaken.

Carsie's eyes fluttered, then opened. He looked at his leg then at his mother. "Hi, Ma." His voice was hoarse and barely audible. "How long have you been here?"

"Only a few minutes," she replied as she filled the glass on the bedside table from the pitcher, inserted a straw and held it to his lips. "Take a drink."

"Mmm, thank you. My mouth and throat felt like they were stuffed with cotton. I see they put my leg in traction. Was that really necessary?"

"Yes, I suppose so, because it was out of alignment for a while. If you'd only broken one lower bone, that wouldn't have been the case. The nurse told me that all three bones were broken, and the fibula in two places. How did you manage that?"

"Let me see if I can remember... Oh, I was on an errand to talk to one of the flume crew. I found him just as a log broke loose from the flume. It was coming straight at me, so I tried to dodge out of its way and stepped in a hole. I fell over a large rock, and the log bounced right over me, thank God."

3

A tall, middle-aged doctor with a receding hairline and horn-rimmed glasses came in just then. "Hello, I'm Dr. Clavor. You must be Mrs. Walden. How is our patient doing?"

"He feels a bit warm. Is that because of the internal damage?"

"Yes, there was a tear in the intestinal wall. Luckily, he hadn't eaten for several hours, so there was very little leakage, other than some blood. I had to leave his incision open to let it drain. He'll be on antibiotics for a while to treat the peritonitis and make sure the leg doesn't get infected. There wasn't much debris in it, and I'm confident that I got it all out. As soon as the seepage stops and his fever comes down, we'll stitch him up."

Then he turned to Carsie, "How are you feeling?"

"I'm hurting pretty bad," Carsie admitted. "A little worse than yesterday, actually. But," he managed a grin, "at least my foot is pointed in the right direction now."

The doctor smiled and pulled his stethoscope out of his pocket. "That was a pretty bad accident, but from what I understand, it could have been a lot worse."

Alice brushed a lock of wayward hair from Carsie's eyes. "His guardian angel must have been looking out for him."

The doctor checked under the bandage on Carsie's abdomen, and the leg alignment one more time. "Everything looks good. You shouldn't need the traction more than a couple of days. Then we'll put on a cast and send you home to recover. I'll send the nurse in to give you some medicine for the pain. I'll check in on you tomorrow morning." He shook hands with both of them and bid them goodnight.

Once Carsie was settled down for the night, Alice made her way to the nearest hotel and checked in for a two-night stay. She used their phone to call the Bridal Veil School office to inform her father of Carsie's successful surgery. He assured her that he would pass the news along to the rest of the family and the hotel.

Three days later, Alice stepped off the train and helped Carsie down. Tucker was supposed to be waiting for them. It was Sunday, so he didn't have to take any time off of school to meet them.

Alice scanned the station platform and the street beyond. "Now where is that brother of yours? It's just like him to be late."

"Maybe he's on the other side of the train," Carsie replied. "He has a knack for being in the wrong place. I think I'll sit down and put my foot up while we wait for him." He hobbled over to the bench and sat on one end. Alice helped him put his foot up on the other. "Ah, now that's better!" he sighed, as he handed his crutches to Alice, who propped them against the wall of the station.

"This reminds me of the time your father came home on crutches from the high camp right after the New Year," she said.

"Yeah, I remember that. How old was I then?"

"Well, let me see... I seem to remember that it was just after the Indian funeral. We moved to West Linn the next summer. So you were about six or seven."

Carsie chuckled, "Oh, yes, West Linn. I remember that house!"

Alice stiffened-a look of disgust on her face. "Don't remind me! That house will haunt me the rest of my life!"

Carsie broke into his infectious laugh, holding his belly. "Oh, that hurts!" Alice tried to stay stern, but his laughter soon won her over, and she couldn't help but join in. They shared memories as they laughed. They were wiping tears from their eyes when she heard a familiar voice behind her.

"I didn't know a broken leg could be that funny."

She spun around to receive a bear hug, which she returned. Then she stood back and looked her friend over. "Mattie, you look wonderful! How *are* you?"

"Just fine. I'm a nurse now, too. I have a job waiting for me at the hospital in Portland, and was just returning from nursing school in Boston. I thought I'd stop by in Bridal Veil to look you up. I ran into an old friend of yours, a Dr. Williams, who said you were living here now. How are you doing? I heard about your husband. I'm so sorry. Is this your son?"

"Yes, my oldest son, Carsie. His brother was supposed to be waiting here to take us home. Now I'm glad he's late. How long will you be here?"

"I start my orientation the day after tomorrow."

"Then you shall stay with us while you're here. And I won't take no for an answer!"

Carsie interrupted, "Here comes Tucker now."

Tucker pulled up in his grandparents' buggy. It was a four-seater, and could accommodate six in a pinch.

"Gramma thought Carsie would be more comfortable in this rig than in a rented wagon. Besides, it's cheaper," he stated matter-of-factly. He offered no explanation for his tardiness. Alice and Carsie just looked at each other and shrugged their shoulders.

Tucker didn't ask about Mattie, but hopped down and loaded the baggage. He and Alice helped Carsie into the buggy. Then he remounted the wagon and waited for the women to climb up.

Mattie looked at Tucker with a puzzled expression. She'd expected him to offer to help her and Alice up. Carsie hadn't noticed-he was busy trying to get positioned in such a way as to leave room for both of them. Alice was used to Tucker's ways, so she was already climbing up. Once she was seated, she offered Mattie a hand.

Tucker started off at his usual pace and had to be reminded to slow down for the comfort of his passengers.

The half mile trip to their house went rather quickly as they chatted. Mattie asked about Carsie's leg. Then she told Alice about the schooling she'd gotten from the nuns, and how she'd decided to become a nurse because of their and Alice's influence. She had no romantic interests so far.

"So, what have you been doing, besides taking care of your family? Are you doing all right?"

"The last couple of years have been difficult," Alice replied, "But God has given us the strength and grace to meet our needs." Then she filled her in on the births of Little Frank, Lafe and Doley, the forest fire, and Frank's illness.

"Ilda got married last month. She met her husband Albert at a friend's party last Christmas. He inherited his uncle's farm near Portland. Their wedding was a simple family affair held at his parent's home in Bridal Veil. They moved onto the farm immediately after the wedding.

Carsie is a camp foreman with the logging company in The Dalles."

Then, as the buggy lurched to a stop; "Here's our house. It's no mansion, but it meets our needs. It's also a little crowded, but we'll find space for you somewhere."

Mattie's eyes took in the small size and weathered exterior of the house, in contrast to the neat garden. "No need to apologize. It's better than Andy's shack, or the house you were in when we met. If I remember correctly, it was fancy on the outside, but the walls were stuffed with newspapers-what there were of them."

Carsie chuckled, "That was a *mansion* compared to the one before it!"

Alice shook her head and rolled her eyes. "Let's not start in on that again!"

"Mama! Carsie!" Lafe came running out to meet them.

"Welcome home!" Ercyline came in the back door, wiping her hands on her apron as Alice and Carsie came in the front door.

Alice noted that her father had obviously been napping. A book lay on the floor next to his chair, and Doley was in his lap, just rousing. "Look who we found at the train station while waiting for Tucker."

Alice made sure Carsie got through the narrow door and around the end of the sofa to the water closet, then introduced Mattie to her parents.

Grace came in the back door with Little Frank and a basketful of garden bounty. "Welcome home, we thought you'd enjoy a nice fresh salad and some cobbler, after eating hospital and hotel food for the last couple of days."

"Oh yes, thank you!" Alice replied.

Then Grace turned from the sink, where she had deposited the vegetables. "I see you picked up an extra person while you were gone."

"Grace, do you remember Mattie?" Alice asked her.

"I don't think so."

When Carsie came out of the hallway, Ernest relinquished the old comfy chair, and Alice went to prepare some laudanum tea for Carsie. She'd noticed that he was trying valiantly to hide his pain. While she was in the kitchen, he related his incident with the rogue log.

Then Grace, Ercyline and Alice busied themselves with dinner preparations, while Carsie sipped and snoozed, and Mattie related the story of her rescue from the junkyard to the rest of the family.

"So, what are you doing here in Bridal veil?" Ernest asked.

"I have a job waiting for me in Portland and was just returning from school in Boston to get started. I met Dr. Williams there, and he told me where Alice was living now. So I thought I'd stop by and see how she was doing and thank her for changing my life in such a positive way."

Alice was listening from the dining room as she set the table. "You're very welcome, dear. Dinner's almost ready. Go wash up, everybody."

The dinner conversation was lively and varied. They told Mattie the stories of Ka-teen ha, about Tucker and the moonshine, and the cabin that Frank Sr. had built for them.

After the meal, the girls stacked the dishes and Alice went to the linen closet for some fresh towels and bedding. Mattie followed her. "You've had a lot of interesting adventures, haven't you?"

"Did Doctor Williams say what he was doing in Boston?" Ercyline asked as she came into the living room for Carsie's tray. He had stayed there with his foot propped up, and was still on a restricted diet, due to his abdominal surgery.

"He was going there to visit his parents, whose health is failing. He's been offered a position there at the school."

Alice looked thoughtful, "We'll miss him if he accepts the job. I hope a suitable replacement can be found for him here.

"Now, where can we put you up for the night? Carsie usually shares Tucker's bed when he's home, and I doubt that will work out very well. We'll have to fix Tucker up on the sofa and have you sleep with me."

"Why don't we take Lafe and Little Frank home with us," Ernest offered.

"That's a good idea." Ercyline agreed. "They can stay as long as needed. Then Carsie can sleep where he's used to and Tucker can have the boys' bed."

"Yay!" the boys danced over and hugged their grandmother. "Can we, Ma?"

"Well I suppose so, as long as Grandma and Grandpa promise not to spoil you too much."

"Who, us?" Ernest feigned innocence, and Ercyline flashed a guilty smile at her daughter.

Alice looked over at Carsie as he chuckled, his eyebrow doing its usual acrobatics. Then he was off to sleep.

After the rest of the family was abed, Alice and Mattie got caught up with the details of their lives since parting those many years ago.

"The nuns at the hospital and at the convent school were so nice and helpful," Mattie told Alice. "They made sure I got a good education, taught me good manners and all. I even considered becoming one of them, but couldn't shake the feeling that God had a different plan for my life. I would love to have a family of my own."

"I'm intrigued by the Indian woman that you mentioned at dinner. Tell me more about her story."

Alice told her all about Ka-teen-ha and her grandmother's funeral. The subject eventually turned to Frank. Mattie hadn't gotten any details from Dr. Williams, so Alice recalled the sad details:

Chapter Two

GOODBYE DARLING

Saturday, May 15th, 1906 promised to be a beautiful, sunny day in Bridal Veil, but not in the hearts of Alice and her family. They had just released their beloved husband and father, Frank, into the arms of Jesus and would have to wait a long time to see him again.

Alice had shed many tears, but always in the privacy of her bedroom. She told herself she had to be strong for the little ones. How else could they be expected to believe that their Papa was better off where he was, instead of here with them. And she had to convince them that they would all learn to be happy again without him. He had always been the sunshine in their lives.

After the forest fire had claimed their home four and a half years earlier, Alice and the children had gone to stay in Bridal Veil with her parents. Frank had stayed behind to help arrest the remains of the fire and give moral and spiritual support to the other men, all of whom had lost their homes and some, their family members, to the consuming flames.

Frank had rejoined his family after a week, with a nagging cough that was resistant to all the herbal remedies that Alice had in her arsenal. The doctor at the hospital in Portland had nothing to offer either, except advice to "Not exert yourself, and stay here in the Pacific Northwest, where the weather is usually mild and humid." Frank had worked as a foreman at the sawmill for the next two years, until his breathing got so labored that he had to retire to menial jobs at home, while Carson and Alice supported the family.

His last two months, he had been bed-bound, but still cheerful. He knew where he was going and that his family would be all right. Jesus had promised that He would never leave or forsake them. He passed away quietly, while the three youngest ones and Tucker were asleep, Carsie was at the mill and Alice, Ilda and Grace said their goodbyes.

"Mama, Tucker's back with the buggy!" Grace was at the kitchen sink, wrapping up the flowers for the grave, while Alice and Ilda got changed.

Tucker hitched the horses to the fence post and came inside, forgetting to wipe his feet, as usual, just as Alice emerged from the bedroom. "Stop and think about what you're doing, Tucker!" she chastised him, pointing at his muddy feet. He gave a little shuffle on the entry rug and proceeded to the kitchen to look for a snack. He grabbed an apple from the bowl on the table and bit into it. Then he ambled off toward the bedroom he shared with his younger brothers, wiping the juice from his chin on his sleeve as he went. He nearly ran into Ilda as she exited the hallway with her three youngest siblings in tow.

"Hurry up and get changed," she told him. "We need to be at the cemetery in an hour. Grace ironed your blue shirt and black slacks and tie while you were gone."

He changed quickly and was struggling with the tie a few minutes later. "I'm no good at tying these darn things! Ma! Do I have to wear a tie?" he complained. "They're so uncomfortable!" Grace came to his aid, "Yes, and the jacket, too," and helped him tie the knot. Carsie drove up with Ernest and Ercyline just then. Alice and Ilda finished getting Little Frank, Lafe and Doley ready, while Tucker and Carsie got the buggies loaded up with the rest of the family and the supplies. Alice helped the little ones up after Ilda, then turned to look at the house, remembering how much joy it had contained just a year ago, before Frank had gotten too sick to play or sing with the children. Then she stepped up into the carriage and took a seat beside her mother.

Four-year-old Doley, as she had been dubbed by Little Frank and Lafe, sat on Ercyline's lap with her head resting on her grandmother's shoulder. She had contracted yellow fever the year before, and had been sickly ever since.

Little Frank had made it his mission to look after her and protect her. They would enjoy a close relationship the rest of their lives, just as

Carsie and Ilda did. Lafe transferred his attachment from Little Frank to his Grandpa as soon as they had arrived in Bridal Veil after losing their home in the forest fire.

Carsie was 20 years old now, and quite independent, but made a point to come home for weekends whenever possible. He was the youngest foreman that the logging company had ever hired. He knew all the procedures and equipment and most of the workers because he'd started so young. Every penny he could spare went to helping his mother pay for medicine and doctor bills.

Ilda had graduated from high school with honors, and then dived headlong into caring for the household while her mother worked a second job to keep food on the table for her growing family.

Grace, though only fifteen months older than Tucker, was much more responsible than he, and looked out for him; making sure he didn't cause any more trouble than Alice could endure in her busy life. She was also Ilda's helper.

The ride to the church was a quiet, somber one. Little was said, other than Tucker complaining about the hard seats and his tie.

The memorial service was held at the little church in West Linn, where Ilda and Carsie had surrendered to the Lord and been baptized. Carsie dusted off his old violin a few months earlier, and had been practicing Frank's favorite hymns in preparation for this day. He played "Amazing Grace" and "How Great Thou Art", then took a seat with his family.

Stephen Thatcher was honored that they'd asked him to officiate at the services. He mounted the platform and surveyed the assembly. Loggers were standing along the side and back walls of the little church, and all the pews were full. He greeted the crowd and introduced himself.

"Thank you, Carsie. I'm glad you got some use from that violin I gave you. How long ago was that; ten years now?"

Carsie nodded, "That sounds about right."

Stephen continued, "I got to know Frank and his family quite well while they lived here in West Linn. Their family was sizable then, and they've added two more in the interim.

"I'm not surprised to see so many people here to say goodbye to such a wonderful man. Frank was always cheerful, generous to a fault, devoted to his family, and a hard worker. He was an asset to our church, and we were sad to lose him and his family when they moved.

"When Alice wrote me that he was very ill and wouldn't be with us much longer, I was surprised, to say the least. He seemed to me to be invincible; always youthful and strong. But I've learned not to question God's reasons for taking any of his children home early. And Frank was surely one of God's most precious children. He served as a deacon, sung in choirs, and was always willing to share his strength, his home and the Gospel with anyone who needed them.

"I met his boss, Mr. Harney, and he said the logging company had so many requests for leave to attend this service that they decided to close the whole shebang down for the day. As I look out at this crowd I must say, I've never seen so much plaid flannel in my whole life!"

When the laughter died down, he continued, "Frank was a 'man's man', but also quite a ladies man in his early years. Then he met Alice. He was smitten, and so was she. When he told her about his past exploits, he thought he'd lost her. He'd already lost his family and his inheritance. God had taken hold of him, turned him upside down and given him a good shaking.

"How many of you have done that to someone who offended you or owed you money? Come on now; be honest."

First one, and then two, then several hands went up as their owners blushed and looked sheepish.

"Don't feel too bad. I did it myself a time or two before God turned me around. Then I learned that offences toward people are offences toward God.

"In Matthew, chapter twenty-five, starting at verse thirty-four, Jesus is quoted, 'Then the King (meaning God) will say to those at his right hand, come, you blessed of my Father, inherit the kingdom prepared for you from the foundation of the world. For I was hungry and you gave me food, I was thirsty and you gave me something to drink, I was a stranger and you lodged me. I was naked and you clothed me. I was sick and you visited me. I was in prison and you came to see

13

me. Then the just will answer him. Lord, when did we see you hungry and give you food or thirsty and give you drink? And when did we see you a stranger and welcome you, or naked and clothe you? And the King will reply, Truly, I tell you, in so far as you did it for one of the least of these my brethren, you did it for me. Then he will say to those at his left hand, be gone from me you cursed, into the eternal fire prepared for the devil and his angels. For I was hungry and you gave me no food, I was thirsty and you gave me nothing to drink. I was a stranger and you did not welcome me. I was naked and you did not clothe me, I was sick and in prison and you did not visit me.'

"Think of it this way: If some kid bullies your kid or someone is rude to your wife or your mother, you probably get angry and demand an apology at least, right? Why do you feel that way? It's personal, because they're family. You love them and feel their hurt. Well, that's how God feels about each of us.

"Maybe you were taught that you have to earn your way to heaven by following the Ten Commandments. The problem with that view is that you would have to follow *each and every one to the letter* your whole life. The only one who ever did that is God's son, Jesus. Maybe you were taught that God is some big meanie sitting on his throne, watching and waiting for us to make a mistake so he can throw a lightning bolt down and turn us to ashes. No, he is love, but he is also perfect. And perfection cannot dwell in harmony with imperfection. They are like water and fire. He *will* forgive us for our failures, though, if we'll only ask.

"In the start of John's Gospel he writes, 'In the beginning was the Word. And the Word was with God and the Word was God. All things were made by him and without him was nothing made that was made.' And then a few sentences later, it says, 'And the Word became flesh and dwelt among us. That Word it is referring to is capitalized. It means that the Word of God is Jesus and that Jesus is the creator of all things.

"I don't know about you, but I think it's amazing that the creator of the universe loves us so much that he left heaven for a short time, was born as a human baby in a manger and then *voluntarily* suffered and died a horrific death on a Roman cross to redeem us. He paid our debt so that we could spend eternity with God.

"But that forgiveness is not automatic. We have to accept his free gift, turn away from our sins and ask his forgiveness. And he *will* give it. In John 3:16 it says, 'God so loved the world that he gave his only begotten son, that whosoever believes in him will not perish but have eternal life.'

"If you ask him, he will come to dwell in your heart and make you pure in his eyes, so you can live in his presence for eternity.

"Would you bow your heads and close your eyes, please. If you would like to accept his sacrifice for your sins and ask his forgiveness, you can repeat this prayer silently.

"Jesus, I'm not worthy of your love and presence in my life, but I believe that you love me and that you died for me. I'm sorry for turning away from you and doing things that displease you. Please come into my heart today and cleanse me from the stain of my sins."

After the service there was a reception. Bettina Thatcher outdid herself, as usual. She'd baked and slaved over the stove all that morning and the day before, making sandwiches, cakes, pies and salads. Several other ladies who remembered the Waldens did the same. During the service they had set up tables in the church yard for the feast, complete with white table cloths and vases filled with lilacs, daisies, azaleas and irises.

As Alice stepped outside on Carsie's arm and saw all the food and flowers, tears filled her eyes. Then she turned to Bettina. "Thank you for arranging all of this." As she started down the steps, she breathed deeply. "Their heavenly fragrance is almost enough to make a butterfly swoon."

"It's a good thing the Lord provided us with a beautiful sunny day," Bettina replied. "We couldn't have accommodated this many people and tables inside the building."

Mary, Alice's old friend and assistant came over to talk to Alice as soon as she was seated. Her daughter, Sarah Jane was with her, holding her young son, and obviously pregnant again. Helen was there, also, along with her husband.

Alice was pleased to see and talk with Grace and Andy, whom she hadn't seen since they'd moved to Seattle to take another job.

Carol and Hank Engen, along with their youngest son Terry, Becky and Jim Ingeborg, Mr. Henner and several friends from Bridal Veil were there. There were many men from the logging company, some of whom Alice didn't recognize, as well.

Mr. Harney took an opportunity to talk with Alice after the meal. He introduced his new wife, Clara, then remarked, "I'm so sorry for your loss. I feel partly responsible for Frank's illness, since you wrote me that you think the smoke and ash from the fire's aftermath were to blame for his illness."

She put her hand on his. "I told you it's no one's fault, John. Frank volunteered to stay behind and help. That's just who he was."

"Yes, he was a good man; one of the best workers we've ever had. I've missed working with him, and you, too. Are you doing all right? You look a little tired."

"I've been holding down two jobs to keep a roof over our heads. I don't know what I'd do if Carsie weren't contributing. Also, my father's health is declining. I'm concerned about him."

"I noticed that the children and your mother seem to be doing well, Harney interjected. I've seen Carsie a few times since you moved back to Bridal Veil, but haven't had a chance to get back there myself since the fire. I understand the town has grown somewhat."

"Yes, it has," she replied. "The school board is convinced that my father and I are the reason. I may have been partly responsible for getting him here, but he did the rest. We're very proud of our schools."

"Are you working as a nurse, still? he asked.

"Yes, but only part-time. Some of the folks who knew me from before ask for me occasionally. And I pitch in to help Dr. Williams when a crisis arises. But mostly, I work in the hotel laundry, and cook for them when the regular cook is sick or away. It's not good money, but we have a garden, pick wild berries and glean from Mr. Goodwin's orchard every summer. The girls have gotten quite adept at canning, and have become good little homemakers.

"Now that Frank's gone, our medical bills will shrink some. I just wish I knew what to do about Little Dolores. She contracted yellow fever when it came through here last year, and she's been sickly ever since. But then, she and Tucker never did thrive like the others."

Harney checked his watch, stood up, and put his hand on her shoulder. "If you ever need a job or personal reference, you can count on me to provide one. Now I have to collect my crew and catch the train. We have a contract to fill by next week. Take care and keep in touch."

He whistled for the men to come together. They said goodbye to Alice, then mounted the wagons and pulled away.

Although they corresponded, Alice would never see John Harney again.

Frank was buried in the Bridal Veil cemetery. After the funeral, the family went back to some semblance of normalcy; as much as they could muster. The house seemed cold and empty without Frank, despite the temperature outside.

Grace took over the running of the household when Alice was working. Doley stayed with Ercyline while the other children were at school. Alice threw herself into her work to keep occupied, so she wouldn't have time to feel the Frank-shaped hole in her heart. She left the running of the household to Ilda and Grace. Grace was assuming more and more responsibility, though, as Ilda had taken a job as a maid at the hotel.

Ilda had been invited to a Christmas party the year before by one of the other maids, where she'd met a gentleman from Portland, named

Albert Newman. He'd approached her and asked for a dance. "I'd be happy to," she'd replied.

He was a little shorter than she, with her two-inch heels, but was a polite and humble man in his mid-twenties. They were instantly attracted to each other. As they spent the evening together, they found that they had a lot in common and had the same values.

His father, who had been a preacher, had died when Albert was ten. After his father's passing, his mother used to send him to her brother's farm for the summers.

"I loved working the farm and always hated going back to the city every autumn," he said, "even though I missed my mother while I was gone. I would never tell her," he leaned in and whispered, "but my aunt was a much better cook than my mother."

"My uncle is very sick now, my aunt died a few years ago and their children have all moved on to pursue their own goals. I've been working the farm for him the last two months, and he says he has willed it to me upon his death.

"A good neighbor is keeping an eye on things while I take a break to visit my family here in Bridal Veil."

They danced almost every dance together, and corresponded every week after he left. Their romance blossomed more with each letter. His uncle passed away in his sleep a few months later. Albert gave himself a month to grieve.

Then one day in June, he appeared at the Walden's doorstep with a ring and a proposal.

"I don't have much to offer you, except a home, hard work and my devotion, but would you do me the honor of becoming my wife?"

Tears welled up in Ilda's eyes as she nodded her head and held out her hand to receive the ring. Then he stood up and gave her a kiss as her family, listening from inside the house, came spilling out to congratulate them.

They were married in the church in Bridal Veil after Sunday morning church service a week and a half later. Everyone was invited to stay for the ceremony.

Ilda's friends from school were there, as well as Albert's parents and a couple of his friends. Naturally, the entire Walden clan was there. Albert's cousin and Grace stood up with them.

Afterward, they went to Albert's mother's home for lunch. Then Albert's horse was hitched to the preloaded wagon that they had been given as a wedding present. Then the newlyweds were sent on their way amidst a hail of birdseed and wildflowers.

They couldn't afford a honeymoon, but settled right into farm life about ten miles southeast of Portland.

The morning after Carsie came home from the hospital, the children went off to school. Then Alice showed Mattie around town, while Grace took over Carsie's care. Mattie's train wouldn't be leaving until one thirty.

Their first stop was the medical clinic, where she left a message for Dr. Williams to contact her upon his return from Boston. Then they browsed in a couple of stores and stopped at her parents' home for a chat and a cup of tea with her mother. Their last stop was a tour of the schools, led by her father, who was still principal of both schools. He treated them to lunch at his favorite restaurant, then drove them to the train station after picking up Mattie's luggage at Alice's house.

The train was just coming into view as they crossed the tracks next to the depot. They hugged goodbye on the platform and promised to keep in touch.

Carsie's leg healed nicely, but took longer than he'd hoped. When the cast came off eight weeks later, he'd expected to be back at work within a week. Alice knew what to expect and had scared up a cane for him to use. It was two weeks before he could walk far enough to leave the house and another month until he could walk without the cane.

"A blessing in disguise," Alice teased him, "At least we know you'll be home for Christmas this year."

Carsie's position at the logging camp had been filled while he was recovering, but another one opened up at the mill near Portland a couple of months later. Ilda and Albert had no trouble convincing him to move in with them. He appreciated the exercise he got helping Albert with the farm chores, and Albert appreciated the help.

A few months after Carsie moved in, Ilda presented Albert with a beautiful, healthy baby girl. They named her Faye, after Albert's mother.

Chapter Three

THE DELIQUENTS

One Saturday morning in early May, 1908, sixteen-year-old Tucker was nowhere to be found. His bed hadn't been slept in. It wasn't unusual for him to be out late with his new friends, now that the weather was warm and the days were long, but he'd always come home before. He finally stumbled in the door, just as Grace was putting breakfast on the table, and went straight to bed without a word.

Grace was glad that their mother wasn't home to witness this. She had left early for work at the hotel. They were worried about Tucker: his grades never were very good, but they'd gotten worse lately. He'd been acting even more elusive than usual, and coming home smelling of cigarettes, ever since he'd made friends with the Barton brothers.

Not long after the Barton family had moved to Bridal Veil, things started mysteriously disappearing all over town. At first, no one thought anything of it; they were just a few small, inconsequential items that no one noticed were missing for a while, or whose owners had thought to have been misplaced. When more expensive items started disappearing, and property was being vandalized more than usual, people started talking about it and complaining to the sheriff. At the next town council meeting, it was the first issue for discussion.

The mayor banged his gavel down to quiet the people assembled at City Hall. "Ladies and gentlemen" he called out with authority, "will you please take your seats!" When everyone was seated and quiet, he continued, "The first order of business will be addressed by Sheriff Gowrie.

"Benjamin, you have the floor." The mayor sat down, and the sheriff mounted the platform.

"Ladies and gentlemen, I have received numerous complaints regarding thievery and mischief from all parts of town, in the last few months. When I started interviewing shopkeepers and residents, I uncovered a larger problem than I had previously thought.

"Someone has been committing acts of vandalism, and stealing various items from businesses and homes in town. This person or persons must be caught and dealt with. Does anyone have any clue as to who the culprit or culprits might be?"

Several hands shot up and the sheriff called on Mr. Clark first.

"I seen the Smith boys snoopin' 'round my place th'other day. Coulda been them."

The mayor stood up to declare that wild assumptions based upon personal opinions weren't helpful. He knew that Mr. Clark and Mr. Smith disliked each other, and that the Smith boys were rather mischievous, but harmless. Mr. Clark sat down and some of the same hands were raised again. The sheriff called on Mr. Orand.

"I saw the Barton boys and Mrs. Walden's oddball son out behind the livery during school hours last week. They were smoking and had something sticking out of their pockets."

"I've seen them out past Conner's farm at odd hours, too," said another.

"I've seen them around during school hours, too," someone else volunteered.

"They seemed so polite and mannerly, and had a good excuse for being out of school, so I never suspected them," said the sheriff's wife.

"Mr. Beebe, were you aware that your grandson has been doing any of these things?" the sheriff asked the school principal.

Ernest stood to answer the question. "Two of his teachers mentioned, in passing, that Tucker might get better grades if he didn't miss classes as often. When I approached Tucker about it, he said he didn't feel well after lunch a couple of times. I know that he dislikes, and has always struggled in school, but he's never lied to me before, so I took him at his word.

"His mother is a widow who works very hard to keep food on their table and a roof over their heads, so I didn't want to burden her with this issue. I had no idea it was this bad.

"As for the Barton boys; they have been frequent truants, ever since they moved here. Their father has never answered any of my summons. I wasn't aware that my grandson was associating with them."

"And why is that?" someone asked.

"You must understand that I have two whole schools, full of students and teachers to deal with. It's impossible to keep track of them all.

"I am dismayed to think that his teachers haven't come to me with this problem, just because he's one of my family. I will have a talk with my staff, and ask them all to keep a closer eye on Tucker and the Barton boys, and report any problems to me, personally. I'll also have a serious talk with all three of the boys."

"Let me know when, and I'll be there, too," the sheriff replied.

On Monday, Ernest called Tucker into his office, where the sheriff was waiting. Ernest told him about the discussion at the council meeting.

Tucker sat slumped in his chair and wouldn't meet his grandfather's gaze.

Ernest made the boy stand before him, and took Tucker's face in his hand, forcing his grandson to look right at him. "I don't want to worry your mother about this, but I will, if you don't straighten up, and stop skipping school. I'm going to talk with your teachers, and keep a closer eye on you and your friends from now on."

The sheriff was next. "The town council is convinced that the three of you are responsible for the crimes the town has been experiencing lately. If I find that you've been involved, I guarantee you will be punished. I'll be easier on you if you tell me what you know, and how much you may have been involved."

By now Tucker was shaking, and tears pooled in his eyes. "I went along, and it was fun to be with them, but all I ever stole was an apple or two from Mr. Conner's orchard and a jack-o'-lantern from a front porch, like some other boys do. They shared some of their stolen food and cigarettes with me, and I helped them push Mr. Lansing's outhouse over. But that's all, I swear."

"Do they have a secret place you can show me, where they might keep some of the things they've stolen?" the sheriff asked.

Tucker nodded. "But I'm afraid I'll get beat up if they find out I ratted on them!" he sobbed.

"Do you know if the Barton boys are in class now?" he asked Ernest. "I'd like to go with Tucker to see the hideout right now, if they are. We won't let on that Tucker told us anything.

"Does that sound okay to you, Tucker?"

The boy nodded and dried his tears.

"Let me go check," Ernest said. "Why don't you take Tucker to the nurse's office while I try to collect them? I'll keep the brothers here, if they are."

As it turned out, they were both in class, and Ernest personally escorted them to his office. The sheriff peeked out of the nurse's office, and saw them go by. As soon as they were out of sight, he and Tucker left.

Tucker led him to an old shack, hidden in the woods, adjacent to the Barton's property. The shack looked as if it could fall down at any moment. It stunk of cigarettes and whiskey, dust, vomit and rodent droppings. The little critters could be heard squeaking and scratching around in the rafters and corners.

The sheriff made an inventory of all the stolen items he found in the shack. Then he asked Tucker if he knew where they'd come from.

"It never occurred to me to ask. I never saw 'em take nothin' but candy and such from the store."

"How about the whiskey jugs; did they tell you where they came from? Did you or they drink any of it?"

"They did, but I don't like it. I think they slipped some in my soda pop once, though, 'cause I fell asleep here one night and woke up with a headache in the mornin'".

Meanwhile, Ernest was having a heart-to-heart talk with Jake and Jeff Barton. He didn't mention the council meeting or the crimes, but talked about their family. He said he was concerned about their truancy and that their father never answered his requests for a meeting.

The boys both sat, looking at the floor, and only glanced at each other once or twice. After a long, awkward pause. Jeff, the older of the two, finally spoke. "Pa ain't been the same since our ma died a few years ago. When he ain't at work, he drinks. We been pretty much takin' care of ourselves ever since."

"I'm concerned about your welfare and your future," Ernest told them. "Do you eat well enough?"

"Ma taught me how to cook before she died," Jake, the younger brother, answered.

Ernest noted that the boys were starting to relax and open up to him.

"Do you have enough to eat?" He was fishing for a confession.

"Pa does some shoppin' on Saturdays, and we scrounge around for stuff sometimes," Jeff admitted.

"Does your father ever mistreat you?"

"Oh, no!" Jeff suddenly got defensive. "He only whips us if we're bad or yells at us if we're lazy. Mostly, he just keeps to himself."

"That's fine; not to worry," Ernest reassured them. "I was looking at your records, and was wondering why you skip class so often. I'm certain that your grades would improve quite a bit, if you would apply yourselves to your lessons and do your homework."

Both boys looked down at the floor again and shrugged.

The lunch bell rang a moment later, and Ernest asked them if they had brought lunches to school with them. His question was answered by their silence. He stood and said, "Let's go get you something to eat. I'll bet you're hungry. I know I am!"

He escorted them to the cafeteria, casually so as not to embarrass them and went into the kitchen to talk to the cook. "I'm going to buy two more extra lunches for the remainder of the school year, and thought I'd better let you know in advance."

"Mr. Beebe," the woman sighed, "you already pay for four kids that I know of here. I bet you feed some at the grammar school, too, don't you?"

"Full bellies make for good students," Ernest replied with a grin.

Ernest had asked the brothers what time their father usually came home from work. Their answer was: "If he comes straight home, usually about five or five-thirty. And dinner needs to be ready for him or he yells, whips us and goes straight to the bottle," Jeff admitted.

"On Friday and Saturday nights, he may not come home at all. When he does, it's real late, and we're usually asleep," Jake added.

Ernest made arrangements with his pastor and the sheriff, to go to the Barton home a couple of days later. They arrived as the family was finishing dinner, and the boys were clearing the table. Mr. Barton hadn't had time for more than one beer, so he was sober enough to grasp the weight of the situation. He met the men at the door, and greeted them with trepidation. "Evening, sheriff, what're you and your friends doing here?"

"Hello Butch. This is Ernest Beebe, the school principal, and Reverend Dennis Cole. May we come in to talk with you for a bit? It's rather important."

Mr. Barton was scared and angry now. "Just a minute," he said, and closed the door, leaving the three men outside. They heard him yell at the boys, "What kind of trouble have you gotten into now? Go to your room and don't come out till I tell you to!" They heard the boys running, and a door slam. Then Butch opened the door and let the men in.

The first thing they noticed was the odor of alcohol, garbage and sweat that permeated the place, then their strong visual impression, that the house hadn't been cleaned since they'd moved in.

Butch cleared spaces for them to sit, and pulled up a chair for himself. Though it was a comfortable temperature in the room, Butch was sweating profusely. He pulled out a filthy handkerchief and wiped his face, as his visitors took their seats.

"Butch," the sheriff began, "As you suspected, we are here to address a problem with your boys. Our town has been experiencing more crime and mischief, since your family moved here, and when I looked into it, I found evidence that your boys were behind the crimes."

Butch started to turn angry again, and defensive. "I don't know what you want me to do about it." he replied. "Their mother's been dead three or four years now, and I got to work to keep food on the table and a roof over our heads. I can't keep track of a couple of active boys."

"I know it's been hard since your wife died, but that's not all."

"Ernest, tell him what your concerns are."

"Mr. Barton," Ernest began, "The boys' grades have been very poor and, though his teachers and I have tried numerous times to meet with you about their absences and neglect of homework assignments, we have yet to receive a reply from you. I interviewed the boys, and am convinced that they are basically good boys, but lack proper nutrition and guidance. I'm concerned that they'll have difficulty supporting themselves as adults.

"Another boy has been consorting with them, and his truancy and grades have followed theirs."

"I fear their crimes will escalate, until they end up dead or in prison for the rest of their lives," the sheriff added.

Butch stood up suddenly and ordered them out of the house. "I don't need nobody to tell me how to raise my boys!"

Ernest and Reverend Cole left, but the sheriff stayed outside and listened, to intercede if necessary, on the boys' behalf. He heard some yelling, two belt whippings, crying and door slamming. Then it grew quiet. He heard the boys comforting each other, and a cork popping out of a whiskey jug. Confident that Butch's anger had been vented for the night, the sheriff left.

Ernest took the truant brothers under his wing and invited them to his home for an occasional weekend meal. He also called a teachers' meeting the next week and recounted what had transpired, not going into details or naming names. He figured that the Barton brothers' and Tucker's teachers would recognize who he was talking about, and trusted that they would come to him if and when they needed to talk or take action regarding this matter.

The crime rate went down, and the Barton boys stopped skipping school, but still, their homework assignments weren't being completed. Ernest knew they would all have to repeat their classes the next year, and hoped the Barton family wouldn't move away before their problems could be resolved.

Two weeks after school let out for the summer, Sheriff Cole called Ernest at home on a Saturday morning. "Ernest, I have Butch Barton in my jail for assault and attempted murder. He's awake now and very distraught. Can you and Reverend Cole come over here?"

"I'll call him, to see if he's available. Where are Butch's boys; are they all right?"

"They're with my wife, at my house."

Ernest talked to Ercyline, and then called his pastor's house. Mrs. Cole picked up on the second ring. "Hello? Ernest, how good to hear from you! We just finished breakfast. Did you want to talk to Dennis?" She turned the phone over to her husband, and went into the kitchen.

"Ernest, I was just about to go to my office and review my sermon for tomorrow. I suppose you have something important to discuss?"

"Yes; do you remember the Barton family that we visited a couple of months ago, with Sheriff Gowrie?"

"Of course I do. What's happened?"

"Butch is in jail."

"Do you think he's reached some crisis, so that he may be open to receiving help?"

"That's what Benjamin and I are hoping. He's there for some serious crimes."

"My sermon can wait. I'll be there in thirty minutes."

He hung up the phone, and went into the kitchen. "Betty, I'm needed at the jail. I don't know how long I'll be gone."

"I'll be praying for you all," she said, then gave him a kiss and resumed her task. As he went out the door, he heard her on the phone, talking to someone. "Yes, someone in a crisis of some kind down at the jailhouse... Thank you, dear."

Ernest was waiting outside the jail when Dennis arrived. "Let's pause and pray, before we enter the battlefield, Ernest." When they had finished praying, they steeled themselves before opening the door.

Sheriff Gowrie filled them in on the details leading to Butch's arrest. "He was stinking drunk when Deputy Jim Harris stopped in to check on things at McDougal's, as is his routine on Friday and Saturday nights.

"The bartender said Butch was being loud and abusive toward the waitress and some of the other patrons. He didn't know what set him off; said he's usually pretty quiet and keeps to himself.

"When Jimmy approached Butch and asked him if he could take him home, Butch got belligerent and combative. When Jimmy tried to cuff him, he grabbed a whiskey bottle and hit Jimmy in the head, knocking him out cold. Then he stole Jimmy's pistol, and ran off.

"The bartender called me to report the incident. I went looking for Butch, and found him on the road to his house. I feared for his boys' lives, so tried to stop him before he got home. He shot at me, but thankfully, was too drunk to hit the broad side of a barn. Then he stumbled and fell. He lost hold of the pistol, and I was able to overpower him and bring him in.

"After I locked him up, I got a visit from Mr. Waldron, claiming that Butch had shot someone at the other bar. That man was taken to the medical clinic for treatment. It looks like he's going to pull through."

"Does Butch remember any of this?" Reverend Cole asked.

"Were the boys home: did they witness their father's arrest?" Ernest added.

"I didn't see the boys, but a light came on, so I knew they were home. I went back for them after bringing their father here.

"Butch seemed to remember some of what happened, but when I told him that he was headed home with a loaded gun, he started shaking and crying. He's been curled up in a fetal position, weeping like a baby ever since. That's why I called you in; I think he's finally hit bottom and is ready to listen."

He took them to the back room, where the jail cell was. Butch had fallen asleep, but woke up when the sheriff unlocked the door and it creaked open.

"You have some visitors," the sheriff told him.

Butch sat up slowly and looked at them with bleary, bloodshot eyes. When he focused enough to recognize the men he started to get agitated again. "Whatta you want? I told you I don't need your help!" Then he remembered what the sheriff had told him about the previous night and the color drained from his face. "I love my sons; really I do," he sobbed. "I don't want to hurt them no more." Then he buried his face in his hands and moaned, "Oh God, I coulda killed 'em!"

Ernest sat on one side of the bereft man and his pastor on the other. "Would you like us to pray with you?" the minister asked.

Butch nodded and bent low, with his forehead resting on his hands.

Ernest and Reverend Cole put their hands on his back and took turns praying for strength, guidance, protection and wisdom for Butch and his sons. Then they talked to him about Jesus and that he needed God's strength to conquer his addiction.

"Since the beginning of time, men have tried to live without God," Ernest told him. "I know; I was one of them. But when my world fell apart, much as yours has, I finally turned to him and was restored."

"Jesus loves you, in spite of everything you've done," Reverend Cole assured him. "He wants to be your father and friend. Do you want him to restore your life and release you from your bondage of sin?"

"I tried drowning my pain in whiskey, but it just made things worse. I don't know how to get free of it." He turned to Reverend Cole. "I don't know how to pray. Can you help me pray, Rev?"

"Of course." Reverend Cole kneeled, and Butch followed suit. While they prayed, Ernest went out to talk with the sheriff.

"What do you think will happen to him, and to the boys?" Ernest asked.

"It's up to the judge and possibly a jury," the sheriff replied. "I'll be sending him to Portland in a day or two. Depending on which judge he gets, his penitence could help quite a bit toward his sentencing. If the man he shot wants to press charges, that could go against him.

"As for the boys; I'll talk to my wife about them. She may or may not want to continue looking after them. Our kids are all grown and out on their own."

"I'd like to continue my relationship with them and mentor them in the faith, if possible," Ernest told him. "Please keep me informed about their situation."

"I'll be sure to do that, my friend."

Reverend Cole came out of the back room and informed the sheriff that his prisoner was ready for some food.

"That's a good sign. He hasn't touched a bite since he got here last night. I'll see what I can drum up for him."

"Thank you both for coming. I had no idea what to do with him; he was such a mess."

"You're welcome," they both replied, then walked out.

"I'm going home for a bit." Reverend Cole said. "I told Butch I'd be back a little later, Ernest."

"I'll try to stop by to visit him after the service tomorrow," Ernest said. "I'll see you in the morning, Dennis."

The Barton brothers stayed with the sheriff, and started attending church with Ernest and Ercyline.

The man that Butch shot recovered, but did press charges against him. Butch was convicted on two counts of first degree assault and being drunk and disorderly. He spent five years in prison, then was reunited with his sons, who were already graduated from high school. The youngest was attending college in California, and the elder was working at a mill in Klamath Falls.

Chapter Four

MATRON OF HONOR

In early February, 1909, Alice received a letter from Mattie, saying that she was engaged to a doctor at the hospital:

> We're planning an early autumn wedding. We haven't chosen an exact date, yet. Charles' parents live in Seattle, so it will most likely be held there.
>
> I wanted to give you advance notice and ask you to be my matron of honor. Charles comes from a large, close-knit family, so it will be a big wedding. His brothers, sister, cousins, nieces, nephew and our best friends will be the other attendants.
>
> His grandfather will officiate. He's a retired pastor.
>
> Of course, your whole family is invited. Let me know if you can come, and how many train tickets you'll need. His father will cover all the costs.

Alice sent a reply the following week:

> Dear Mattie,
>
> I'm so happy for you! You deserve the very best in life. I'm pleased that you chose me to be your chief attendant. If you'll send me the fabric and pattern, I'll be glad to make the dress myself.
>
> We'll need five train tickets. Mamma, Papa and Tucker are staying behind to "hold down the fort".
>
> Papa is very busy with school functions that time of year, and Carsie can't afford to take time off of work, because he was off for several months after his accident.
>
> Ilda can't travel right now, because her second baby is due about then.
>
> I can hardly wait to meet Charles and his family.

In April, Alice received a package from Mattie with a dress pattern and the most beautiful emerald green brocade she'd ever seen. Also included was a very generous check to cover the cost of clothes, notions, new shoes, etc. for the whole family. The date for the nuptials was three O'clock, Saturday, October fourth, at the Trinity Parish Episcopal Church in Seattle, Washington. The train tickets would follow later.

Alice borrowed her mother's new, electric sewing machine, and cleared the Kitchen table to cut the fabrics. She and Grace kept the table, the iron and the sewing macine busy for a couple of months, measuring, ironing, cutting, basting, marking, sewing, readjusting and hemming, to make sure every garment was flawless.

The children's clothes were made last, to make sure they wouldn't outgrow them before they were needed. By the time the sewing projects were all finished, they had all grown accustomed to eating in the living room and not going barefoot, to avoid stepping on pins.

The boys had to step up to the plate and do some of the women's chores, and frequently had to go fruit-picking without them that summer.

On the afternoon of October second, Tucker drove his mother, brothers and sisters to the train depot in Bridal Veil. They would be travelling to Portland and then transferring to a passenger train with Pullman and dining cars.

Tucker was quite uneasy when they got near to the train. Alice noted this, and her mind went back to the time he'd wandered off and almost been killed by a train when he was little. "I wonder if he even remembers why he is so fearful of them?" she thought. He dropped them and their luggage off as quickly as possible, and hurried off.

Doley wasn't too thrilled with the train, either. It was big, smelly and noisy. When they arrived at the Portland depot and maneuvered their way through the crowd, she became distressed. She had never been anywhere as noisy, or with so many strangers. Once they had stowed their baggage, found where their bunks were, and took their seats, she calmed down and started watching the scenery and asking all kinds of questions, as did the boys.

Frank and Lafe were so excited by the whole adventure, that Alice feared they would be awake all night. She was prepared, with an herbal tea to help them all relax. She wondered if she'd have the opportunity to use it, and would it be enough?

As it turned out, the cabin boy was willing and able to brew the tea for them and, even though they were excited by the trip, the movement and rumbling of the train was conducive to sleeping, and they had no trouble getting to sleep. Doley slept with Grace, and the boys shared a bunk. Alice had a bunk to herself.

At seven o'clock in the morning, the whistle blew and the conductor came through with the announcement, "Tacoma, Washington in five minutes, breakfast in fifteen minutes, Seattle in one hour!" They all piled out of their bunks, along with everyone else in their car, jostling past each other.

"Oops, sorry."

"Coming through!"

They went to the restrooms to get dressed, then to the dining car for a continental breakfast. While the children were eating, they chatted excitedly, firing off more questions as they peered out the windows at the passing scenery. They were awed by the tall buildings as they approached Seattle.

It was raining lightly as they exited the train. They were expecting to be met by Charles' father at the Seattle depot. What they weren't told was that he would be riding in a shiny black carriage, replete with footman and driver in top hats and tails!

Their host was a rather large man; modestly dressed; a down-to-earth sort. "Mrs. Walden, I'm Charles' father, Harold Brown. You can call me Harry. I usually don't stand on so much formality," he said, gesturing at the carriage, "but I rented the rig for this special weekend, knowing I'd need the extra space for your large party and others."

Doley was a little afraid of the horses, so big, black and shiny. The boys were enthralled by them. None of the children had ever seen such a splendid team or rig, having been born and raised in and around frontier towns. Alice was reminded of her trip to St. Louis with Annabelle.

They drove through the streets of Seattle, commenting on the tall buildings and all the hustle and bustle of the big city. They were soon climbing up First Hill. Near the top, the carriage stopped in front of a large, but modest home. Alice had expected a mansion. To the children, it was just that. They had never seen so grand a home in their short lives.

Their luggage was carried inside by a strapping young man, introduced as Daniel. "If you need anything during your stay, don't hesitate to ask me or Jenny, the maid," he said. When they entered, they were met in the parlor by a short, pudgy, but well-dressed woman.

Harry introduced them. "This lovely flower is my wife, Clara."

"Dear, this is Mattie's friend, Alice, and her children... whose names I... can't seem to remember. I'm sorry," he apologized to Alice, "I must be getting old."

Alice introduced them. "This is Grace, Frank, Lafe and Doley."

"You're lucky we didn't bring the rest of the family along, too!" quipped Lafe.

"Is that so? And how many more are there?" Clara asked him.

"Let me see..." He counted on his fingers. "There's Carsie, Tucker, Gramma and Grampa..."

"Don't forget Ilda, Albert and Faye," Grace whispered.

Lafe thought hard while he recounted. "Seven!"

"And where's your father?" Clara asked him.

His face clouded and he looked down, then up at his mother.

"He's in heaven," volunteered Frank. "I was named after him. He was a big, strong logger. I'm going to be *just* like him!"

Lafe's mood changed back instantaneously, "Our brother Carsie is a logger, too! But he's not as big and strong as Papa."

Just then, Jenny came in to announce that lunch was ready. Harry ushered them into the dining room. When Alice saw it, her mind was immediately transported back to her Uncle Minot's plantation in Illinois. The room wasn't as large or as grand as her uncle's had been, but it was furnished in a similar style and color.

They were served a lovely green salad for the first course, then beef and barley soup with assorted sandwiches. Dessert was vanilla ice cream atop a choice of Dutch apple pie or chocolate cake. Alice and Grace ate daintily, refusing second helpings, but Doley and the boys ate as if they hadn't eaten in days. "The food on the train wasn't to their liking," Alice told their hosts.

After lunch, Harry asked, "Who wants to go sightseeing?" The boys started jumping up and down, shouting, "Me, me!" while Doley was rubbing her eyes and yawning.

Clara informed her husband that she and Alice had preparations to make for the wedding. Grace said she'd love to go along if she wasn't needed.

"Doley needs her nap, so I'll keep her here with me," Alice told him.

"Think we can all fit in my flivver?" Harry smiled at the boys.

They looked at each other, confused. Then they asked, "What's a flivver?"

"Wait on the front porch and I'll show you," he said over his shoulder, as he hurried out the back door.

The boys ran excitedly, chattering the whole way, "Maybe it's a special kind of carriage." When they got to the porch and heard the motor, Frank exclaimed, "It's an automobile!"

Harry came motoring around the end of the house in a 1904 model A Ford. It had the optional rear seat and rubber top.

The boys were speechless and their eyes were as big as saucers, as they ran to look inside. They'd seen autos for the first time on this trip, on the streets of Portland and Seattle.

"Hop in! Lafe can sit with me where the view is better, while you two take the back seat."

Clara brought their coats out. "You'll be needing these before you're back." As they were getting seated, she reminded Harry to be sure to be back by seven for dinner.

He drove them back down the hill toward Elliot Bay, pointing out some of the tall buildings that his company had designed. He took them to Pioneer Park and Square, and the brand new Pike Place Market, where he bought them all treats and souvenirs. Then they went to a family-friendly show at the Paramount Theater. It was a day never to be forgotten.

That evening there was a large dinner for the wedding party and relatives, most of whom had arrived the day before and were staying at nearby hotels-those who weren't resident Seattleites.

The next day started early, with flapjacks, fruit and sausages, as there was much yet to do before the ceremony. The men kept the children occupied, while the women were busy primping.

Right after lunch, they climbed into the carriages and cars and proceeded to the church. Clara and the children stayed at the house until the second trip.

The church was decorated beautifully, but simply, with local, seasonal flowers; chrysanthemums and roses mostly, and emerald green ribbons, perfectly matched to the bridesmaids' dresses.

Harry's father ran them through a rehearsal. Then Clara arrived with the children and started bustling about, making sure all the ladies and the flower girls were in place, while Harry lined up the groom, the ring-bearer, the best man and the ushers.

Mattie's gown was fashioned of white brocade in the same pattern as the bridesmaids'. It had a modest-length train trimmed with lace. She wore white roses and small orange mums in her hair. The flower girls were similarly dressed, but in a soft pastel green. The men all had black tuxedos with matching green bow ties and cummerbunds. The bachelor's buttons in their boutonnieres matched the ones in the ladies' bouquets, varying in color, from dark red to yellow. The groom's included a white rose. Grace had made new dresses for herself and Doley, using Alice's pattern, but modifying it slightly. They were embellished with leftover fabric from their mother's dress.

The church was packed by the time the ceremony was to begin. Mattie was understandably nervous, but Charles was used to crowds, having come from a large, well-to-do family. It was a very lovely ceremony, complete with candles and communion.

After the wedding and a simple reception, family members and honored guests retired to the Brown's home, where the gifts were opened. Then they were served a feast of roast turkey and pork with all the trimmings. After dinner, all but the youngest children enjoyed games and dancing until nearly midnight.

After brunch the next morning, the newlyweds, the Waldens and some others were taken to the train station to start their honeymoon trip or return home.

Three days after the Waldens returned from Seattle, word came from Albert that Ilda had presented him with a healthy baby boy, whom they'd named Frank.

That holiday season was reminiscent of the one when Frank was absent due to his accident in the woods many years before. Alice had to force herself to be cheerful for the children's sakes. Her parents were a big help in that regard. Ernest taught the boys how to whittle, and took them fishing on weekends. Ercyline taught Doley how to cook, bake and sew.

They tickled, kidded and played with them and took them to visit with friends.

One beautiful spring day, Ernest and Ercyline took the children on a picnic. Alice and Grace were working at the hotel and Carsie was at the lumber mill, but Tucker was available to go with them.

They took the buggy and went to a forest clearing next to the river. It was peaceful there. They enjoyed watching the birds and squirrels, and the children splashed in a shallow pool, chasing fish and frogs and catching crawfish. Tucker watched them, while Ercyline and Ernest rested in the shade. They dozed off for a while when the children were being quiet.

Ercyline was awakened by a fawn's wet nose touching her cheek. She thought it was Ernest kissing her until she opened her eyes. She was startled, but not enough to scare the fawn away. She sat up very slowly and reached out to touch it. It sniffed her hand and licked it. Then she tried talking to it in hushed tones and petting it. She noticed, then, how skinny it was. "I'll bet you're an orphan."

Just then, Doley came toward them and saw the deer. She didn't know what to think at first, but when she saw how gentle and tame it seemed, she followed her grandma's instruction to approach slowly and quietly. She was delighted when the fawn allowed her to pet it and nibbled at her clothes. Then the boys saw what was going on, and slowly approached. Soon the young doe was surrounded by children and loving the attention, nuzzling and sucking at their fingers. "She's hungry," Ercyline told them. "She must have lost her mama."

"Oh, poor baby," Doley cooed at the fawn. "Can we take her home? She'll die without our help." By this time Ernest was awake and saw what was transpiring. He knew it would be a mistake to try to make a deer into a pet, but he also knew how helpless he and Ercyline were to ignore the pleas of their grandchildren. He tried to reason with them, but knew it was useless.

So the children brought the fawn home with them. Ernest bought a bottle and Grace got some goat's milk from a neighbor who kept several nannies for his children who couldn't drink cow's milk. "What are you going to do with it?" Alice asked when she came home.

"If we leave her outside, the dogs will get her," the children reasoned, with pleading eyes.

"Oh, no; she's not coming in this house!"

"It'll just be for a couple of weeks, until she's weaned." Frank reasoned.

"She can stay in our bedroom at night," Lafe added.

"I'll clean up after her," Tucker volunteered.

"We'll keep an eye on her outside in the daytime," Doley said.

"Please," they all begged.

"Oh, all right, she can stay," Alice surrendered.

"Thank you!" they all cried, and hugged their mother. Then Dottie proceeded to relieve herself on Lafe's shoes.

No one got much sleep that night. The children all took turns feeding Dottie and cleaning up after her every two or three hours. She wasn't used to being indoors, so she was restless and uneasy, just like the family members.

They all settled down to a routine by the second night, and the word got out around town by the third day. All the children in town came to see Dottie the deer.

Two weeks turned into four as Dottie filled out and started eating grass and clover. Her spots started to fade and she was getting into everything, including Alice's garden.

"That's it!" Alice said with resolve, when she found that Dottie had eaten her pea plants. "It's time to take her back to the woods. She's weaned and ruining my garden!"

The children hated to see Dottie go, but knew their mother was right. They had promised to release her once she was weaned. By now she was too big and strong to be taken in the buggy, so they borrowed the neighbor's wagon for the trip.

Everyone but Alice went along to say goodbye to Dottie. It took most of them to control the wiggling fawn during the trip. When they reached the spot where they had found her, the children all hugged her and cried. It was a moving scene that made even the adults a little misty-eyed.

Dottie was getting restless, so Ernest said, "It's time for her to go home."

They all stood back and watched as their temporary pet bounded into the woods.

Chapter Five

THE NEW OLD DOCTOR

Doctor Williams had been searching for a replacement for himself in Bridal Veil for over a year, so he and his wife could move back East. His father-in-law had passed away a few years before, and his mother-in-law had become frail and weak. His wife had no relatives who were able to care for her, so he and his wife had felt obligated to move back home. His parents lived in that same city, and were needing more and more help, as well. He had found a new position at a rural hospital about fifty miles outside of Boston.

His replacement, Dr. Alexander, was what one would call "old school". He was in his early fifties-thin and tall, with a full head of graying hair. He'd been trained at a small school in the Midwest and had worked with a superstitious old doctor in Minnesota until his wife got tired of the extreme weather and threatened to leave him if he stayed there. She was from Louisiana and never could get used to the cold and snow. Both of their parents had already passed away, and they had no other close kin to keep them in the Midwest.

Alice's first dealings with Dr. Alex, as he came to be known, were in November, 1909, when Bridal Veil was hit with overlapping epidemics of measles and chicken pox.

The primary school was hit particularly hard-so much so that her father took Alice's advice and closed it down for the time being.

Dr. Alexander hadn't even had time to get settled in before the first patients' families called upon him. It wasn't long before he had so many cases that he was forced to ask for help. He asked the mayor for referrals to as many nurses and aides as he could supply. Naturally, Alice's name was first on that list.

By the time he came calling, she had suspended her work at the hotel to treat several patients of her own, including Doley, Frank and Lafe. The boys were over the measles before they got the pox, but Doley had them at the same time.

"I've been told that you are not formally trained, but the mayor and several others have given me very good reports of your work," he told her, as he examined Doley.

"I've begun to get concerned about her," Alice said. "She seems sicker than my other patients."

"How old is she?" he asked, as he exited the bedroom.

"She turned eight recently," Alice replied. "I know what you're thinking. She's small for her age because she's been rather sickly all her life."

"What other illnesses has she suffered?" he asked, as he pulled a tablet and pen from his pocket and sat down on the sofa.

"Let me see… rubella, yellow fever, croup, pneumonia-three times, and every cold and seasonal flu that comes down the pike. I'd keep her home all the time if I could, in order to protect her from being exposed."

"Were there any complications with the pregnancy or her birth? Was she born premature?"

"Not at all. In fact, she was the largest one of them all-twelve pounds."

The doctor raised his eyebrows in surprise. "Hmm, well, let me think on it." Then he checked his watch, rose from his seat and pocketed the tablet and pen. "I'm off to see your neighbors' children. You're already doing everything right for her. I'll check in on her again when I get back this way."

When Alice was gone caring for other patients, Grace had to step up and care for Doley and the boys. One night, Alice came home to find Grace asleep on the sofa. She went to check on Doley and found her seizing, due to a high fever. "Grace, come quick!" She pulled the covers off the little girl as Grace came running in.

Grace froze when she saw Doley writhing on the bed.

"Go fill the dishpan with cold water, and get me some towels," Alice directed her. "Then chip up some ice from the ice box."

Grace just stood there, staring at her sister. Both girls were as white as sheets. "Go!" Alice shouted.

Grace roused from her trance and rallied to her mother's aid. They both worked constantly for two hours before they got Doley's fever down enough to stop the seizures. Then Alice examined her more thoroughly. "We'll have to keep a closer eye on her. She's been scratching her pox, and now they're infected."

"Would you mind taking over here while I get some food and rest? I've been up for over twenty-four hours with scarcely time for more than coffee and a couple of doughnuts."

"Of course, Mama."

Alice went into her herbal remedy box, chose one herb to fight the infection and another to help ease the itching. She instructed Grace on how to use them.

She scrambled some eggs, split an apple with Grace, brushed her teeth and put on her nightgown. "Wake me at eight," she said, yawning on the way to her room.

The next morning, Dr. Alexander came knocking while Alice and Grace were washing the breakfast dishes. He examined Doley while Alice got dressed and Grace explained what they had been doing for her sister. He met Alice in the kitchen when he was done.

"I don't understand how you do it, but it seems to work. Your patients seem to fare better than most."

Alice observed how tired he looked, so she poured him a cup of coffee and topped hers off. They sat down at the table.

"I think this epidemic is starting to wane," he mumbled between sips.

"I hope so," she replied. "I need to get back to work so we won't starve this winter."

He nodded, "I understand. It can't be easy raising a family the size of yours all alone. I think I can help you there. I was talking with Mrs. Caufield yesterday. She and her husband own the store on Third Street. Her husband's health is starting to decline. He's having trouble with coordination and tremors in his hands, as well as heart problems. She asked me if I knew any young men who could use the work. Her husband doesn't want to hire anyone, but she says he can't keep going on like he is much longer. And I agree.

"She's small, but strong-willed. She says if she hires someone and puts her foot down, he'll give in. I thought about Tucker. Do you think he'd like to try it? It could turn into a full-time job eventually."

"I think he'd go for that. We could sure use the money, even if it only pays for his expenses. I just hope he can keep his head out of the clouds enough to *keep* the job. I'll send him over there tomorrow morning."

The next time the doctor came over, he told Alice, "I told my wife about Dolores being so sickly, when everyone else in the family is so healthy. She thought about it, and looked through some books for the answer. She says she found it in an old book that my grandmother swore by her whole life. It says that Dolores means sadness. She insists that you must change her name if you want her to be healthy."

"You aren't the first one to tell me that," Alice confessed. "It seems far-fetched to me, but," she shrugged and lifted her hands in exasperation, "I've tried everything else!"

After the epidemic was over and life was getting back to normal, Alice told Doley what the doctor had said about her name.

"I never did like my name much, anyway. I've thought about it a lot, and I know just what I want it to be; Cleora!"

"Cleora? How did you come up with that name?"

"Our neighbor's new baby, Clementine, combined with my best friend, Laura. They're both so pretty, and happy all the time."

So Cleora it was from then on, although the nickname Doley stuck with her the rest of her life. Superstition or not, Cleora was not sickly anymore. Just like Tucker, though, she never grew tall like her siblings.

Tucker took the job at the store. The Caufields had met the young man before and had taken a liking to him. Mr. Caufield said he reminded him of his brother, who had drowned when he was about Tucker's age. They had no sons, only daughters, who'd grown, married and moved away. So the young man became the son they'd never had.

Tucker dropped out of school shortly after starting the job, but he seemed happier than ever before, so Alice left him alone to find his own way. She had more important things to worry about.

One day, a few months after the epidemic, Ercyline came racing up in their buggy, just as the children were preparing to go out the door to school, "Your father is very sick. You know that he caught a bad cold a couple of weeks ago? Well, it's only gotten worse. He stayed home from work the last two days because his coughing has kept us both awake all night. Now his breathing is labored and Doctor Alexander is out of town. I'm very worried. Can you come over right away?"

"Of course, Mama. Give me a minute to pack some supplies and talk to Grace."

She directed Grace to go to the hotel and tell them she wouldn't be able to come in. "Would you be able to fill in for me if they need you?"

"Yes, Mama. You go take care of Grandpa. I'll take care of things here at home, too."

Cleora and Lafe protested about going to school. They were worried about their grandpa.

"There's nothing you can do for him right now, except go to school and make him proud of you," Alice told them.

Frank said he'd keep an eye on them after school, if need be. "Don't worry, Mama, we'll be all right."

Alice and Ercyline raced off to her parents' house. Along the way, Alice told her what needed to be done. "It sounds like pneumonia. We'll need to make a steam tent."

When they arrived, Alice rushed to her father's side, while Ercyline brewed the herbs that Alice had brought along.

Ernest was sicker than she'd ever seen him. His face and fingers were a bluish-grey and his eyes were sunken and dull. They rigged up the tent and got the medicated steam filling the air inside it as quickly as they could.

"Now, Mama, I'll take over here while you get a little breakfast and go back to bed. We don't need you down with pneumonia too."

Alice didn't tell her mother, but she feared this was the last straw for Ernest. When the doctor finally arrived later that afternoon, he was gone.

"I'm so sorry, Alice, Ercyline. You did everything I would have done, and more. It just wasn't enough. He was too frail to weather this storm."

He packed up his bag, and as he went out the door, asked, "Would you like me to call the undertaker for you?"

Alice nodded, unable to speak for fear of breaking down and upsetting her mother more than she already was.

Alice stayed with Ercyline until Ernest's body was removed, then took her home with her. "The last thing you need right now is to be left alone in this house," she told her.

The children were real troopers; helping and consoling their mother and grandmother as much as they could.

The pastor of the Bridal Veil church and its members took charge of all the service preparations. Carsie, Ilda and Albert came for the memorial service. They left the little ones with their paternal grandmother for the day.

"Mom is thrilled to spend time with them," Albert told Doley when she showed her disappointment. "You can see them for a short while after the service, but then we have to get back home. We're expecting several important animal births any time now. Perhaps your mother would allow you to come visit us this summer?"

"Perhaps you could *all* come to visit us?" Ilda looked questioningly from Alice to Albert.

Albert nodded.

"Mama, can we, *please?*" the children all pleaded.

"Oh, no, you don't mean it?" Alice asked Ilda. "Where would you put all of us?"

"Our house is large enough, and we can borrow some beds and bedding from our friends at church. Please, Mama?"

"Well...all right, I'll see what I can arrange... after the funeral is over and Grandma is moved in with us. Right now, we have to get going. The service starts in an hour and we still have a few things to do before we go."

She received hugs from all of them.

The service was well attended by church members, town officials, students and their parents. As expected, there were so many people that the church would not have held half of them, so it was conducted in the town theater. Even so, there was not enough space for everyone to be seated. Stephen and Bettina Thatcher and other old friends came from West Linn and Oregon City. The fire marshal looked around nervously the whole time.

The foyer was full, also, so their church, which was nearby, was used as a nursery for the younger children. Most of the businesses closed their doors for the afternoon, and all three restaurants made contributions for the reception.

Ernest was buried near Frank, in the Bridal Veil Cemetery.

Most of Ercyline's belongings had already been moved to Alice's house before the funeral, but Ernest's things and all the other items that she wouldn't need any longer were sold or donated to the church pantry.

The children helped Alice and Ercyline clean the house for the next tenants.

"This house has been my home for twenty years. I'm sad to leave it, but I'm grateful that this happened when the garden was mostly idle," Ercyline mused as they moved some of her plants to their new home in Alice's garden.

The children were glad to have their grandmother living with them, even though they missed their grandfather.

This time, it was the schools that seemed cold and empty. They went the rest of the year with two temporary principals: the high school's history and math teacher, and the grammar school's fourth grade teacher.

Doctor Alexander's "baptism by fire" got him well acquainted with the townspeople. Although he wasn't as knowledgeable as Doctor Williams, they loved his warmth and sense of humor.

His wife, Barbara, was a large woman with a strong will and a rather abrasive manor. Her personality was so opposed to her husband's that Alice wondered what they ever saw in each other, besides being superstitious. She had caught that bug from her grandmother, rather than from the same source as her husband and had run wild with it. But they got along somehow, and even though they didn't show it in public, it was evident that they were devoted to each other.

The Alexanders' first winter in Oregon was the coldest one in many years. There wasn't much snow, but there was an ice storm in early February. The temperature aloft was warmer than at the ground, causing the rain that fell that day to freeze as it hit.

When morning came, the children were thrilled and awed by the sight outside their windows. Everything was coated in several inches of ice. The boys went out and measured the ice in several places and fell down numerous times in the process. They came inside laughing and rubbing sore bottoms.

As they were eating breakfast, it started to snow big, wet flakes. It snowed most of the day, then cleared up and froze solid that night. It was much too cold in the bedrooms to sleep, however, so they made it fun by dragging the mattresses into the living room for an indoor campout. Alice was awake all that night, nervously monitoring the progress of the storm. All night she prayed that no trees would fall on her home or the places where the rest of her family members were. She also prayed for everyone and every business she could think of in the town. She figured that there would be damages and emergencies associated with a storm like this one, and that she would need to be ready at a moment's notice. Soon after sunup, they heard and saw branches and ice start to crack and fall all around them. They were all mesmerized by the spectacle outside. Then a large branch broke off of a tree in their back yard, barely missing the house.

Alice was concerned about their friends and elderly neighbors, but knew it was too dangerous to be out where a branch or large chunk of ice might fall on them. Besides, walking on the frozen ground was nearly impossible. She kept the children busy in the front of the house, playing games, as there were large trees overshadowing the bedrooms.

As the morning wore on, the temperature rose well above freezing and the snow began to melt and get even heavier. The sound of cracking and falling branches and ice chunks intensified. Then the electricity went out.

Alice had planned for this inevitability, setting up candles, matches, lanterns, and pans and buckets of water for flushing, washing and cooking. They always kept a good supply of firewood in and near the house, because the electricity went out every time there was a windstorm. The ice all melted off the trees just in time for the night-time temperature drop, when all the snow and meltwater on the ground began to refreeze.

It was clear and bitterly cold that night. No more branches or trees had fallen in several hours when bedtime came.

Alice was still concerned about Tucker, Carsie, Ilda and the townsfolk, but it was impossible to get out because of the ice. Even if they could afford a telephone, all the lines were down. Two days passed before the ice melted enough to walk outside safely. Then Alice drew up a plan for the children and herself to check on their neighbors.

"I'll go to the clinic and see if the doctor needs me. Frank, you go west and check on the Smiths and the Johansens. Lafe can go east and check on the Van Huskers and the Kruegers. While you're out, look for smoke from all the chimneys. If you find anyone in trouble, do what you can for them and report any injuries or deaths to the clinic. Grace, you can check on the Bakers and the Roemishes. Mamma, you and Doley can stay here and keep the home fires burning. There is plenty of firewood stacked up right outside the back door. I'll have the boys bring some more in before they leave."

Getting around the town was difficult due to all the debris. It took the children all day to check on all of the elderly folks in their neighborhood.

Frank found a dead horse under a fallen tree in the Smiths' yard, and all of their chickens had succumbed to the elements. They were almost out of firewood in the house, so he cut and carried some more in for them.

Lafe saw a home with no evidence of a fire in the fireplace, but when he checked it out, he was relieved to find it empty.

The Krueger's pipes had frozen, and the back yard was full of branches, so they still had no access to their wood supply. They were dehydrated and cold; having rationed what they had in the house.

Lafe cleared a path to their woodshed, brought some wood into the house for them and stoked the fire. He went to their neighbors' for some water to tide them over and shut off their main line. When he was sure they'd be all right, he continued on his rounds.

Grace found Mr. Baker cold, weak and depressed. As she banked the fire, she asked him where his wife was. He started to cry. Between sobs, he related this story:

"Jeanie went out to check on the animals and slipped on the ice. She fell, and couldn't get back into the house. I tried to get out to her with some quilts, but that big branch fell and blocked my path. There was nothing I could do for her. She told me to come in the house and keep warm; that she was ready to meet her maker. I checked on her several times, but it was so cold that she never had a chance. She was my angel. We were married fifty-eight years last June."

Grace held him until he quieted and then made him some soup. He didn't want to eat, but she urged him, saying, "What would Jeanie tell you if she was here?" He was still for a moment, then took the bowl and ate. After finishing, he asked for another.

"I feel a little better now. You should go and finish your rounds. See if there's anyone else who needs help."

"I'll notify the undertaker and send one of the boys over to check on you tomorrow." She gave him a hug and bundled up for the walk home.

Alice came home exhausted two days later, reporting, "One couple and two families suffered frost bite and hypothermia after trees fell on their houses, exposing them to the elements. Six people suffered concussions, skull fractures and other injuries from falling ice and branches. One of them was Fred Blankenship, the Postmaster. He died last night from his injuries.

"The Chumskis' house burned down with them in it. The fire chief said they probably had a chimney fire while they were sleeping. The whole family's remains were found in their beds."

There were multiple homes with burst pipes. For two weeks, every able-bodied man and boy was out cutting limbs to clear roads and wires, or helping neighbors repair damaged houses. Both the churches were utilized for way-stations for the workers. The hotel supplied rooms and meals for the displaced. It was three weeks before power and telephone services were restored.

Ten days later, after the roads were all cleared, there was a mass memorial service for the victims; nine in all. Several years later, the damage from the storm was still evident.

Chapter Six

PORTLAND

On May third 1912, Alice came quietly in the front door of the house, so as not to awaken her family. It was half past midnight, and she was tired from a full day at the hotel. There had been a wedding that evening, and she had been asked to stay to help with the clean-up. She hung her coat up and went to the kitchen and poured a cup of coffee. Then she sat at the table to read the mail. The first one was a pink envelope from Mattie. She opened it to find a card announcing the birth of their first child: a little girl named Alice Marie. Inside the card was a check and a letter:

Dear Alice;

I hope you are pleased that we named our blessing after you. I waited until she was a month old, because I've had two miscarriages and a stillborn birth prior to this. I know how hard you work and how much you care, so I didn't want to burden you with my problems.

Little Alice Marie is such a beautiful baby and hardly any trouble at all. She was born a month premature, but is doing well.

Her father delivered her in our home when I went into labor in the middle of the night. The automobile wouldn't start, and she arrived before our friend came to take us to the hospital.

I want you to come visit us in Portland. I may have found a job for you here, if you're interested. Can you be here on May fourteenth? I've taken the liberty of setting up some interviews for the 15th.

I know you don't have the money for travel, so I've included a check for train fare. Nothing would make me happier than to have my best friend and mentor living nearby.

I hope to hear from you very soon.

Love, Mattie

On May fourteenth, Alice stepped off the train at the Portland depot. Mattie was waiting in the station house with little Alice Marie in her arms.

"Alice, It's so good to see you!" she gushed as she gave her friend a long hug.

"Mattie, you look wonderful!" Alice replied, then turned her attention to the baby. "She *is* adorable!"

"I'm so glad you could come, Alice. Would you like to hold her? I'll take your bag. I left the taxi waiting outside. I have your visit all planned out."

They exited the station and found the taxi waiting, just as Mattie had said. Alice was surprised to see how much Portland had grown since the last time she was there. They left the city proper and traveled along the river road westward, and then took a side street, which went up a slight hill. Halfway up the hill, the taxi stopped in front of a modest home.

"It's exactly as I imagined it would be," Alice remarked as they walked up to the house. "The yard is lovely. Do you do the gardening yourself, or do you have help?"

Mattie smiled, "I'm afraid I don't have your green thumb, Alice. We have a Chinese gardener."

Baby Alice had fallen asleep on the trip and was now awake and crying. As soon as they walked through the door Alice gave her back to Mattie, "Just point me toward the kitchen and I'll make us some tea while you tend to the baby."

Alice filled the teakettle, started the stove and found the tea, sugar, cream, cups, saucers and spoons. Then she went looking for the restroom. When she emerged, she met Mattie in the hallway, carrying a much happier baby. "Did you find everything all right?"

"It wasn't hard; your kitchen is well appointed, and I love your bathroom, too."

After they finished their tea, Mattie stood. "Would you care for a two-bit tour before we start dinner?"

When they entered the nursery, which was all decorated in pink, white lace and flowers, Alice exclaimed, "Oh, it's lovely! My girls would be so envious. They felt fortunate to have a separate room from the boys!"

Then Mattie showed her all the clothes in the closet and the toys in the toy bin. "Charles' family and our friends and colleagues held a baby shower for me. We bought most of the furniture, but most of these were gifts."

Then they emerged from the nursery, "You didn't say anything, but I'm sure you noticed that the rest of the house looks pretty bare. We've only been here four months. I spent the first month decorating the nursery. I barely got it done before my doctor put me on bed rest."

"But it's pink! How did you know you would have a girl?" Alice asked her.

"Charles just knew. He has a knack with that sort of thing. Half of the time, when the phone rings, he knows who's calling before he picks it up."

As they finished the tour, Mattie glanced at the clock, "Would you like to hold the baby while I start dinner? We won't wait for Charles. I never know when he'll be home."

Alice played with the baby, while Mattie fixed dinner and told her about some part-time job opportunities that she had heard about. "The main reason for bringing you here, though, is that we have opened a new midwife program connected with the hospital's obstetrical unit. It was started about six months ago and seems to be quite popular and successful so far. They're accepting new applicants tomorrow morning, and I thought you'd be perfect for the job."

"I *am* getting tired of cooking for the hotel full-time, and I've been getting restless lately. I'm used to moving every few years. It gives me a chance to clear out the cobwebs and try something new.

"Ilda and Carsie are both here in Portland, and Tucker is doing well at the store. I would love to be able to spend more time with my grandchildren."

Halfway through dinner, Charles walked in the door. They passed a pleasant evening visiting. They got up early in the morning, ate breakfast and got ready to go to the interview that Mattie had arranged for Alice at the hospital. Charles was off of work that day, so he stayed home to watch the baby.

When they got to the hospital, Mattie was greeted cheerily by the receptionist and several doctors and nurses as they made their way to the OB/GYN ward. They checked in at the head nurse's office, where several other women were waiting already.

A few minutes later, the head nurse came in and greeted them, "My name is Teresa Bailey. Are all of you here to interview for the midwife positions?" She pulled some forms, clipboards and pens out of her desk and passed them out. Then she introduced Mattie. "She is a nurse here, and has agreed to monitor you while you fill out the forms, and help me rate them. She's also here to answer any questions you may have while filling them out." Then she pulled a timer out of her desk and set it. "You have one hour. I'll return then."

When the timer went off, Mattie collected the papers and sent the applicants to the break room for some coffee and snacks, while she and Teresa looked the papers over. Then the ladies were called back into the office one by one. Two of them were sent home and told to study more before reapplying. Alice and two others were accepted into the hospital's midwife program.

Mattie could hardly contain herself, she was so excited. As soon as they left the hospital, she took Alice to her favorite restaurant for a celebratory lunch.

Charles met them there and brought baby Alice to be nursed by Mattie. Then he took her home, and the women spent the afternoon going to several more interviews. Alice accepted a part-time job offer at a ladies' apparel shop.

The next day, Alice went to visit Ilda and Albert to give them the good news. She was pleased to hear that Carsie was coming for dinner. They were all thrilled to learn that she was planning to move to Portland.

They had a nice afternoon visiting with each other and playing with the children.

"We'll need a place to stay temporarily, until we find a permanent dwelling," Alice told them.

"We have plenty of room here," Ilda volunteered. "Is that all right with you, Albert dear?"

"You can stay as long as you need to," he offered. "Besides. I'll bet Frank and Lafe could be of real help to me here on the farm."

Alice returned home and immediately started making plans to move her family to Portland.

She contacted the people from whom she had rented the house, and talked to the school principal to acquire the children's records. She went to the hotel and the clinic to let them know that she would be leaving, and submitted a change of address form at the post office. Then she marshaled her family to pack up all their belongings and rescue as many plants as they could from their garden, to transfer to Ilda's yard.

Alice, Ercyline, Frank, Lafe, Grace and Doley said goodbye to Tucker and all their friends, and exchanged hugs and addresses with them.

Two weeks after she returned home, the church deacons loaded up one large wagon with the Waldens' durable possessions and plants, and a Conestoga with the breakables, the perishables and the family members. The children talked excitedly, most of the trip, about the adventure they were embarking upon. This would be a new experience for Alice and her family. Although they would be living on a farm, which in itself was a new experience, they would be very close to a big city, which they would be visiting regularly.

Alice would be spending a lot of time at the hospital, meeting with her clients and the doctors. The dress shop was downtown, very near the hospital, so she would be able to walk from one to the other.

The children would be attending school in the city, as well. They wondered if they would fit in and what it would be like milking cows, harvesting crops and going to plays and other cultural events.

"Mama, if we're living on a farm and going to school in the city, how will we get from one to the other every day?" the children asked. "How will you get around to all your jobs?"

"We'll figure that out when we get there," she replied. "I'm sure God will supply some sort of transportation for us. After all, he kept us fed and housed until now, and he supplied a home, employment and good health for this new chapter in our lives."

As they approached Albert and Ilda's farm, Ercyline exclaimed, "Now *this* brings back memories!"

"Did you grow up on a farm, Gramma?" Doley asked.

"No, but your mama grew up on your grandpa's uncle's farm in Illinois; except they called it a plantation. He was quite wealthy, and had a large, fancy home and many servants."

"Do Ilda and Albert have servants?"

"No, they aren't wealthy like Uncle Minot was."

About that time, they saw the cow, horses, sheep and pigs in the field behind the barn and the chickens and ducks in the pen near the house. The children got all excited. "OOh, Mama, look at all the animals!" Lafe shouted. "This is gonna be fun!"

Doley strained to see how many she could identify, as a dog came running out to meet them, barking at the wagonloads of strangers, and some kittens scurried under the porch.

"It won't be all fun," their mother reminded them. "We have to earn our keep by helping with the chores."

"I don't mind doing that," Frank said. "In fact, I look forward to working alongside Albert."

"And I can help Ilda cook and take care of little Faye and the baby," Doley pitched in.

Just then, Ilda came out onto the front porch with the children, and Albert came out of the barn. The wagons pulled to a halt, and everybody climbed down.

After greeting each other, Alice, Ercyline and the girls cooed over the baby, while the men unloaded the boxes with the personal items from the wagons.

"Why don't we put the furniture and the other boxes in the barn for now," Albert instructed. "You can get settled into your bedrooms and rest up tonight. We'll worry about the rest of it later."

Carsie arrived just then and helped them unload the wagons.

Ilda had a feast prepared for them. "I assume you're all as hungry as you are tired."

"It *has* been a long, tiring day," Ercyline sighed.

"I didn't realize just how hungry I was, until I smelled all that good food!" Alice exclaimed, as they entered the house.

"I learned from the best cook I know," Ilda replied with a grin.

After dinner, the deacons bedded down in the barn for the night, and then returned to Bridal Veil the next day.

Alice and Ercyline rested the next day, but the boys were eager to start learning how to be farmers. They both wanted to drive the tractor and ride the horses. Albert showed them how to milk the cow. "Next spring, if you like, I can show you how to shear the sheep," he offered.

Alice watched the baby, while Ilda showed Doley how to feed the chickens and collect the eggs. She had fun playing with the kittens and the lambs but wrinkled her nose when slopping the pigs. She had trouble getting to sleep that night because of an itchy rash on her arms and face. Alice whipped up an ointment to get her through the night, but was stumped as to its cause.

"Do you have any idea what might have caused it?" Alice asked Ilda the next morning. "There are so many new things here that she could be allergic to."

Ilda turned from the stove and looked at the rash. "A friend of mine had one just like this after she handled the sheep," she replied. "She's probably allergic to their wool."

"Oh! Now that you mention it, she never could sleep under a wool blanket or wear wool socks or sweaters. I'd forgotten!"

Albert took Alice to the hospital on Monday, to check in with the head nurse, Teresa Baily. After finding out that Alice had a lot of experience as a midwife, but didn't drive a car or have a buggy at her disposal, she put her on duty at the hospital. As they went on their way to the maternity ward, she briefed her:

"I'll assist you in a few deliveries here, to be certain that your skills are up to par before you take over your official duties. I'm thinking that you would be the perfect candidate to take over as head midwife. Up until now I've been in charge of the program, but it's gotten large enough now to need its own director. If you accept the position, you will report to me every morning. Then you'll have appointments with the mothers-to-be that have asked about the program. We just opened a new office and designated two rooms in the maternity ward for midwife deliveries, so you'll have all the help you need for difficult cases and emergencies.

"When you take over your duties as director, you will assign the new clients to the midwives. You'll need to study maps of Portland, to cut down on travel times; and of course, you will need to get to know the other midwives to try to match their personalities with the appropriate clients. Do you think you can do all that?"

"Yes, I do have experience along those lines," Alice smiled. Then she briefly related the story about the flu epidemic in Bridal Veil. "That's just one of many stories I could tell you; and I have seven children, so I often had to handle them while quite pregnant."

Teresa stopped in her tracks; she was shocked. "Was there no doctor available?"

"The towns were too small and remote to support one at the time."

"It's obvious from your application that you are quite knowledgeable. Where did you train?"

"In Illinois, where I grew up."

"I was born in Illinois too! What town are you from?"

"Lynnville; on my great uncle's plantation. He had an extensive library and an on-site school. The house isn't there anymore. It burned down about twenty-five years ago."

"I can't believe it! Does the name Imelda Beebe mean anything to you?"

This time it was Alice who was surprised. "Yes, she is my father's cousin. You wouldn't happen to be her daughter, would you?"

"Yes I am. So you're the famous Mary Alice that I heard about, growing up!"

Alice blushed. "How funny is that?" two cousins crossed the country and landed in the same place! It's a small world isn't it?"

"It surely is," Teresa said as she gave Alice a hug. "Mother will be thrilled to hear that we've found each other!" Then she glanced at her watch. "I have to get back to work now, but if you'll have lunch with me, I'd love to hear all about your family and life here in Oregon."

"I'd like to hear about your family and how you ended up here, as well."

Alice and Teresa became close friends after that. Teresa picked up Alice on her way to work every morning, as it was only about a mile out of her way.

Alice proved herself by settling into her new position quickly. She screened candidates for the midwife program, held classes for the mothers-to-be, and had clients outside the hospital as well as in. As time went on, women started asking for her. If they lived close to her home or the hospital, she could oblige them. If not, they were matched up with other midwives, according to their locations and personalities.

Clients had the option of delivering their babies with a midwife in or out of the hospital, providing they weren't high-risk, and were counseled on nutrition, exercise and infant care. It wasn't unusual for Alice's clients to ask for her advice about other medical problems, when she saw them for appointments. If they were simple matters, or if they were using the midwife program because they couldn't afford a doctor, she would advise and sometimes treat them.

One example of this, was when the daughter of her neighbors, named Pete and Elsie Dressler fell ill. They were immigrants from Austria and had little money and no family doctor. They didn't own the farm, but were working it for the owner, who was out-of-state for an extended period of time. The farm's owner had introduced them to Albert and Ilda before he departed, earlier that spring.

Albert had knocked on Alice's bedroom door, early one cool autumn morning, and announced that Pete was asking for assistance for their daughter, who was having trouble breathing. Alice quickly got dressed and packed her medicine bag.

They climbed aboard the waiting wagon, and raced to the neighbors' farmhouse. It only took Alice a few moments to determine that the child was suffering from croup. She bundled her up and took her outside for some fresh, cool, moist air. Within a few minutes, her breathing improved markedly. Alice turned her over to her father and followed Elsie into the kitchen, where she gave her some herbs from her bag and instructions on how to use them. "As long as you follow my instructions, she should recover within a few days. Don't hesitate to call on me again if she doesn't improve."

"Ya, dis I vill do. Tank you so much," she replied in her thick German accent.

A few days later, the young family came over to see Alice. They brought fresh produce from their garden, and German pastries with them.

"No money ve haff to pay you for our leetle girl safing, but dis ve do haff," Pete offered humbly, as he handed over the basket. "Goot to us, Got has been since to America ve come. Tank you for his vessel being."

A week before Christmas, Pete came over and invited them all over for Christmas Eve dinner. "Ze rest of our family, ve vant dat you should meet."

"Thank you so much. We'd be honored. May we bring something to contribute to the dinner?" Ilda asked.

"If you vant, but not necessary. Plenty food ve haff. Old family recipes Elsie and her sisters cook."

"We have some of our own that we can share with you," Ilda replied.

Carsie came to the farmhouse after work on the 23rd, and spent the night. After breakfast the next day, Alice, Grace and Ilda got busy cooking some dishes to contribute to their neighbors' feast. When they finished, they changed clothes, while the men got the children and the wagon ready.

As they drove up to the Dressler's farmhouse, they noted one car and two wagons out front. As they pulled to a halt, Pete came out to greet them. "Vilcomen!"

He ushered them into the front room, where he introduced them to his brothers-in-law, John and Carl Bauer and his cousin Henry. The women went into the kitchen, where they found Elsie and two other young women, whom she introduced as her sisters, Caroline and Rose. "It's nice to meet you," Alice, Grace and Ercyline said, as they presented their contributions to the feast.

Elsie was the oldest, and had been in the U.S. the longest. She was also very pregnant. Caroline was the youngest; still a teenager.

The rest of the Bauer family was still in Austria. Caroline was the youngest from their natural mother. After their mother died, their father had married a widow with three children of her own. Together, they had three more, bringing the total to eleven. They had all grown up with little more than love, hard work and faith, just like the Waldens.

Meanwhile, in the living room, the men and children were getting acquainted.

Doley had an instant crush on the tall, handsome John, but she was a very plain young girl, and he was ten years older than she. He and Carl, had only left their homeland two years prior, and had lived in New York until recently. Henry and Caroline had come straight from their homeland to travel to Oregon with John and Carl. They were all frequent visitor to the farm. Doley took advantage of every opportunity to be near John, which he found to be very annoying for several years.

As they ate the meal, they all got better acquainted. Through the course of conversation, the Waldens found out that the name Bauer meant farmer, which is what they had been all their lives. They told stories about their home in Austria, which was made of stones and mortar, with a large central fireplace. The sides and back of the fireplace had sleeping shelves built into them, to keep them all warm on cold winter nights. It was not unusual for them to have deep winter snows, so they had a sleigh for winter transport. They told them how they grew cabbages and pickled them whole, to make the cabbage rolls, which were part of that night's meal.

The Waldens told them stories about the gingerbread house, Ka-Teen ha, Tucker and the moonshine, and the log cabin that Frank Sr. had built for them on the reservation.

They reveled in the new taste experiences, and shared laughter and Christmas stories, then exchanged recipes before parting.

Ten weeks after Christmas, on a Saturday, Elsie went into labor, late in the evening. Several hours later, Caroline, who had been staying with them, got worried, because her sister wasn't making any progress with the delivery. So she sent Pete to fetch Alice.

It was two o'clock in the morning when Ilda woke her. "Mama, Mama, wake-up Mama. Elsie needs you."

"Is she in labor?"

"Yes. She didn't think she'd need you, but they are getting worried now."

By this time Alice had her shoes on and was reaching for her robe. "Ooh, it's cold in here!"

"Really! I hadn't noticed," Ilda said sarcastically, as she stood there hugging herself and shivering. "The fire went out. Albert is tending to it. If you don't need me, I'll go back to bed where it's warm."

"Go ahead-Caroline and Pete will be there to help me, if I need any."

Ilda checked on the children, adding blankets where needed, then climbed into her own bed. She barely had time to get comfortable before Albert joined her. "Before we go back to sleep, I think we should say a prayer for Elsie and Mama," she murmured.

"I agree-that's what I was doing the whole time I was stoking the fire."

Alice didn't bother with her coat. She took the quilt off of her bed to keep her warm on the eighth of a mile trip to the Dressler's home. She went down the stairs and found Pete warming himself by the fire.

"Sorry in the meeddle of a cold night to vake you," he apologized. "Trouble before, Elsie neffer had. A hard time she is haffing wiff diss one."

They went out the front door and were nearly blown off their feet by an icy north wind. "Feels like we're in for a storm!" Alice had to shout to be heard.

He mounted the wagon and helped her up. "Homesick for Austria, it makes me!" he shouted back with a grin.

Alice prayed on the way to their house. When she entered her neighbors' home, she put the quilt on the chair by the front door, and paused to warm her hands at the fireplace. Pete handed Alice her valise. Then she quickly mounted the stairs and followed the familiar sounds of a distressed labor.

"So glad you could come, I am." Caroline was obviously more distressed than her sister.

Alice went to the bathroom and washed her hands, then hurried to Elsie's bedside. She sat on the bed and put her examination gloves on and lubricated them. "Now, let's see if we can fix the problem."

She examined Elsie and listened to the baby's heartbeat. "The problem is that you have two babies vying for first-birth rights, just like Rebecca in the Bible," she told Elsie.

"Two der ver, two munss ago, de doctor said. But a problem, he didn't sink it vould be."

"Normally, it wouldn't be-especially since you had two children before, with no complications," Alice replied.

Elsie was seized with another contraction just then.

"Try to relax and not push until I tell you to. Take short, quick breaths... That's it."

When the contraction was over, Alice told her, "This is going to hurt, but I have to push one of them back in. Go ahead and scream if you need to."

When Caroline heard that, she left the room crying.

"Young and tender-hearted she iss," Elsie explained. Then she took a deep breath and grabbed her pillow tightly with both hands. "Ready, I am."

She uttered a muffled scream between clenched teeth as Alice grasped the protruding leg with her right hand and pushed it in. She held it in place from the outside with her left hand, and deftly maneuvered the second twin's head into position. Then she removed her right hand and kneeled on the bed to push on Elsie's abdomen with both hands to make sure they stayed in position. "Here comes another contraction-go ahead and push."

Just then Pete knocked on the open door, "Any help do you need?"

"Yes, go wash your hands and hurry back," Alice replied. When he returned, she instructed him to stand close by. A few minutes later, the first baby was born. He was a little small and thin. She suctioned his mouth and nose, but only had time to put one clamp on the cord before his even smaller sister arrived. She was bluish in color and limp. While Alice tried to revive the baby, she directed Pete to finish with the first infant, who was starting to cry.

Elsie was upset and had raised herself up to see what was going on. She was torn between wanting to hold her new son and worrying about his sister. Alice tried everything she knew to do, but it was no use-it was obvious that the baby girl was dead.

Pete had swaddled his son and was concentrating on him to try to control his emotions. Alice bit her lip to hold back her own tears as she cut the baby's cord and wrapped her.

Elsie reached for the dead baby and cuddled her close.

Alice cleaned up the bed and disposed of the afterbirths before leaving the couple alone with the babies. She went downstairs and found Caroline in the kitchen.

She had kept herself busy cooking a breakfast feast to help calm her nerves. It was five o'clock and she had just loaded a huge platter with potato pancakes, sausage links and eggs.

"Sitten ze down und eat," she said, avoiding eye contact with Alice.

"Thank you. I think I will. Elsie was very brave and strong. One of the babies, a boy, is doing fine, but the little girl didn't survive."

Caroline gave a plate and silverware to Alice, then reached for a cup. "Coffee? she said with a quaver in her voice.

"There's no need to be embarrassed," Alice said as she gave Caroline a little hug. "I've seen grown men faint at the sight of blood and cry like little babies when their wives are in pain. Yes, I could use a cup right now."

Caroline used her handkerchief, then poured the coffee.

After Pete comforted Elsie, he gave her the live infant and took away the dead one.

After breakfast, he took Alice back home. The sun was up by then and the storm had died down, so the return trip wasn't as cold.

When she came through the door, Ercyline peeked out of the kitchen, took one look at her and said, "You look like something the cat drug in, Alice. How did it go at the Dresslers'? Have you eaten yet?"

"Thanks a lot; I feel just like that. Elsie is doing fine, but one of the twins didn't make it. Caroline cooked up a feast while I was upstairs. I ate there.

"Now all I want to do is go back to bed. You'll have to give my apologies to pastor Parks. I would simply sleep through the sermon anyway. Please ask everyone to pray for Elsie and Pete when you get to church."

She met Doley on the stairs, with Faye in tow. "Have you eaten already?" She asked her mother.

"Yes, I just got home from delivering Elsie's twins. I ate there. I'm going back to bed now."

"Aren't you going to church," Doley asked her.

"Not today; I'm just too tired. You can tell me all about it after you get back."

"Sleep well, Mama."

Chapter Seven

THE ROWLEYS

Grace was preparing to teach her class of second graders one Sunday in March, 1914, when a gentleman came in with his son. "Hello ma'am, I'm Mr. Rowley and this is my son, Gerald. We call him Jerry. We just moved into the area a couple of months ago and thought it was about time to start attending church again. When my wife was alive, she made sure we attended church every Sunday. We have been remiss, I'm afraid, since then, in our church attendance."

"Good morning Mr. Rowley, welcome to our church. I'll take good care of Jerry while you're in the adult service."

Mr. Rowley was a little late picking up his son after the service, so she had some time to talk with Jerry and find out more about him. The boy was the oldest of three brothers being raised by their father alone, ever since their mother died two years prior.

When Jerry's father returned for him, he apologized, "I'm so sorry-I got involved in a discussion with your pastor."

"That's perfectly all right," she replied. "My family won't leave without me. One of us is usually holding up the parade."

Two weeks later, there was a potluck dinner at the church during which, Grace got a chance to get to know the whole family. They all seemed a little sad and lonely, so Grace made it her mission to cheer them up by inviting them-with Ilda's permission, of course-for lunch one Sunday afternoon.

The next Sunday, Grace rode to the farm with the Rowleys. While the women were fixing lunch, Albert took the boys out to the barn to see the baby animals. Faye and Doley went along too. Frank and Lafe went out to check on a section of fence that Lafe had noticed looking slightly askew, on the way home from church.

The youngest Rowley boy, Ronny, only three years old, seemed to like the kittens best. He seemed perfectly content to play with them the whole time. The middle boy, Guy Jr, whom they called Chip, was most interested in the lambs and piglets, wanting to know all about them. Jerry remained reticent, petting the dog and making sure his brothers behaved themselves and treated the animals gently.

After lunch, Alice and Ilda washed the dishes, while Ercyline and Doley took the Newman children upstairs for a nap.

Frank and Lafe took the two older boys with them, when they went to repair the fence, and check on the other animals. Carsie, Albert, Grace and Guy talked, and Ronny napped on his father's lap.

While they were sharing stories, Guy asked Grace and Carsie where they grew up, and about their father. Then told them about his wife. "It's been hard the last couple of years. We had to get out of that house-there were just too many sad memories there.

"I was working for the railroad company in Arizona and requested a transfer shortly after Lindsay died. After eight months, an opening finally came up, here in Portland. I'd been to the Pacific Northwest many years ago, and loved the area-so green and cool. So we packed up and struck out, hoping for a better life in this land of promise."

"What's Arizona like?" Carsie asked him. "I've never been outside of Oregon myself. Grace went to Seattle once, with Mama, Doley and the boys."

"There are some beautiful rivers and rock features there, such as the Colorado River, the Grand Canyon and the painted Desert, but it's mostly hot, dry and treeless-the opposite of Oregon."

Grace spoke up next. "You haven't seen Central Oregon, I take it? Parts of it are a lot like your description of Arizona."

The Rowleys got more and more involved in the church programs, and became frequent visitors to the farm. The boys became more cheerful and sociable. Before long, Guy and Grace's friendship blossomed into a romance.

One day in early May, Guy invited Grace to join his family for a day at The Oaks amusement park. They took the electric train, which was a true marvel to Grace. They had a wonderful day together.

One Saturday evening in early June, they left the boys at the farm and had a romantic dinner at a restaurant. They were just finishing their entrées when the waiter brought her a piece of cake with a surprise on top-an engagement ring! She was speechless.

"I talked it over with the boys," he said, "In fact, they suggested it first. We all love you, Grace. Will you marry us?"

"I love all of you too. Nothing would make me happier!"

They were married at their church two weeks later. Frank and Doley stood with them, as Ilda was quite pregnant again. Faye was the flower girl, Ronny was the ring bearer, and Carsie gave the bride away. Jerry and Lafe were ushers.

The color theme for the wedding was yellow and white. Naturally, Grace's dress was white; a simple knee length, cap-sleeve sheath with yellow patterned stitching and braided cord at the neck and hem. She carried yellow roses with white ribbons. Doley had a yellow dress, so didn't need a new one. She held a nosegay of white rose buds.

The men wore white shirts with dark pants. It wasn't a formal affair, by any means. They served lemon Meringue pie and fresh fruit at the reception.

The happy couple honeymooned at an inn near Bridal Veil Falls for two days, while the boys stayed with Ilda and Albert.

Grace quit her job to stay home with the boys, and make their house into a home. In the six months that the Rowley had lived there, there had been no curtains on the windows, rugs on the floors, or any other homey touches applied to the residence. She wasted no time in cleaning, painting, planting flowers, sewing curtains and pillows, and developing a menu of dishes to fit all their tastes. At least once a month, she would slip in something new and healthy in order to broaden their food repertoire. She was really in her element as a homemaker and mother.

August, that year, was warm and humid. They received just enough rain on a regular basis that summer to keep the lakes, ponds and wetlands at optimal levels. The Newmans and the Dresslers had bumper crops in their fields. The vegetable gardens and fruit trees produced more than ever before, keeping all the ladies busy canning, drying and preserving, so much so, that canning jars became scarce as hen's teeth. Cellars, hay lofts and rafters were full in all the farmhouses. Life was good.

Alice had a very busy summer. She ended up pulling extra shifts at work, because three of her midwives had to pull out of the program for various reasons, and there were several complicated cases, as well. One of those cases involved her friend Mattie.

Alice was in her office one day in March, and was pleased to see Mattie's name on one of the applications. When Mattie came in for her orientation the next week, she requested Alice as her midwife.

"I will do my best, but I can't promise anything," she told Mattie.

"I understand-it's all in the timing."

"And the complexity of the delivery," Alice added. "You're a doctor's wife and a nurse yourself-so why did you sign up for this program?"

"I'm trying to hedge my bets," Mattie replied. "As you know, I've had several tragic experiences in the past, and the one successful delivery I had was a month early.

"Alice Marie is almost 4 years old now. She's old enough to be aware of what's happening with me. It's as much for her sake that I'm taking extra precautions, hoping to benefit from your wisdom, to try to save all three of us from the heartache of another failed pregnancy."

"Well, I'm glad you're here, and I hope our new alliance will be beneficial. I'll keep you in my prayers."

"As you are in mine," Mattie sniffled, as she embraced Alice warmly.

Two months later, Mattie came into Alice's office seeking her advice, "My obstetrician is recommending medication for me, but I would rather use something natural, if at all possible. I had rather unpleasant side effects from this same medication the last time. Can you help me?"

"Sit down and tell me all about it."

After Mattie recounted her symptoms, and what the doctor had prescribed, Alice examined her. "Well, everything looks all right, except for you blood pressure. I have some herbs, diet recommendations and special exercises you can try, but have you talked to your obstetrician or Charles about this yet?"

"No, I came straight from my doctor's office."

Alice wrote down a brief description of her recommendations, and the names of the herbs she would use. Before she gave it to Mattie, she made her promise to talk to Charles and her doctor before deciding which treatment plan she would follow.

When Mattie came in for her usual midwife appointment a week later, she said that she had permission to go with Alice's treatment plan. "My doctor and Charles are both skeptical, but agreed to let me try it for a month, to see if it works better than the conventional medicine, which seemed to do as much harm as good. Maybe I can carry this baby to full-term, with your help."

Mattie followed Alice's program strictly, and did seem to do much better under her supervision and treatment plan. Her symptoms weren't eliminated entirely, but she had no side effects, so was given permission to continue with it.

On a Wednesday in early June, Alice was at work, when she was notified that Mattie was being brought in by ambulance. Alice was tending to another client, but as soon as she could, she went to see what had happened.

When she entered the emergency ward, she was informed that Mattie was in surgery. When she arrived at the waiting area, she found Charles pacing the floor, obviously upset. "Oh Alice, I'm so worried."

"What happened? She seemed to be doing so well."

"She was fine, until our friend's dog tripped her up on the way out of her house today. She said it was her own fault-that she wasn't looking where she was going. She fell down pretty hard. What will I do if she doesn't make it-if *they* don't make it?"

"I'm sure they're doing all they can. Is Alice Marie all right?"

"Yes, she's still with our friend, at her house."

Then he asked her if she would keep an eye on Mattie, while he went to the chapel to pray. "They told me to stay out of the operating room-that I would just be in the way."

After he left, Alice scrubbed up and entered the operating room. The surgeon was so intent on his task, that he seemed not to notice her arrival. Mattie was being prepped for surgery, and when she saw Alice, she reached for her. "Alice, I'm so... glad... y..." Then she was asleep and the anesthesiologist told the doctor to proceed. Alice stepped back out of the way and observed the operation, all the while praying for Mattie and her baby.

Ten minutes later, the limp, silent baby was rushed next door to be attended by a pediatric team.

Alice was torn between staying with Mattie and going next door to check on the baby. Mattie's condition was touch and go for a while. She lost a lot of blood and her uterus had to be removed because it was so damaged. She decided to stay with Mattie until the operation was over and she was taken to the recovery room.

Alice then inquired about the baby. "He is alive," the nurse told her, "That's about all I can tell you. You'll have to check with the pediatrician handling his case."

Just then, Charles entered the ward and walked up to Alice, "Is Mattie all right? Is the baby all right?"

"There was a lot of damage," Alice told him, "They had to do a hysterectomy, but I think she's going to make it. The baby is alive, but they can't tell me any more about him than that."

Charles turned to the nurse, "Which doctor's care is he under?" He wrote the information on a notepad, and gave the page to Alice, along with a note for the doctor, to fill Alice in on the baby's condition. "I'll stay here with Mattie. I don't want her to be alone when she wakes up. Would you go and see how the baby is doing, and then return and give us a report?"

"Of course. I'll be back as soon as possible," Alice replied as she spun on her heel and rushed off.

Dr. Baumgartner read the note Alice gave her, and led her into the nursery annex, where they kept fragile infants needing extra care. She approached one bassinet, whose occupant looked very small and frail. He was hooked up to oxygen and an intravenous tube.

She looked at the patient chart, then lowered it and sighed, "If this child survives, he won't have a normal life. He was deprived of oxygen too long. His heart and lungs are not fully developed, either. All we can do for him now is support and monitor him. The rest is up to God. I don't envy you the task of reporting this to his parents."

"Thank you, Doctor. If you are a Christian, we would appreciate your prayers."

"I am, and I will. I wish I could have given you better news."

Alice prayed as she waited in line at the cafeteria. Then she returned to Mattie's room. She peeked in the door to see if her friend was awake, yet. Charles saw her, gave Mattie a peck on the forehead, and came out to talk to Alice. "She just went back to sleep," he reported. "What did you find out about the baby?"

"I brought us both some coffee. Let's have a seat." Her mind was spinning-how to tell him? She searched his face for some clue as to how to proceed. He was a doctor, and used to giving negative diagnosis, not receiving them.

"It's not good news, I'm afraid. He's very sick. His heart and lungs aren't fully developed, and there may be brain damage as well. They are doing everything they can for him, but ultimately, it's up to God whether he lives or not."

Charles took a deep breath, closed his eyes tightly and bit his lip to control his emotions. After a moment, he let out a quavering sigh, "What am I going to do, Alice? She'll want to know, but how can I tell her?"

Alice put her arm around his shoulders. "You stay here and pray for strength and comfort. I'll go sit with Mattie. We won't tell her any more than necessary, until her doctor thinks she's strong enough, all right?"

"Okay." He grasped her hand and gave it a squeeze, "Thank you so much. I'm going to call our pastor, then go back to the chapel for a while. I'll be back when I collect myself."

Mattie's eyes fluttered open an hour later. She looked around the room, "Where's Charles," she asked Alice.

"He'll be back any minute."

"How is the baby, is he all right?"

"He's in the nursery. They're taking very good care of him. You can see him when you're feeling better."

"My belly hurts. Did they have to…?"

"Yes, I'm afraid so."

"Does Charles know, yet?"

"Yes, but what's most important to him, is that you're going to be okay. It was touch and go for a while."

Charles walked in the door, just then. Alice gave Mattie's hand a squeeze, stood up and left the two of them alone. She went to the chapel to pray:

"Dear Lord, I don't know how to pray for this baby. If he lives, they'll love him but he'll be a burden. Only you know how long he'll live and what quality of life he'll have. I know that all things work together for good to them that love you, but it's hard to imagine any good coming from this."

Two days later, Alice stopped by on her way to her office to find Mattie's bed empty. She inquired at the nurse's station and was told that Charles had taken her to the nursery. When Alice got there, she found the little family together.

"It's good to see you up and about, even if it is in a wheelchair," Alice remarked.

"She's going to be as right as rain in a couple of weeks," Charles replied, "It's this little guy that we're not too sure about. He does seem to be improving a little, though."

"Let me know if there's anything I can do to help," Alice said. "I'm on my way to work now. I'll see you again tomorrow morning."

"You're such a good friend," Mattie said as she opened her arms for a hug. "Dr. Kelly said I should be able to go home within a week. Charles' mother arrived yesterday, to take care of us while I'm recuperating."

It was two months before Little Harry was well enough to go home. He remained frail, sickly and small for his age. By the time he was six months old, it was obvious that he was mentally slow, also. No one was surprised that he was only as strong and coordinated as a healthy child of two months of age. Mattie and Charles took this in stride, and loved him all the more, as did his big sister, Alice Marie.

Autumn turned dry. They had no rain the whole month of October.

One evening in early November, ominous storm clouds gathered over them, and a cold wind blew in from the north. Everyone was looking forward to rain, but they got dry lightning instead. All the adults kept an eye out for lightning strikes as the rumbling got closer and closer. The radio station reported that there had been several lightning strikes in the area, already, two of them causing small fires.

Alice thought it would be a good idea for them to take turns keeping watch that night. "Ilda shouldn't be included, because she'll be up every few hours to feed the baby, and can check on whoever is keeping watch."

"I doubt any of us will get much sleep tonight, with all this thunder," Albert added.

"Make sure to look closely out every direction, the whole time you're on watch," Alice directed Frank, when he relieved her at midnight. Half an hour later, the whole household was awakened by a loud CERACKK!!! They jumped out of bed, expecting that something terrible had happened.

"Boy, that was close!"

"Where did it hit?"

"Is everything still in one piece?"

"I saw the flash over that way, towards the Dressler's"

"You're right. I think I see flames over there." Albert opened the door to get a better look. He smelled smoke, and confirmed what he'd seen: their barn was on fire.

"We'd better get over there as quickly as possible, to help save the house and the animals," he said as he pulled on his coat. Frank was already heading for the barn. As soon as Alice and Lafe came out, Frank and Albert had the horses hitched to the wagon, which was quickly loaded with every bucket and blanket that Doley and Ercyline could find.

It was only a few minutes from the time the fire started, until their wagon pulled into the neighbors' yard. The barn was fully engulfed in flames, and Pete was leading the cows out. The horses could be heard screaming inside. Elsie had to stay on the porch to make sure the children were safe, so she was very relieved to see her neighbors come to the rescue.

Albert and Frank ran into the barn to help get the horses out. They had to knock a wall down, to give them safe egress. Alice and Lafe used the blankets and buckets to put out spot fires, caused by flying embers. One bit of burning hay flew to the house roof. Frank saw it as he was coming around the corner of the barn, and ran up the stairs, to the window nearby, with a bucket of water. Lafe was right on Frank's heels, while Albert was helping Alice with the spot fires, and Pete was leading the animals safely away.

Just then, the sky opened up, and the rescuers all got drenched. The house was saved, but the barn and everything stored in it, were a total loss. Alice and Albert treated Pete's and his animals' burns. Thankfully none were very serious.

When a head count was taken the next morning, it was discovered that two piglets had been trampled to death, and three kittens were missing. The mother cat had burns, they supposed, from trying to save her kittens. She had managed to rescue two of them.

All their neighbors banded together, and supplied the Dresslers with feed from their surplus, and helped them put up temporary shelters for the animals, until a new barn could be built in the spring. Under normal circumstances, they would have rebuilt it right away, but the rain and wind were relentless that fall and winter.

Chapter Eight

DESTINATIONS

Tucker didn't move to Portland with the rest of the Walden family-he had a store to run. He was doing fairly well, even though Mrs. Caufield had to keep reminding him to keep his mind on his work. She did most of the customer dealings, only leaving Tucker alone when she had to tend to her husband.

Mr. Caufield had gotten so feeble that he was forced to turn the whole operation over to his wife and Tucker. Their residence was above the store, and he couldn't manage the stairs anymore. Because he was cooped up alone so much and almost completely dependent on others, he became very depressed.

He had been a pipe smoker most of his adult life, and fell asleep with his pipe lit one evening-or so it was reported. His wife was gone on a short errand, and Tucker was visiting a friend.

When Tucker turned the corner coming home that evening, his senses were assaulted by smoke, noise, crowds and firemen. As he came nearer, he saw that the store was burning. It was fully engulfed in flames. Mrs. Caufield was across the street, wailing and clinging to a friend. The firemen had already given up any hope of saving Mr. Caufield or the store, and were trying, valiantly, to save the neighboring stores and residences. They battled the fire for several hours. In the morning, Tucker and Mrs. Caufield returned, to find the store and all of its contents burned beyond recognition.

Mrs. Caufield told Tucker, in confidence, that she thought her husband had set the fire on purpose, hoping that no one else would be hurt. Tucker kept that to himself until after putting Mrs. Caufield on the train to go live with her oldest daughter and son-in-law.

Before he became incapacitated, Mr. Caufield had opened an account at the bank, to help Tucker get a new start. Tucker used some of this money to buy a horse and wagon, then headed for Portland. Mrs. Caufield received the life insurance payout.

On the afternoon of September 5th, Ilda was very surprised to see Tucker standing on her front porch when she answered his knock, "Tucker, what are you doing in Portland? Don't you have a business to run in Bridal Veil?" She stepped aside to let him in.

"Not anymore," he said, matter-of-factly, as he looked around. "The store and Mr. Caufield got burned up. I'm hungry; got anything to eat? Where is everybody?" he asked as his nose led him to the kitchen.

Ilda closed the door and followed him. "Is Mrs. Caulfield all right?"

"Yeah, she's off to live with her daughter in Iowa."

Ilda was saddened by the news that Tucker had so casually mentioned, but not too surprised at his reaction.

"I was cooking dinner when you showed up. Mama is at work, and Doley and Lafe are at school. Grandma is upstairs with the children, and Albert should be in any time now."

Faye had crept downstairs and was peering around the doorway at this stranger. Her little brother, who wasn't shy at all, came around her, toddled right up to Tucker and grabbed his leg. Tucker bent down and picked him up, "What's your name, little fella?"

"His name is Frank," Faye said as she came into the room, "but we call him Buddy. My name is Faye. What's yours?"

"This is your Uncle Tucker," Ercyline answered as she came in. "We've talked about him before. Do you remember? Tucker, it's so good to see you!" She exclaimed as she embraced him.

"He'll be staying with us for a little while; until he finds a place of his own?" Ilda directed this last part to Tucker, while she set the table and her grandmother took over at the stove.

He didn't answer, but went with the children into their bedroom, where they showed him their favorite toys and books.

When Albert came in from the field a few moments later, he asked Ilda, "Who does the wagon out front belong to?"

"It's my brother, Tucker's. He's upstairs with the children."

Then she told him what Tucker had said about the store, and his reaction to it. "It looks like he's going to be staying for a while," she said with a sigh. "He's my brother and I love him, but..." She shrugged her shoulders.

"Whoa, Tucker! Good to see you! What are you doing here?" Lafe almost collided with his brother at the bottom of the stairs. They went into the living room together, where he managed to get the whole story out of Tucker.

"So you used some of the money to buy a wagon and a horse?" Lafe asked.

"And new clothes," Tucker answered. "I lost everything in the fire- not that I had that much."

Doley and Ilda came out of the kitchen with steaming bowls of food. "Go wash up; dinner's ready."

Ercyline called after Tucker, as he followed Lafe to the washroom. "Some of you might want to wash more than just your hands!"

When they were all seated and holding hands, Albert asked Tucker to say grace for them.

Tucker paused a moment, then bowed his head and said, "Thank you for my family. Thank you for the meat. Thank you for the spuds and gravy. Good God, let's eat!"

The children giggled, Albert said "Amen," and Ercyline and Ilda gave Tucker dirty looks. Tucker didn't notice; he was focused on the food.

"Careful how much you take," Ercyline told them all. "We didn't plan on this many people for dinner when we started cooking. There's another dish in the oven, that should be ready in about ten minutes."

"And an apple pie for desert," Ilda added, "with whipped cream or cheese to put on top."

"Yum, yum!"

"I'll definitely be saving room for that!"

"Uncle Tucker can have my vegetables, if he wants," Faye volunteered.

"No, we fixed plenty of those."

"It figures."

After dinner, the children took Tucker by the hand and pulled him out to the barn to see the animals.

As soon as the dog saw Tucker, he started to bark. "Shush, Barney," Faye scolded. "He's family."

Tucker crouched down and called to the dog. In no time at all, they were best buddies. Next they introduced Tucker to their faithful mouse catcher, whiskers, then their horse, Dotty, and cows, Blanche and Gertrude. "We didn't name the pigs or the chickens," Faye told him. "Daddy said not to get attached, because they'll end up on the dinner table someday. The pigs stink too much anyway. So do the sheep. We don't eat them, usually. Papa sells their wool and milk, just like he sells the cows' milk that we don't use."

When Alice came home three hours later, Tucker was already asleep on the sofa.

Tucker had finally found his calling. He wasn't much of a farmer, but seemed to have a way with animals, and got along with them much better than he did with people. When the rest of the family went to church on Sundays, Tucker usually stayed behind to keep an eye on things.

Ilda presented Albert with another baby girl a month after Tucker moved in. They named her Elsie May. She was a pretty baby, but colicky. Ilda and Ercyline spent many nights walking the floor with her the first month or so. Because of this, Tucker moved to the barn loft, until Ilda and Alice discovered, through trial and error, that the baby did much better on goat's milk.

In order to help avoid getting pregnant again right away, Ilda donated her breast milk to the hospital's maternity clinic for as long as she could. She would pump it several times a day, store it in the ice box and send it to the hospital with her mother. This would become a very important service that she, her sisters and the Bauer women would carry out whenever possible, especially in the desperate years to come.

During breakfast one Saturday morning in early November, 1914, after a particularly hard work week, Alice announced, "This commuting into Portland every day is getting old. And I love you all, but it's hard to get a good night's sleep or a much-needed nap in a house full of people, especially rambunctious little ones. Teresa told me of a bungalow near the hospital, coming available soon, that I can move into."

Everyone started talking at once.

"How big is this place?"

"Will you be living there all by yourself?"

"Are you sure you can afford it?"

"Don't go, Grandma!"

Alice stood up to shush everyone, "I've made up my mind," she stated, in a tone that defied anyone to argue with her. "I've already signed the lease and put a deposit down. I can move in at the beginning of the month."

"We'll all miss you terribly between visits," Ercyline said, "but I suppose you're right. I've noticed how tired you've been lately, and how you hate the winter commutes, especially."

Everyone pitched in to help Alice move into her new home on December first. It was a quaint little house-just big enough for one or two people, and within easy walking distance of the hospital. She missed her family during the week, but appreciated the peace and quiet, save for occasional sirens and such of the city.

In no time at all she had the little house looking like home, with colorful curtains, pillows and rag rugs in nearly every room, and herbs and flowers lining her south and west-facing window sills. She talked Tucker and Lafe into preparing a garden bed for the next spring.

Carsie started picking her up on Sunday mornings, for church services, and then to the farm or the Rowley's for the rest of the day.

Just after midnight on February 26, 1915, Ilda heard the baby crying, but had to use the water closet before tending to her. She was reaching for the doorknob to exit the WC, when she heard a scream and a series of thumps. Albert, Lafe and Doley came bursting out of their bedrooms to investigate.

They all rushed to her side. The baby was all but forgotten, when they found Ercyline unconscious at the bottom of the stairs. Her arms and legs were splayed at odd angles, and blood was trickling from her mouth and ears. They moved her gently onto the couch, and then Doley was sent to tend to the baby.

In her distress, Ilda couldn't think of what her mother would do in such a situation. Albert and Lafe went out to the barn to hitch the horses to the wagon.

Ercyline was taken to the hospital, where she was diagnosed with internal injuries and countless broken bones, including two skull fractures. She never regained consciousness, and passed away a few days later.

The ground was frozen, so her body was cremated, and her ashes put in an urn, to be buried in Bridal Veil on Easter weekend.

The day before Easter, Albert and Guy stayed behind to care for the farm and the youngest children, while the rest of the family traveled to Bridal Veil for the funeral. Her ashes were buried with Ernest, in the Bridal Veil Cemetery,

John had been working in a bicycle shop, owned by a Polish immigrant. He had been saving his money, and bought the shop from the owner's widow, upon his death.

Just after harvest time that same year, Pete and Elsie's landlord returned from his travels and sold the farm. Pete landed a good job and moved his family to Beaverton, Oregon.

Doley had been spending as much time as possible at the Dressler farm, hoping to get closer to John, as he was a frequent visitor, along with the rest of the Bauer clan. Once the Dresslers moved, this became impossible. In order to continue her close friendship with the Bauer clan, she convinced Alice to let her move in with her.

"Faye is old enough now to help with the new baby, and Tucker is real good with little Frank. Besides I'm getting too old to go to school smelling like horses and pigs," she reasoned with her mother.

By this time, she was starting to develop into a young lady, and John wasn't finding her so much of a pest anymore. It was a short bus ride from her school to his shop. The grocery store that they frequented was also one block away, and she found excuses to go there after school and on weekends, so she could stop and visit with him. She did her best to make herself useful, and he found himself relying on her math and people skills, more and more.

In April, 1915, she hatched the idea to give Alice a special Mother's Day gift. She had read an article in the newspaper about a woman named Hulda Klager in Woodland Washington, about twenty-five miles north of Portland, who had a beautiful garden on her farm, featuring lilacs, some of which were cultivars that she had developed herself. She and her family and friends had been working very hard to restore it ever since it was flooded by the Lewis River a year and a half earlier.

It had become a tradition for her to open her gardens, at no charge, to the public every spring, when the lilacs were blooming. People came from far away to tour her gardens every year, taking in the sights and scents, learning about gardening in general and lilac breeding in particular and sharing lemonade on the front porch with this amazing, self-taught woman and her family. Doley plotted with her siblings to surprise Alice with a visit to the garden.

Carsie had purchased an automobile a couple of years before. Daniel had one, also, and volunteered to drive.

On Mother's Day, it wasn't unusual for the whole family, including Tucker, to attend church services with Alice. When she exited the church that Sunday, she was surprised to see the Bauer clan drive up; the children piling out of the cars as soon as they stopped. They had three picnic baskets, and gave one of the baskets to Alice.

"What's all this about?" she asked.

"It's a surprise," Doley answered, as Tucker pulled up in the wagon. "Tucker, Pete, Guy and Albert will take the children to the farm, or fishing for the day. We're taking a road trip!"

"A road trip, to where?"

"You'll see when we get there!" Carsie replied with a grin. "Hop in, we're burning daylight!"

Doley arranged to sit with John in Carl's rumble seat for the trip. Seven-month-old Elsie May and three-month-old Elizabeth Dressler came along, too, as they were both still breast-feeding.

They ate lunch and sang hymns and silly songs on the way. When they crossed the Columbia Bridge, Alice was beside herself with curiosity. "Won't you give me a hint, at least?" she pleaded. Everyone just grinned and kept on singing.

Then the cars left the main road and started down a country lane, between the railroad tracks and the Lewis River dike. Alice breathed deeply, "What is that heavenly fragrance, is that lilacs?" Then she saw a line of cars parked along the fence. "What in the world?" Then the sign, KLAGER LILAC GARDEN.

"Oh, what a wonderful surprise!" Alice couldn't believe her eyes. There were dozens of people walking down the road and streaming in the gate, and many more strolling around the grounds. They had to park almost a quarter of a mile away-there were so many cars crowded onto the narrow lane.

It was the most wonderful Mother's Day that Alice had ever experienced. She got to tour the garden with Mrs. Klager herself, while the men watched the babies or talked with Hulda's husband, Frank. The farmers among them, were definitely interested in the science of the garden, if not the flowers themselves.

There was also a large vegetable garden and an orchard on the farm. John and Alice were interested to learn how she had developed her own apple cultivar, as well as several daffodil varieties and fourteen different lilacs.

Hulda told them she had started with daffodils and other flowers, then started on the apples, because she wasn't happy with the ones she had. "The flesh was too soft and the skins were too tough," she told them. "I didn't plan the lilacs-the first ones were a gift from my children. One thing led to another and," she spread her arms, "it developed into this!"

"You must have a lot of help to keep this all going," Alice remarked. "Do you open to the public every year?"

"We have a small army of family, students that we board, and bucket boys to do the watering. And no, we had some flooding a year and half ago, and spent all last year cleaning up the debris, replanting and restoring what was damaged or lost. We had the foresight and the manpower, thank God, to lift the lilacs and put them on rafts tied to trees, to save them from the river."

"That's very inventive-where did you learn to do that?"

"From experience, living thirty years on a floodplain. The soil is excellent here, but we are between two rivers that flood every few years. When they put the railroad tracks in on the Columbia side a few years ago, and planned a dike on the Lewis River side, we thought our worries were over. The dike came one year too late."

Rose's new husband, Daniel sneezed almost the whole time they were there, "I must be allergic to lilacs," he sniffled.

After their tour, they congregated on the porch and were served lemonade and cookies, while they rested. As they were leaving, they saw a sign next to a bucket. "Free lilac starts," they read, and noticed a can, half full of coins on the fence post. They dropped some coins in the can, and selected six lilac cuttings to take home.

They ate at a diner in Woodland while they talked about the day's adventure:

"Tank you for asking mit you to come. A wonderful time ve had, ya?"

"Vunderbar!"

"Ya, danka!"

"Achoo, sniffle, very nice"

"Hahaha"

"Did you know that her husband is a dairy farmer?"

"German immigrants dey are."

"She developed all those new colors and scents through trial and error."

"Can you believe that she uses a turkey feather or a paintbrush to selectively pollinate the flowers?"

"She must be very patient woman."

"Und a hard vorker."

"Yes, and her husband must be very devoted to her."

"Dat he iss. Two cows he sold to buy for her, plants from France."

They got home rather late, and all of the children, Tucker and Albert were already asleep. Before collecting their boys, Grace and Guy sat down with the others for a cup of coffee and a cookie offered by Ilda. Before serving anyone, Ilda stood before them holding the tray, "Out with it," she said to Grace, who blushed.

"We have good news," Guy said.

"I bet I know what it is!" Doley exclaimed.

"I thought I noticed a special glow about you," Alice added.

"A baby?"

"Congratulations!"

"When?"

"Do the boys know?"

"Whoa, one at a time!" Guy exclaimed, then turned to Grace. "You tell them, dear."

"The Doctor estimates the middle of November. We didn't tell the boys, yet-we wanted to surprise you on Mother's Day, and were afraid they'd spill the beans."

"This is one Mother's Day I'll never forget!" Alice exclaimed, as she hugged Grace and Doley.

Ilda and Grace each planted one lilac starts on either side of their front porch. Alice planted hers on either side of her front gate. Several years later, Alice would discover one of Hulda's Apple cultivars at the local grocer.

Frank was very bright and had always gotten good grades in school. In this, his senior year, he was faced with new challenges, but not the kind that he was used to. His social studies teacher, a Mr. Frost, took an instant disliking to Frank. The man was an unapologetic atheist, and Frank was equally enthusiastic about his faith in God.

Frank had been a favorite of many of his teachers when he was younger, because of his honesty and helpfulness. He didn't know what to do about Mr. Frost. The man seemed to go out of his way to make everything as difficult as possible for poor Frank. He treated good students decently, but played favorites with popular students whose parents had money and influence. The underachievers and the poor, he treated with disdain; calling them lazy and stupid.

Mr. Frost had given his students an assignment; to write an essay about the slave trade and its impact on our society and then to present it to the class in oral form after his perusal. Frank's paper was heavy with scripture quotes, pity for the victims and condemnation for the slave traders. The day after he turned it in, he was asked to stay after class. He stood before Mr. Frost's desk waiting for his onslaught.

The teacher sat with his hands clasped and his head down; chin on thumbs. Then he peered over his glasses at Frank. "Young man, I've had enough of your proselytizing. This is a social studies class not a Bible study."

He picked up the report and tore it in two. Then he stood and leaned on the desk, so that his face was inches from Frank's. Between clenched teeth, he growled, "Either you rewrite this with *no* reference to the Scriptures, or I will flunk you from this class." Then he sat down and dismissed Frank, with a flick of his wrist.

Alice and Frank met with the school counselor a couple of days later, to try to get him into a different class, but was told that it wasn't possible.

"There is only one other teacher in the school, who teaches that course," she told them, "and her classes are already full in all the time slots available to Frank's schedule. If he had another year to go, he could sign up for Mrs. Foster's class next year, but Frank needs this credit in order to graduate. I'm sorry."

"What should I do?" he asked Alice on the way home, "I was taught to respect my elders, but also, not to compromise my faith for any reason or anyone. I've done my best to do both. But I've never been faced with such a stubborn, godless teacher before."

"I can't make that decision for you, son. Continue to pray about it, and follow your heart. Remember that God can bring a good result from any situation, if you will keep your mind and eyes on him."

Mr. Frost wasn't Frank's only problem, though: Mr. Bailey, the new coach, and boys' physical education teacher, had a favorite; the center on the football team, who could do no wrong in his eyes. They were both bullies and overachievers, who insisted that all the other boys be as aggressive as they were.

Frank was a good athlete, but a pacifist; wanting only to have fun and get some exercise on the playing field. He believed in playing fair. All Mr. Bailey and the jock wanted was to mold everyone else into their images and win games.

It wasn't unusual for Frank to come home from school with bruises from Bruce's and others' elbows, knees and equipment strikes. The other boys got them, also, but Frank especially.

One day, Alice got a call from the school nurse, informing her that Frank had been brought in for a blow to the head, which had rendered him unconscious for a few minutes.

Frank was awake when Alice arrived at the school, but he had a knot on his temple and a black eye.

"What happened?" she asked him.

"I'm not sure," he answered. "We were playing soccer, and I was running down the field with all the others. Then I woke up here with a nasty headache."

When he tried to sit up, he found that his wrist was painful, as well. She took him to the hospital, where a doctor examined it and sent him for an x-ray. They were relieved to hear that it wasn't broken.

Alice took him home for the night in order to keep an eye on him, in spite of his objections that he would be just fine.

At his first convenience, Frank talked to Guy privately, about getting a job with the railroad. "I'll do anything they want me to do," he told him. "Will you put in a good word for me?"

"Of course I will," Guy answered. "Are you looking to start after you finish school? That's still six months away."

"No, I'm ready right now. I have two teachers who hate my guts, and I can't get away from them. They're making my life miserable."

"What does your mother think about this?"

"She says I'm old enough to make my own decisions. Besides, you, Carsie and John didn't finish school, and you're all doing okay."

Two weeks later, Frank dropped out of school and started his new job as a janitor and messenger boy at the railroad station. When he got offered a better position, on the same schedule as Guy a few months later, he moved in with the Rowleys. He did a very good job; gaining the respect of his boss and fellow workers, although some thought he was daft or annoying for his beliefs. Just like his brothers, he never went back to school, but prospered, as long as he kept his heart tuned to his Savior's voice.

Chapter Nine

DIVINE INTERVENTION

In the autumn of 1915, the newspapers reported that Germany was amassing a huge army and weapons of war, and had invaded Poland. Rumors and speculations about their intentions and next possible target was the main topic of conversation everywhere Alice went and on the front page of every newspaper she saw.

Hot on the heels of the war news, was that of a flu epidemic spreading across Europe, claiming many more lives.

The Waldens' pastor called for extra prayers and scheduled special meetings once a week to pray for victims and their families of both the war and the epidemic.

"Brothers and sisters," he said from the pulpit, "Europe is in a bad way right now, and it will probably get much worse before it gets better. We need to pray for them-for the victims and for the German military personnel, also."

Several people gasped at this last comment, and a murmur arose in the congregation.

He paused a moment, waiting for his flock to quiet down, then continued, "I know that this is not something that comes naturally to us, but Jesus told us to pray for our enemies. We need to pray that they will see the error of their ways and turn to him. Satan and his minions are hard at work, so we must be, too. Most of all, pray that the war and the flu epidemic will end soon."

The whole family was in a somber mood the rest of the week-in fact, it was as if there was a black cloud hanging over the whole country.

On December first, the Waldens' spirits rose when Grace gave birth to a nine-pound baby girl, whom they named Ercyline Rose.

Guy had come knocking on Alice's door as she was starting to prepare for bed. Normally, she would have been asleep three hours earlier, but she had dozed off while knitting a sweater for the baby, after a stressful day at work.

She knew exactly what to expect when she opened the door. "Come on in while I collect my bag and shoes."

He took her coat off the rack and helped her put it on.

"How long ago did her contractions start?" she asked him as they went out to the car.

"Not long; maybe half an hour; just long enough to determine that it wasn't another false alarm."

"Is someone with her?"

"Yes, I woke Jerry before I left. I hope the baby holds off until we get there. I understand that you delivered most of your children very fast."

"If she takes after me, Jerry will have quite a story to tell his family and friends."

Fortunately, Grace wasn't quite as efficient as her mother and sister. Jerry was happy to turn over the reins to Alice, after reporting his timing of Grace's contractions.

Guy, who had delivered his youngest son, stayed with Grace and Alice, while Jerry went to the kitchen. He was too wound up and nervous to sleep.

He had been up, studying for a test the next day, and had gone to sleep half an hour before his father woke him. He was concerned for Grace, knowing that this was her first birth, and that she might deliver before his grandmother arrived. He had seen puppies and lambs being born, and knew that problems could arise, which he wouldn't know how to handle.

He was also concerned that he would fail his test and/or doze off in history class. He was a good student, but struggled with math and science. He did well in art, English and grammar. The test he'd been studying for was in math class.

He didn't have long to wait. He was drinking a glass of milk when the baby's cry startled him, so that he spilled milk down the front of his pajamas. He had pulled the dish towel off the stove handle and was drying off, when his father came out of the bedroom. "It's a girl," he told him.

"And Grace; is she okay, too?"

"She's just fine. Do you want to visit before you go back to bed?"

"Uh, huh," Jerry nodded as he mopped up the milk on the table.

"Your grandma said she'll be ready in a few minutes. I see you spilled your milk. Why don't you change while you're waiting?"

While Jerry was changing, Ronny and Chip came out of their room, rubbing their eyes. "We heard a baby crying," Chip said.

"You have a baby sister." Guy told them. "But you'll have to wait your turn. Jerry gets to meet her first."

Jerry came out of his room as Alice exited the master bedroom. "They're ready for visitors now; only one at a time, except for Papa."

Alice prepared a bottle of sterilized sugar water for the baby, while the boys were meeting their new sister. She knew that no one would get any rest until Grace's milk started to flow. The baby was getting her mother's colostrum, or first milk, but it wouldn't satisfy her hunger for long.

By the time the boys went back to bed, Alice had the bottle filled and partially cooled. She took it in to Grace. Guy took the bottle and placed it on the side table. "The baby's asleep right now. It'll keep until she wakes, won't it?"

"Yes. It's much too warm right now. It should be about the right temperature when the baby is ready for it.

"I'll need to examine you both once more before I go home," she told Grace. "Or I could stay and nap on the sofa and go home later."

"I'm beat," Guy replied, "and I have to go to work in a few hours. My backup man came down with the shingles last week. I could drop you off on my way to work."

On March 18, 1916, Alice was walking home from the bus stop with a bag of groceries when she noticed a girl, perhaps fifteen or sixteen, standing in the doorway of a bakery. She looked hungry, frightened and cold. Alice stopped on the other side of the doorway, being careful not to get too close or look directly at the girl. She waited a minute to see if the girl would speak to her. She did not, but her gaze swung between the bakery counter and Alice's groceries.

Without turning her head, but her eyes only, Alice asked, "You're hungry aren't you?"

"Yes ma'am," The girl answered, shyly and quietly.

"Do you have nowhere to stay-no one to take care of you?"

"No, ma'am."

Alice turned to face her, then noticed that the girl appeared to be pregnant. "I have a daughter about your age. I live only two blocks away. Why don't you come home with me for a hot meal and a bath, at least?"

"You don't know me. Why would you help me?" Now she was staring intently at Alice's grocery bag.

Alice pulled an apple out of the bag and held it out to the girl, "Because it's the Christian thing to do. You can't stay on the streets in your condition."

The girl blushed and lowered her gaze, "Thank you-I *am* hungry and cold." She took the apple from Alice, with both hands, and bit into it greedily. Alice put her arm around the girl's shoulders and led her to her home.

When they walked in the door a few minutes later, Doley was at the stove, and the table was already set for two. When she saw the girl, she said not a word, but got out another place service and started fixing more food.

Alice showed Linda to the restroom, so she could wash up. Then she washed her hands at the kitchen sink and told Doley about Linda's situation.

"After dinner, while she's in the bathtub, I'll make up the couch while you wash the dishes, and then we'll find her some clean clothes."

"I think I have some warm clothes that would fit her, Mama. We might have to make some maternity clothes for her, if she stays very long, though. How long do you think she'll be staying?"

"I don't know, honey-we'll cross that bridge when we get to it."

After a long, hot bath, a good night's sleep and a couple of good meals, Linda was feeling more like herself, and her trust and gratitude toward Alice and Doley caused her shyness to melt away, so that she opened up to them-revealing her whole, sad story.

"My mother died six years ago, when I was only nine and my brother was fourteen. Daddy took to drinking heavy, I suppose, to try to kill the pain of Mama's death. He was hardly ever home, and then he was sleeping. My brother had to get a second job in order to support us, because Daddy lost his job.

"With Daddy drunk all the time and my brother working, I got terribly lonely and depressed and took up the company of our preacher's son a couple years ago. We got real close, and one thing led to another...

"I figured out that I was pregnant about two months ago. I told Daddy last week, when he was nearly sober. He got mad, called me some horrible names and told me to pack a bag and be gone when he got home. Then he stormed out the door.

"I love Mike too much to put him and his father through the shame they'd face, once people found out. My brother gave me some money for bus fare and a hotel room for a couple of nights."

"What did you tell him and Mike?" Alice asked. "Surely they would have done more for you if they knew the whole story."

"I told them that I had a friend in Portland who had offered me a job."

"So they don't know about the baby then?" Doley asked her.

"No-it isn't my brother's problem. Besides, I wasn't thinking straight, I guess."

"You can stay with us until we find a better arrangement for you," Alice said as she patted her hand.

Linda stayed at the house, while Alice and Doley went to work and school. She puttered in the garden, pitched in on the housework and made clothes for herself and the baby. She had learned how to do all these things, out of necessity, after her mother died, she told them.

Alice called in a favor, and a week after Linda's arrival, she got some surprise visitors.

They had just finished eating lunch on Saturday, when Mattie and Charles came to visit.

Linda started heading for the bedroom when she heard their knock, but Alice stopped her, "No, stay here. I hope you don't mind-I asked this couple here to see you."

Linda sat back down, uneasily, on the kitchen chair, as Alice let her friends in, "Mattie, Charles, Sweet Pea, come on in." Then she bent down and addressed Little Harry in his stroller, "And how are you, young man?"

The little boy smiled, flapped his arms and gurgled at her.

Alice closed the door behind them and turned to face the teenager, "Linda, this is my old friend, Mattie, her husband, Charles and their children."

Linda stood and shyly shook the hands that were offered to her. "We're pleased to meet you, Linda," Charles and Mattie both said.

It was a nice day, so Doley took the children out to the yard, while the others talked in the living room.

Alice sat facing Linda, pulling her chair close, "Charles is a doctor and Mattie is a nurse. I hope you don't mind, but I told them about you, and that you had received no prenatal care, as yet."

Linda's countenance changed from uneasiness to near panic, "I can't afford a doctor!"

Mattie quickly reassured her. "We owe Alice a debt of gratitude. Many years ago, when I was about your age or a little younger, I was in a situation not much different from yours, when she rescued me and turned my life around."

"Alice is concerned about your health and your baby's," Charles pitched in. "When you're comfortable with the idea, I'd like to examine you to make sure everything is progressing properly. I'm not an obstetrician, but I know what to look for. And Alice, being a midwife and nurse herself, knows just how important it is."

"Would I have to come to your clinic, or could you do it here?" Linda asked him.

"In this setting, Alice could probably do as good a job as I, but because of your circumstances and age, I would like you to come to my office for a more thorough exam."

"Would you stay with me during the exam, Alice?"

"Of course, dear," Alice said as she squeezed her hand. Then she turned to Charles. "When can you fit us in?"

"My first appointment is at nine. Can you be in early Monday, say 8 o'clock?"

They spent the afternoon playing with the children and getting to know each other better. Linda fell in love with Little Harry. She asked Alice about him after they left, and expressed genuine compassion for the family.

Monday dawned cold and wet. Linda was nervous about being seen in public, but relieved to have an excuse to hide her swollen belly under bulky clothes. When they got to the hospital, the woman at the front desk greeted Alice in the usual manner and nodded at Linda.

The janitor also, leaving for home, did the same, and merely smiled at Linda.

Alice stayed with Linda and held her hand during the exam. Charles was as gentle with Linda as with a newborn baby. When the examination was completed, he instructed them to meet him next door in his office when they were ready.

"Everything appears to be fine, but we won't know for sure until the lab results come back," he told them, "I should have them by the end of the week. Would you like to come to our house for dinner on Friday night-all three of you? We'll discuss the test results and any recommendations I may have."

"Doley may already have plans for Friday night," Alice replied, "but I should be available." They both looked at Linda, who smiled and nodded.

On Friday afternoon, when Charles left his office, Alice and Linda were waiting for him. He led the way to his car and drove them to his home. Mattie was just putting dinner on the table as they walked in the door.

"I hope you like ham, green beans and scalloped potatoes," she said, "I know it's Charles' favorite. I fix it for him every Friday night, and he never tires of it."

Linda started to cry.

"What's wrong, honey," Alice asked as she gathered her into her arms.

"That's the same meal that my brother always asked Mom to fix for his birthday."

"You must miss them very much," Mattie commiserated.

"Let's sit down and eat before the food gets cold," Charles said as he passed Linda his handkerchief. "I'm hungry. I don't know about you!" He smiled at Linda and then seated her at the table.

"Aren't the children going to eat with us?" Alice asked, "I hear them in the other room, so I know they're here."

"They ate nearly an hour ago," Mattie answered, "They're in their pajamas already."

They had a pleasant conversation while they ate-sharing happy memories of their early years.

"Oh, Alice," Mattie prompted with a grin," did you tell Linda about the gingerbread house, yet, or the one that Carsie mentioned at the train station? I never heard you talk about that one."

"No," Alice nearly choked as she put her fork down, "and you never will," she dabbed her mouth with her napkin.

"Oh, come on," Mattie goaded, "we want to hear the story, don't we Charles?"

"Maybe after our food has settled," Alice sighed, "I don't want to ruin that scrumptious dinner."

The other three chuckled. "Does anyone have room left for chocolate cake?" Mattie asked, as she stood and started collecting the dishes.

"I'm stuffed!" Charles answered.

"Maybe later," was Alice's reply.

"Thank you, but I'm watching my figure," Linda said with a gleam in her eye.

They all laughed, and then the other three retired to the living room, while Mattie checked on the children.

"Well," Alice asked Charles once they were comfortable, "what were the results of the lab tests?"

Charles directed his answer at Linda. "They indicated that you are a little anemic and could afford to gain a few pounds, but I'm sure Alice's cooking will remedy that," he turned to Alice. "if it hasn't already."

On Easter Sunday, Alice convinced Linda to attend church with them, and then to dinner with the family. "If you want, you can sit in the back corner of the church. I'll even fix you up so you look older. You don't have to talk to anyone there if you don't want to."

"How about your family; will they accept me as I am?"

"They already have-they're looking forward to meeting you."

"All right, I'll go. I've really missed attending church these last few months. Before Mama died, we went together as a family every Sunday. My brother and I were both baptized there. When Daddy took to drink and stopped going, we would go without him whenever we could."

The church was full that Sunday, and there were many new faces in the crowd, so Linda was able to remain anonymous. The service was very moving, and she felt reconnected with God.

"I think I'd like to go back there again," she told Alice on the way to the farm. "I know now that God forgave me for my bad choices, but in my despair, I forgot how much he loves me. Thank you for accepting me and taking care of me. I know God will reward you for it."

When they got to the farm, she was a little overwhelmed by the number of people there. They all welcomed her with open arms and hearts. Linda doted on the littlest children most of the afternoon.

Two weeks later, Mattie and her children came over for lunch. While the girls were washing the dishes, Mattie pulled Alice aside,

"With your permission, I'm going to talk to Charles about asking Linda to stay with us. She loves Little Harry and I think he loves her, too. It would be nice to take a break once in a while to go shopping, and perhaps volunteer at the hospital part-time, while someone else watches the children. And then she won't be alone so much, while you're at work and Doley is at school."

"That sounds like an excellent idea-I think Linda would be amenable to that idea."

"I think Charles will go for it, too."

They were both right. Charles picked up Linda at Alice's house on his way home from work a few nights later.

Mattie convinced Linda to write to her brother and boyfriend to tell them the truth. "Honesty is always the best policy," she told her, "and you never know what good may come of it. God works in mysterious ways, as you and I can attest, by the way he brought us into Alice's life and care."

A week later, the telephone rang while Linda was home alone with the children. She immediately recognized the voice on the other end of the line, "Linda, I love you and I miss you. Why did you run away?"

"I didn't want to ruin your life," she sobbed, "I love you too."

"It's my baby too. I'm at least as much to blame as you are. I talked to my father, and he said you are welcome to come back after I finish school and get a good job to support you. That is if you want to get married, and if you leave the baby behind. He said if it was up to them, they would welcome you both back with open arms right now. But he's concerned that we're not ready to be parents, and that some of our congregation and the rest of the town wouldn't be so kind and accepting."

Linda dried her tears, "I want to keep our baby, but I think he or she would be better off with someone more mature and responsible than the two of us."

"I agree. Can I come see you next weekend? Father and mother said they'll bring me to visit."

"I don't know-let me think about it and talk to my friends, first. Call me back in a few days, and I'll let you know then."

When Mattie came home a little while later, Linda told her about the phone call. "I'll talk to Charles tonight and Alice day after tomorrow, when I take Little Harry in for his doctor appointment. I wouldn't know what to tell you, but Charles has more experience, and Alice-well, Alice is so wise and practical. I am convinced that she has the Lord's ear and he has hers. I value her opinion very much."

When Mike called back, Mattie answered the phone. "Hello?... Oh, you must be Linda's young man. She's in the nursery with my children. I'll go get her."

Linda came into the kitchen and picked up the phone. "Mike? Yes, I talked to them and they agreed that it would be best for all concerned if you didn't come to see me, at least until the baby is born and adopted. They are concerned that we'll get too attached, which would make it even harder to give it up."

"I understand" he replied, sadly, "My grandmother said much the same thing when I confided in her. Do you know when the baby is due?"

"My friend is a midwife, and estimates sometime in late July. Why don't you give me your telephone number, so I can call you back at that time."

At Linda's next checkup, Charles was pleased to report that she was indeed healthier and stronger, and gave her permission to at least attempt a home delivery, "Providing Alice is available, since she's very experienced and is the one that's been coaching you. If there are any problems at all, or if Alice isn't available, you must promise to come straight to the hospital."

"I promise," Linda replied.

The adoption agency was researching and interviewing two couples interested in adopting her baby, but no decision had yet been made.

While Linda was getting stronger and bigger, Little Harry was getting weaker and thinner. His pediatrician said that his heart was not working correctly and could not support his growing body. He was diagnosed with pneumonia on July 20th, and was admitted to the hospital.

Because Linda's time was near, and Mattie and Charles were spending most of their time at the hospital with Little Harry. Linda was staying with Alice and Doley and Alice Marie was staying home with Charles' mother, who had come from Seattle to lend her aid.

On Sunday, July 27th, at 9 PM, Linda's birth contractions started. Alice had all the needed supplies ready and waiting.

Her labor was long, but uncomplicated, and she gave birth to a perfect seven-pound baby boy, at 2:00 the next afternoon.

After Alice got Linda and the baby cleaned up and settled, she took a shower, got dressed and went to the hospital. She checked in at the nurse's desk in the maternity ward. and then to her office to take care of some paperwork. After half an hour there, she went to the children's ward to see how Little Harry was doing. When she entered the room, she saw that he wasn't hooked up to any tubes or wires. Mattie was holding him, and Charles was holding her. They were both crying. Alice looked questioningly at the nurse, who shook her head, sadly.

Charles glanced up at Alice and whispered in Mattie's ear. Mattie looked up at Alice, and with a weak smile said, "God must have needed another angel in heaven."

"I'm so sorry," Alice said, and gave the little boy a kiss. Mattie gave the baby to Charles, stood and embraced Alice for several minutes, while Charles took the baby away.

"When did it happen?" Alice asked him when he returned.

"He was a trooper," Charles said, "he fought all morning, as if holding out for something to happen first. He opened his eyes, smiled an angelic smile and surrendered at 2 o'clock."

"Oh my God!" Alice exclaimed, shocking them both, "That is exactly the time that Linda had her baby-a healthy boy!" She didn't broach the subject then, because their wounds were too raw, but was convinced in her heart that Little Harry had been waiting for his replacement.

Linda named her little boy Daniel, "after my mother," she told Alice, "her name was Danielle." She and Little Danny remained with Alice and went with her to Little Harry's Memorial service the following Sunday afternoon.

When Mattie saw the infant, she fell in love with him instantly, "I don't believe it!" She gushed, as her eyes filled with tears, "He looks exactly like Charles' nephew!" She gathered the baby in her arms, and Alice knew that her friend's heart had been healed, and that this baby was meant to be hers.

Linda and Danny moved back to Mattie's and Charles' home a few days later, and remained until the next summer, when Mike came to take her as his wife. The adoption paperwork was started the week after the funeral. Mike and his parents signed them and sent them back soon after receiving them six months later.

Linda and Mike kept in touch with Mattie and Charles for another three years, when they sent a birth announcement. They rarely corresponded after that.

Chapter Ten

THE HOBOS

The Walden family gathered for lunch after church services on September 12, 1916.

Guy stood behind Grace with his hands on her shoulders as she sat at the table. Albert stood behind Ilda with his arms around her waist, "If I could have everyone's attention, please!" Albert said. "We have an announcement to make."

"Another baby?!" Faye and Doley exclaimed together.

"No," Guy said, "two babies."

"At least," Grace added. "I'm only three months along and already starting to show."

Alice spoke up next, "if you all keep up at this rate, we'll have to rent a hall to gather us all together."

"Or trade places with the animals and gather in the barn." Tucker added, looking and sounding entirely serious.

They all looked at him with puzzled expressions, then most of them looked at the person across the table from them and shrugged their shoulders. When they all burst out laughing, Tucker was the puzzled one.

Grace turned out to be right in her assumption. Two weeks later, at her next doctor appointment, she was informed that she was indeed carrying twins.

In February, her doctor diagnosed her with edema, "If I remember correctly, you told me that your mother is a nurse?"

"Yes, but since moving to Portland a few years ago, she is the head midwife at the hospital."

"Well, then, I suppose she knows as much as I do about this condition and what to do for it."

"Yes, indeed-she had the same problem when she was pregnant with my sister. There was no doctor practicing nearby, so she treated herself, successfully."

On March twelfth, just after returning from the usual Sunday dinner on the farm, Grace went into labor. Because the possibility of complications was doubled and she had suffered from edema the past month, Guy bundled her up and took her to the hospital. Three hours later, he was ushered into the room to see his wife and twin daughters.

"We needn't have worried," she told him. "Their births were uncomplicated."

"I'm still glad we came here," Guy replied as he bent to give her a kiss, "Better safe than sorry."

They named the girls Virginia and Alice. They had red hair and were very sweet babies. It wasn't long before they were dubbed Ginny and Ginger. Now Grace and Guy had a houseful, with three boys and three girls.

Then, on April twenty-seventh, Ilda gave birth to another boy, whom they named Cleo.

One day in June, Alice arrived at the hospital and was informed that a friend of hers had arrived during the night. The nurse ran her finger down the roster of patients, "Ah, here it is-Rose Koch, in room 305."

She went to see Rose before her shift started. "I only have a few minutes before work," Alice told her as she entered the room. "How are you doing?"

"Not so goot," came the reply, as tears started to gather in Rose's eyes. Elsie walked in just then and explained to Alice as she comforted her sister. "Another baby she lost. Why again, the doctor does not know."

"You carried both babies to full term, didn't you?" Alice asked Rose.

Rose nodded, "Ya, und not too difficult boff birfs ver. Alice, can you help? Vatever you say, I vill do."

"I'll look through my records of past cases. I seem to remember one like this many years ago. I can't promise anything, but I'll give it a try."

Not long after that, Henry Krausse, the Bauers' second cousin who had come from the old country as Caroline's chaperone, proposed to her on her 17th birthday. She said, "Yes," and they were married in September.

Just after Christmas, Rose found out that she was pregnant again. She was worried, and rightfully so, that history would repeat itself and she would be always pregnant, but never a mother.

Alice monitored her diet, daily activities and environment. She prescribed lavender and chamomile to help keep Rose relaxed. But the most important thing she practiced and prescribed was prayer. With Rose's permission, she added her name to the prayer chain at the Walden's church. Elsie had already put her request on the Bauer's church prayer chain.

This pregnancy had a happy ending. Rose gave birth to a healthy set of opposing twins the next summer.

The day before Thanksgiving that same year, Tucker and five-year-old Buddy had taken the wagon into town to get some supplies. It was a cool, drizzly day, but they were dressed warmly. They were both in a particularly good mood that day, looking forward to the family gathering and all their favorite foods the next day.

Thinking back on the Sunday school lesson at church three days before, Buddy was on the lookout for someone to bless. Then he spied a hobo camp near the railroad tracks. He pulled at Tucker's sleeve and asked him, "Why are those men there? Don't they have homes and families?"

"I don't know about families, but they wouldn't be there if they had homes to go to."

"Why not," Buddy asked.

"I don't know," his uncle replied as he stopped the wagon.

"My Sunday school teacher said that we should help those who can't help themselves. Do you think there is a man there who can't help himself-a man who wants to work, but can't?"

"I suppose-why don't we go talk to 'em?"

Buddy's face lit up with a big grin as Tucker shook the reigns, but his countenance changed as they grew closer to the camp. The men looked so rough and dirty. His nose wrinkled at the smells emanating from the camp, and some of the men didn't look very friendly. Buddy clung to Tucker's arm, in fear.

The most respectable looking of the men approached the wagon and held up his hands, signaling Tucker to stop. Then, seeing Buddy's apprehension, he came alongside, next to Tucker.

"Are you looking for someone?" he asked.

"No one in particular," Tucker replied. "We were on our way back home from picking up supplies for tomorrow's Thanksgiving dinner, and Buddy here was wanting to know about you men, and if there was some way that we could help you."

"Yeah, you could get us some women!" One of the other men blurted out. The others laughed or nodded agreement.

"Watch your mouth!" The first man ordered. "This is obviously a sensitive young man. He came here to see if he could do some good."

Then he turned back and addressed Buddy, "My name is Bradley, but you can call me Brad," he said as he held out his hand to Tucker. Tucker shook his hand and introduced himself.

"What did you have in mind, young man?" Brad asked Buddy.

"I don't know," Buddy answered. "My Sunday school teacher said we should help those who can't help themselves." Then he thought a minute. "Jesus fed hungry people.

"You seem like a nice man. Maybe you could come home with us for Thanksgiving dinner tomorrow. Of course, you'd have to get cleaned up first. I don't think Mama would let you in the house the way you are."

Brad chuckled, "You're probably right, but Gary here needs more help than I do. He's a nice man too, but he needs more than food-he needs a doctor." Then he turned to Tucker and asked, "Could you help him with that"

Buddy brightened and said, excitedly, "My grandma is a nurse-maybe she could help him!"

Tucker added, "She told me she was the only medical help in some of the logging camps we used to live in. She's good friends with a doctor too. If she can't help him, maybe her doctor friend can."

Brad walked over to a sick old man lying under a tarp. He and one of the other men there, helped him up and into the back of the wagon.

"Why don't you come along with him," Tucker asked Brad.

"Are you sure?"

"Come on, get in!" Buddy answered for him.

Albert was just coming out of the barn as the wagon pulled up. "Tucker, Buddy, who's your friend?" Then he got a whiff of them and noticed Gary. He helped Brad get him off the wagon and into the house.

Tucker took care of the horses and the wagon, while Buddy ran ahead and opened the door.

"We're home, Ma!" he called out.

Ilda came out of the pantry and stopped in her tracks when she saw the men. "What in the world?" When she saw how sick Gary was, her motherly instincts kicked in and she sprang to action.

"Bring him into Tucker's room," she directed. "Take his clothes off while I make preparations to get him cleaned up.

"Faye, please call your grandma at the hospital and ask her to come over as soon as she can."

While Brad and Albert were getting Gary's clothes off, Ilda filled a bucket with warm, soapy water and another with rinse water. "Buddy," she directed her son, "I'm going to put you in charge of changing these buckets out when they get dirty. Do you think you can manage that?"

"Yes ma'am. Anything else I can do to help?"

"You can show-what's your name?"

"I'm Brad and this is Gary," the younger man answered.

"You can show Brad to the bathroom, so he can wash himself."

Tucker came in a minute later and Albert directed him to find some clothes to fit Brad and then take their dirty things outside. "Ilda needs my help here."

Faye kept dinner warm for her parents and helped Tucker keep an eye on the younger children until Alice arrived an hour later. By this time Gary was washed, and Ilda had found out something about him from Brad. Albert and Brad had just finished eating dinner. All the men and the children were preparing for bed.

Grace came in with her mother to see if there was anything she could do to help.

"No," Ilda told her sister. "I think we have things under control, unless Mama wants to take this man to the hospital."

"Give me a few minutes to examine him, then I'll have a better idea," Alice said.

Grace went to check on the Newman children and fed little Ercyline Rose, whom she had brought along, then checked back in with her mother.

"Are you going to need me to transport him to the hospital, Mama, or should I go on home?"

"You might as well go home," Alice replied. "There's nothing anyone can do for him now, except keep him comfortable. I'll be surprised if he lasts the night."

Then she pulled out a pen and tablet. "Let me give you a list of things I'll need, that you can bring with you tomorrow."

Tucker bunked with Buddy, and Brad insisted on sleeping in the barn that night. "I'm used to being outside and don't want to put you out any more than I already have."

Alice was spot on with her prognosis. Gary passed away quietly just before breakfast.

Everyone was saddened by the news. Brad wasn't surprised, but wanted to know what had killed his friend.

"A combination of old age, exposure to the elements and organ failure," she answered.

"There's also a good chance that he had diabetes, too. Did you know that he had gangrene in his toes and was nearly blind?"

"He had been showing signs of pain in his feet lately and had become uncoordinated the last few months, but he never let on that he couldn't see," came the reply. "It all makes sense, now. He was a proud, foolish old man and never let me check his feet or take him to the hospital."

"Pride can be a very destructive enemy," Albert commented. "It claimed my grandfather's life when he was only forty-four."

"I never knew that," Alice remarked as they sat down to eat. "What happened to him?"

"I never knew him, but Grandma said he fell off the roof and went to bed soon afterward with some gut pain, never to wake up. She said he forbid her to call the doctor for him; saying he'd be fine after a little nap."

"It was probably a ruptured spleen," Alice said.

"Grandma said it didn't matter; that he was a victim of his own pride. They buried him in the family graveyard out back the next day and my father brought her home to live with us. My uncle Randal took over their farm, and when he died, he willed it to me."

"Didn't he have a family to pass it on to?" Brad asked.

"One son who had put himself through college and became a lawyer, two daughters, one of whom died as an infant and the other moved to California when she married. His wife passed from cancer a few months before he did."

"It was evident that he'd been either ill or suffering from depression, by the run-down nature of the farm," Ilda chimed in. "It still needs more work than we can afford to give it. But the Lord supplies us with enough to live on and be content."

Albert got up from the table and excused himself, "The cows won't milk themselves. Hope you can stay for dinner Brad. We'll bury your friend tomorrow, if you like."

"Thanks, but if you'll show me where the shovel and the graveyard are, I'll do the job myself today." He rose from the table and went with Albert, Tucker following close on their heels, stuffing an apple in his pocket.

While Alice looked after Buddy and Elsie May, Faye helped her mother clear the table and start on the dishes. "Mama," she asked, "I thought Daddy milked the cows before breakfast. Why did he say that the cows wouldn't milk themselves?"

"Oh honey, it's just an expression, meaning that they needed to get back to work."

"I'm glad I'm not Uncle Tucker," Faye remarked as she picked up the food scrap bowl for the pigs in one hand and the egg basket in the other and headed for the door.

"Why is that?" her mother asked.

"Because I don't think I could sleep in a bed that somebody died in."

"Somehow, I don't think it will bother your uncle Tucker."

Half an hour later, Brad came in with Tucker to carry Gary's body out to the barn.

"Albert said he has some scrap wood I can use to make a coffin. I think Gary would appreciate it if I made him one. Then maybe we can have the service for him tomorrow, like Albert said."

"That's so nice of you to take care of him the way you did," Alice said.

"Oops, here comes Grace and her family. Perhaps you should slip out the back door with the body before they come in. It might be a little awkward to pass them on the porch with the children and the food."

"Whew, what's that smell?" Jerry asked as he came in the front door a moment later. "Did you burn dinner?"

Grace came in behind him. "Here are the things you asked me to bring you, Mama."

"Thank you dear. Maybe we should build the fires up a bit hotter and open some windows to clear the air."

"Mama's patient died this morning," Ilda told her sister, just as the rest of the family came in the door.

"I'm not surprised," Grace remarked. "He was pretty sick, and I never smelled anything like him before."

"His feet were gangrenous," Alice informed her.

"Is his friend still here? Grace asked.

"Yes, he's building a coffin out in the barn. He'll be joining us later, for dinner. He cleaned up fairly well. I can't help but wonder why he was homeless to begin with. He's such a nice man-hard-working and pleasant."

Jerry was listening and said, "Why don't we ask him?"

"This isn't the right time for that," his grandmother replied. "His memories may be too painful. We'll wait and see if he wants to tell us."

"If anyone asks, he's just Buddy and Tucker's new friend, okay?" Guy directed.

"Okay."

Brad seemed to enjoy himself at dinner. He was charming and witty when he did talk, but was quiet most of the time; watching his hosts' family interactions and playing with the children a little. It was evident that he was a believer, but Alice perceived a sadness hiding behind his smile.

After dinner, while the children were playing out in the barn and the women were cleaning up and putting things away, the men sat talking in the living room. John, not knowing anything about Brad, asked him, "From around here are you?"

"No, not originally. I grew up in Idaho and came here to take a job eighteen years ago."

"What kind of work do you do?" Lafe asked.

"I guess you could say I'm in between jobs right now," came the reply.

"I might be able to get you a job at the lumber yard, if you like," Carsie chimed in. "Of course, it wouldn't pay much to start with and would be pretty demanding, if you're up for it."

This time it was Tucker who spoke up. "He *is* a hard worker. You should have seen him today, making that coffin."

"Coffin?"

"Yeah, for his friend, Gary. He died this morning. Buddy and I found them down by the tracks yesterday."

Alice overheard from the dining room and called, "Tucker, would you come and help me with something, please?" She knew that Tucker would embarrass Brad even more if she didn't intervene. She sent him on an errand to get him out of the house, while Brad tried to repair the damage he'd caused.

"Gary was sick, but wouldn't let me take him to the hospital. They met us there while doing an errand." The other men could tell by his downward gaze, that it was a touchy subject, so they ceased their questioning and went on to other topics.

Before Carsie and Lafe left that evening, Brad pulled Carsie aside and told him that he appreciated his help with finding a job. "I think it's about time I got back to work again."

"How long have you been out of work, if you don't mind my asking?"

"Four years now, ever since I lost my family."

"Oh, I'm terribly sorry. Those kind of wounds are hard to recover from, I know. I saw what my mother went through when my father died. She put on a brave face, but I could sense the pain for years afterward. They were very devoted to each other."

"I'll ask around and let you know if there are any job openings."

After his friend's burial the next day, Albert asked Brad, "Will you be attending church services with us this Sunday?"

"I haven't been to church since I lost my family. I think I would like to start up again. Time has healed some of the wounds, and being with your family has reminded me of what God once meant to me."

Brad rededicated his life to Jesus that weekend, moved in with Carsie temporarily and started work at the lumber mill two weeks later. He became a good friend of his for many years, and dedicated all his spare time to an outreach for the homeless in their area.

Brad remained single, and didn't come back to a family gathering at the farm because he kept very busy with work and ministry.

Chapter Eleven

MORTAL ENEMIES

Lafe got hired on at the lumber mill and moved in with Carsie. The two brothers, because of the fourteen-year difference in their ages, didn't have a close relationship. Even though they were quite different, they got along with each other and became good friends. Many years later, after they had gone their separate ways, Lafe would name a son after his oldest brother.

Most of that winter the news had been dominated by war reports from Europe and speculation as to the United States' possible involvement. Almost everyone agreed that our country would step up to the plate and help our allies. They prayed and waited for an announcement from the president.

There were also reports, though not as prominent as those about the war, of a virus which had been dubbed the Spanish flu marching across Europe even more relentlessly than the German army.

In April, 1917, the announcement came: The United States had joined the Great War. Within a week of our first troops' arrival in Europe, dreaded telegrams started arriving all over the country. This was a global disease that Alice had no medicine to treat. She felt helpless and useless. Even the soldiers who returned, injured from battle, wore scars that were untreatable to all but the expert medical personnel. Wounds such as lost limbs, and invisible ones of the mind and spirit.

Hot on the heels of the returning injured soldiers, came the Spanish flu to our shores. Men who had survived battle injuries, were succumbing to the flu, as were veterans' hospital employees. From there, it spread to the general public-multiplying day by day, week by week and state-by-state, westward. It was also decimating the troops in Europe so much that, in October, the war Department announced the requirement for all male citizens between seventeen and fifty years of age to register for the draft.

One Monday evening in late June of 1918, Frank and Lafe came to visit their mother. The whole time she was fixing dinner, they engaged in nervous small-talk. When they finished eating, Alice started collecting the dishes, when Frank reached over and put his hand on hers.

"Mama, I think it's about time we told you what we're here for."

"I think I already know," she said, sitting back down. "I've been on pins and needles, waiting for this day. When are you leaving and where will you be going?"

"Somewhere on the East Coast for training-next Monday," Lafe replied. "After that, who knows?"

Alice swallowed hard and took a deep breath to hold back the tears. "I've been dreading this day and praying that when it came, you wouldn't have to go overseas into battle."

"I suppose that's possible," Frank said. "And I hope we don't, too."

Lafe cleared his throat just then, "Well, Frank, are you going to tell her the rest?"

Alice perked up. "Does this have something to do with your romance with Mary?"

"Yes, we're going to get married on Thursday. We made arrangements with her Pastor this morning. It will be a simple affair at her parents' home-just close friends and family."

Alice sprang to her feet. "Well then, I had better make arrangements to be free that day and check my wardrobe for a suitable dress to wear!"

Thursday dawned dark and rainy, with a slight breeze.

"I've heard it's supposed to be good luck if it rains on your wedding day," Mary sighed, gazing out the window, while her mother zipped up Mary's prettiest dress.

"Smile, it's your wedding day!"

"I know, and I'm happy to be marrying Frank, but I can't forget that he's leaving on Monday, and there's a good chance he won't be coming back. Cousin George got married just before shipping off to the Spanish-American war, and got himself killed the first week out."

"I know dear, and I had a bad feeling when I'd heard that he was going, but I have a good feeling about it this time. I feel certain that Frank will return safely to you."

"I sure hope you're right, mother."

"Aren't I always?" She gave her daughter a kiss on the cheek. "Now sit on this stool, while I pin your hair up."

When the pastor arrived, half of the Walden clan and Mary's close relatives were already there. Mary's sister and Lafe stood up with Frank and Mary. After the ceremony, the newlyweds were sent off in a borrowed skiff. They camped on a small remote island in the Willamette River, where Frank had done some fishing with his friends and brothers the last few years.

On Monday morning, those family members and friends who were available, said their goodbyes to Frank and Lafe inside the depot, then Frank and Mary went out to the train. Lafe stayed inside, with the family, until the last second, to give the newlyweds some privacy, then kissed Alice and ran out, just as the train started to pull away. Frank held out his hand to pull his little brother in, and they waved goodbye to everyone, now on the platform, as the train picked up speed.

It was almost a month before letters started arriving from the boys. Alice hadn't been too worried-she knew they were still stateside, but wondered why it had taken so long. "It's probably the war slowing things down," Carsie said, after dinner that Sunday.

In mid-July, the first letter arrived from Frank, saying that he could not tell them where he was, but that it was hot and humid there.

> The training has been very intense. They are training troops so quickly, that I fear most are quite unprepared for what they are about to face. Lafe is stationed at the same base I am. I spent the day with him yesterday, and he said that he'll write to you in a couple of days. I'll let him tell you what he's been up to. They are sending me to another base soon, to work with the postal service.
>
> We're both fine, and hope you are the same. I will write again when I get settled at my new base. God bless you all. Love, Frank

Lafe's letter arrived three days later;

> Hello everybody,
>
> Frank and I are at the same base for now, but will be going our separate ways, soon. He's staying stateside, while I'm going to be somewhere in Europe. I don't know where, yet, but I won't be shooting at anyone. I'm going to be in a combat support unit, and will have to carry a rifle for protection only. I don't know what kind of work I'll be doing yet. I know we're in your prayers, as you are in ours.

The government and the newspapers downplayed the flu reports in order to prevent panic, and the war reports eclipsed it. Teresa and Charles heard more details about it from their colleagues, and warned Alice and the other nurses and midwives, that it would most likely be arriving on the West Coast, soon.

"We'll be needing the assistance of every nurse and their helpers once it arrives," Alice relayed to her staff. "We need to be vigilant to uphold the strictest rules of prevention, starting now, to assure that none of you or your family members get sick, so that you will all be available to continue working.

"It is an extremely contagious and deadly strain, and the casualties are mounting, quickly."

Here was yet another global disease-and it was striking close to home-too close for comfort. It was spreading so fast, that no one could calculate the numbers of the infected or the dead.

Alice had to do all she could to protect herself and her family. She advised them to avoid public places, as much as possible. She stocked up on food staples from the grocer and made sure to wear a gauze mask, when in public. She warned all her friends and helpers, and drilled her family on the importance of washing their hands frequently and washing everything that came into their homes and workplaces, that might harbor the virus. "Anything coming from outside, that can't be washed, such as mail and newspapers, should be read and then burned outside," she told them.

This process went on for the whole fall and winter seasons, as the flu pandemic hit Portland. A few members of the Walden family got sick, in spite of Alice's directives, so in late October, they got worried when they hadn't heard from Carsie for two weeks. Alice went to the lumber mill to inquire about him. There weren't many men working there. The holding pond and the river were jammed with logs. She found the foreman and asked about her son. The man looked quite ill; as if he could fall over at any moment. She was careful not to touch anything, unnecessarily, and kept her distance.

"I sent 'im upriver to a couple of logging camps last week to tell 'em to slow down the flow of logs," the man mumbled. "Figured he was either too busy, or he's caught this blamed flu, like everybody else. Anyway, I ain't got time to worry 'bout it. Half my crew's out sick, and I ain't feeling too good myself."

Alice went home and prayed extra prayers for Carsie and his workmates.

The camp was isolated. No one had been in or out for about two weeks, before Carsie arrived, and as yet, no one there had shown any signs of the flu. And they wanted it to stay that way. They had only heard about the pandemic recently, and didn't know that it had arrived in Oregon. There was a lot of disagreement about what to do to protect themselves. Shad quit felling trees when Carsie arrived, and were starting to get restless. Tempers were flaring, o Carsie and Fred Miller, the camp foreman, decided to hold an informal meeting.

All the men and some of the women gathered together in the town square. Fred stood up and called the meeting to order.

"Mr. Walden and I put our heads together and came up with two options to solve our dilemma. Number one: we take our chances and send someone for food. Number two: we close down the road, post a guard to keep people out, ration the food we have, and pray it holds out until the epidemic is over. Since we'll not be working much, if any, we'll have lots of time to go hunting."

Everyone started talking at once, and the discussion heated up. Fred gave a sharp whistle to get everyone's attention and motioned everyone to be quiet. "We're not going to get anywhere if you keep this up! Raise your hand if you want to talk."

At once, several hands flew up. "The chair recognizes Randy Kelso."

"I wanna know more about this flu. How much danger are we in?"

"Mr. Walden's mother is a nurse, and he came here from Portland, so he's seen and heard more about it, Fred replied."

He sat down and Carsie stood. "Okay, I'll give it to you straight: It's bad and it's at our very doorstep. From what I've heard from my mother, this is a new strain of the flu. Everyone is susceptible. People are dropping like flies, and most of the casualties, for some unknown reason, are the healthy young adults.

"My mother and sisters have enforced strong rules of cleanliness in their homes. They've all but quarantined themselves, and wear surgical masks and gloves when they *do* go out."

"Can we get those here?" Fred asked.

"We don't have access to surgical masks and gloves out here, and there's no way of knowing if someone arriving from the outside is a carrier, who just hasn't come down with symptoms yet. We don't know how long it takes for the symptoms to show up after exposure to the virus, but my mother says it's usually no more than twelve days."

"How do we know you didn't bring it in, then!" someone yelled.

"You don't. But I've been closely following my mother's advice, and she works with sick people all the time, without getting sick herself."

"I say we set up a quarantine to keep it out!" one man stood up and shouted.

"I say we lock *Walden* up till we're sure *he* ain't sick!" yelled another.

Everyone started shouting, and several of the men started pushing toward Carsie. Fred and some others blocked him in to protect him.

"Sit down!" yelled Fred. "We'll never get anywhere this way!"

Slowly, everyone took their seats, and order was restored.

Carsie sat down. He was worried about what might happen to him, if someone pressed the issue of his being a possible carrier of the virus.

"But what if we run out of food?" Asked another. "What'll we do then?"

"We'll have to go hunting and ration what we have here." Fred told them.

"For how long?"

Fred turned to Carsie.

"I don't know; could be a month, could be six." Carsie admitted.

"How do we enforce the quarantine?"

"We'll have to post guards on the road."

"What if someone sneaks in on foot? What would we do with him?"

"We can discuss that later," Fred said. "Right now, we're trying to decide if we want to enforce a lockdown or not, and what other options we may have."

The discussion went on like this for half an hour before they decided to quarantine the town against the virus. Carsie volunteered to be isolated for two weeks, to protect himself and allay their fears that he might be infected. Fred chose a man he could trust, to select and assign guards.

While the men who volunteered for guard duty were coming forward and everyone else was leaving, Fred led Carsie away.

"I'm about as sure as I can be that I'm not a carrier," Carsie told him, "I'm doing this more for my own protection. Some of your men looked pretty threatening."

"Yeah, I know the guys you're talking about."

"Just do me a favor and make sure that they aren't put on my guard duty."

"They won't be together on the road guard either. I don't want anyone shot, if I can help it."

"Me neither," replied Carsie, as his eyebrow shot up. "Especially if it's me!"

Fred chuckled. "We have an empty cabin down at the end the road here. We *were* going to move a new family into it, next week, so it's all set up with basic furniture and kitchen utensils. When the first guards come, I'll have them bring bedding, food and firewood."

"Thank you. I was only planning to spend a couple of hours here, so I'll need soap, toothbrush and such. Oh, and could you arrange to have them bring me a deck of cards, a Bible, and pen and paper, too? I don't want to die of boredom, either."

"Sure, just let us know what you need, and we'll make sure you get it."

Half an hour later, a pleasant, attractive young woman arrived with the promised supplies and a plate of hot food in a box. She stood about two yards away. "My name is Gretchen. My parents run the camp store. I hope you like venison stew. I brought along a notepad to write down special needs you may have, and anything else you need. I'll be back in the morning, to bring breakfast and collect the box. How do you like your eggs? Do you prefer hash browns or toast? I would offer you both, but like you said; we need to ration our food supplies."

Gretchen made it a point to be the one to bring Carsie's meals and any supplies he needed. Everything was left on a table right outside the door. Three times a day, she would place a box on the table and back away, after knocking. She waited for him to open the door and remove the plate from the box. They would exchange pleasantries while he ate. When he was done eating, she retreated with the box, loaded with the dirty dishes.

When Carsie had opened the door to her first knock, he'd noticed that there was a middle-aged man with a rifle, standing guard a few yards outside the door. He had a kind face and tipped his hat at Carsie. "My name's Hank. I'll be here for four hours 'til Tim and Sam arrive to relieve me." He noticed Carsie eyeing his rifle, and lifting it said, "Relax; It's Pete, Sam and the flu *I* don't trust."

Every day, from breakfast until lunch a young red-haired fellow with a Norwegian accent, named Eric, stood guard. A tall, dark, bearded German took his place from lunch until dinner, then Tim came with his sister, Gretchen, to bring his dinner. During the wee hours of the night, Carsie would sometimes awaken and hear two other men talking, quietly.

121

The days were long and the nights were even longer, as Carsie waited out the two-week quarantine. He spent his time reading, writing, praying and playing solitaire with the deck of cards Gretchen had brought him. He looked forward to her visits more and more eagerly as the days wore on. The last few days were the hardest, as they were developing a romantic interest in each other.

On the morning of the twelfth day, Carsie was awakened by a heavy knock on the door. He was perplexed, as he wasn't expecting Gretchen for another hour, at least; and she never knocked that hard. He shivered as his feet hit the floor. He took the blanket off the bed and wrapped it around himself as he went to the door. The cabin was colder that morning than it had been on previous mornings.

When he opened the door, he expected to see Gretchen six feet away and his breakfast on the table, as usual. He almost fell backwards, as Fred's large frame loomed in the doorway. "Fred, is everything all right?"

"I know we agreed on two weeks for your quarantine, but since you haven't showed any signs at all of the flu, we thought we'd let you off a couple days early." He was holding a cardboard box, which he handed to Carsie as he spoke.

He stepped inside and Gretchen pushed past him. "I'm so glad you're all right!" she gushed, as she gave Carsie a hug. Then she blushed and backed away. "Not that I ever doubted it, but I would be very sad if anything bad happened to you."

"You're free to go," Fred told Carsie. Then he shook his hand and left the two of them alone.

Carsie put his hands on Gretchen's shoulders. "What can I do to thank you for all your kindness?"

"Would it be too forward to ask for a kiss?"

The words were barely out of her mouth, when he drew her close and pressed his lips to hers. Something stirred inside him, that he'd never felt before. She felt it too. They backed away from each other, breathless.

"I guess I'd better gather my gear and be on my way," he said nervously.

Gretchen opened the door, then turned and asked, "Would you like to come home with me for breakfast, first? My parents would like to meet you. Besides, we can't send you off hungry, can we? It's quite a drive back into Portland."

"That sounds like a fine idea. I'd like to thank them, too."

"I'll step out for a minute while you get dressed."

After he dressed and let her back in, she helped him strip the bed and collect all the other items. Then he picked up the box, and they walked to her cabin, hand in hand.

Her mother was at the kitchen sink, which had a view of the road. She saw them walking and smiling at each other. She grinned and called back over her shoulder, "John, I think I hear wedding bells!"

They had a pleasant breakfast. Her parents were very impressed by Carsie's manners and the way he got along with their two younger boys. "He has six younger brothers and sisters," Gretchen told them after he left.

After insisting that he help Gretchen wash the dishes, he stole a kiss, when they were alone in the kitchen. He needed to touch bases with Fred before leaving town, but had a hard time tearing himself away from Gretchen. They exchanged addresses before he left, but no mail was going through, because the town was closed down.

When Carsie returned home, his family sensed something different about him. "I met a girl at the mill," he told them. "Her name is Gretchen. I think I'm in love, and I'm sure she feels the same way."

He had a hard time concentrating on his work, and there was a lot to do. The epidemic had claimed the lives of many of the workers, and there was still a demand for lumber for the war effort.

Carsie and Gretchen had both written several letters to the other; saving them for later. It helped to ease their longings, some. They poured out their hearts to each other on paper; hoping and praying the epidemic and the war would end, soon.

The old saying "absence makes the heart grow fonder" was very true in their case. If Carsie hadn't been needed so much, he would gladly have spent another year in the cabin, to be near Gretchen again.

The war ended that November, but the pandemic worsened. Then one day, just after Christmas, Frank, who had just returned from military service, came sauntering into Carsie's office, with a sly smile. "Ma sent me over. Guess who showed up at the hospital today."

Carsie stood so quickly that his chair almost fell over. His heart began to beat again as hope stirred in him. "Gretchen? What brought her down from the camp in the middle of winter?"

"How did you guess so quickly?" Frank was smiling from ear to ear. "She had an appendicitis attack."

Seeing the cloud cross his brother's face, he quickly added, "But she's okay; it didn't rupture. She had surgery this morning and is doing just fine. She's asking for you."

Carsie had put his coat on, while Frank was talking. He scribbled a note for his boss and ran out the door with Frank hot on his heels. He drove as fast as he dared, through the streets of Portland. He stopped at the emergency entrance, left the motor running and flew into the hospital. Carsie inquired at the front desk about Gretchen's whereabouts, then rushed to her room and burst in unannounced. "I came as soon as I heard!"

The nurse was taking Gretchen's pulse, and turned to face Carsie, "Young man," she scolded, "You're supposed to knock before entering a lady's room!"

Carsie ignored her and went around to the other side of the bed.

"I hoped you'd be here soon," Gretchen whispered. "I missed you so much."

He sat down and took her hand in his and brushed it with a kiss. "Did you have to get appendicitis to come see me?" He teased her.

"Yes, I planned it all out weeks ago," she countered. Then the smile left her face and she pulled him close for a passionate kiss. "I couldn't stand not seeing you, or even corresponding."

They were so wrapped up in each other, they didn't even notice the nurse leaving.

"I haven't been much help at work, either," he admitted. "You were all I could think of, way up there in the mountains with limited resources, for who knows how long."

"And all I could think about was you down here, surrounded by flu germs."

"I'll be all right. My mother taught us how to protect ourselves from being infected. At least I knew you were safe up there."

"I don't care about the flu or the quarantine. All I care about is being here with you."

"As soon as you get out of here, will you marry me?"

She threw her arms around his neck, "Yes, yes, yes!"

Just then, her parents walked in, "Does this is mean what I think it does?" Her mother asked.

They looked at her, then each other, and answered together, "yes, yes, yes!"

Gretchen was released from the hospital three days later. Two days after that, they were married in Alice's living room, with a bare minimum of attendees, due to the risk of spreading the flu virus.

Gretchen and her parents had left the logging camp so quickly that they'd brought only the basics with them. They had no nice clothes to wear, but Gretchen was nearly the same size as Ilda, and was offered one of her dresses to wear. It needed but a few minor alterations to make it fit perfectly. The bouquet she carried was made of winter pansies tied together with ribbons. Doley found some snow drops behind the house and put them in Gretchen's hair.

There was no honeymoon. The newlyweds spent one night alone in the cabin, while Lafe stayed with the Newmans. "We'll have a honeymoon when the epidemic is over," Carsie promised his bride.

Gretchen's parents stayed with some friends in Tigard.

Two weeks into the new year, Carsie was sent, on assignment, to another camp, and Gretchen went to stay with her parents, while he was gone.

Carsie's trip to the camp was difficult and prolonged, because of heavy snow in the mountains.

One week after Carsie left, Gretchen and her mother's friend came down with the flu The next day, her father fell ill. Her mother tried to take care of all of them, but eventually succumbed herself.

When Carsie returned three weeks later, his Gretchen was gone-another victim of the cruel pandemic. Her mother was still very sick and her father was weak but improving.

"It's best you weren't here," Gretchen's father told Carsie. "It was heartbreaking, the way she suffered."

"But I could have comforted her," Carsie sobbed.

"Possibly. But then we might have lost you, too."

"How can I go on without her?" the broken-hearted Carsie asked his mother, when he saw her the next day.

"It's not easy; I've been there. As hard as it is to believe right now, life does go on. It gets a little easier almost every day. And then one day you'll find yourself laughing and enjoying life. Some day you may even fall in love again, and Gretchen will be happy for you."

Carsie took comfort in his Lord and the Scriptures, his family and his faith that Gretchen was in heaven, waiting for him to join her someday. His sunny disposition couldn't be kept at bay very long. The nights were still long and lonely, but by springtime, his days were full of joy and laughter again.

He went on fishing trips with his brothers and nephews, helped Albert with farm chores, and played with the children on weekends. He and Lafe got involved in a Bible study on Wednesday evenings. On Tuesday or Thursday evenings, they usually helped out at the Salvation Army Mission.

They met so many people there that were far worse off than they had ever been. They had many occasions to comfort grieving widows, widowers and orphans, left behind by the pandemic. They shared the gospel with them, just as the other volunteers did, and helped them to find hope, jobs and homes. Some of the orphans were placed with family members and friends, temporarily, until a permanent home could be found for them.

The Newmans took in a brother and sister, aged four and two, whose parents had fallen victim, after saving their children from the virus. The children had been rescued by a neighbor, after the parents had died. They had been brought to the shelter for help, because the neighbors didn't have the resources to care for them.

The police couldn't care for them either; they were short-handed and overwhelmed in the wake of the war and the flu.

Carsie must have looked like their father or some other relative, because the children took to him, immediately. He and Lafe knew that Ilda would take the children in and care for them, as long as necessary. She, Albert, Buddy and Faye all welcomed the orphans, with open arms and hearts. Elsie May and Cleo were ambivalent. They didn't know quite what to think about these strange, troubled, and needy children. When rivalries started to spring up, Ilda or Faye had to step in quickly, to avert trouble.

The older of the two, who said her name was Nini, was stoic, withdrawn and over-protective of her little brother, Jojo, most of the time, but ignored or bullied him at others. She had nightmares almost every night for two months. Then less frequent, until they almost stopped, by six months. Her moodiness slowly disappeared, as well.

Jojo wasn't toilet trained, and had a bad case of diaper rash when he came to them. Cleo, who was about the same size and at a similar stage of development, had been trained for several months. So Ilda enlisted his example and Faye's help, to train the little boy.

The children welcomed Carsie enthusiastically when he came to visit and cried when he left. When anyone else visited, they hid. So the Newmans didn't host or attend family gatherings for a while.

The children got used to the other family members, little by little, as they came to visit the farm during the ensuing weeks. By the time the children had been with the Newmans for four months, they seemed to be well adjusted most of the time and were able to tolerate small gatherings and attend church services. At first, they stayed with Ilda, Guy and Faye in the auditorium, then in Cleo and Elsie May's classes.

Six months after their arrival, there was still no word on any relatives. So Ilda and Albert left the children in Faye and Tucker's care one day, and went to inquire about the search. They were ushered into an office, after a lengthy wait, and were told by the matronly woman behind the desk, that they could do one of two things: "Start adoption proceedings, with no guarantee of approval, as some relatives may yet be found, or surrender the children to the state, to be placed in an orphanage."

Albert and Ilda looked at each other and knew, without talking, that they would try for adoption. They were given the papers to fill out at home and instructed to return them unsigned within a week. "Your signatures will have to be notarized," the woman said.

When they returned home with the news, their children's reactions were as varied as they were. Faye was thrilled, as she had become quite attached to the pair. Buddy didn't care one way or the other. Elsie May and Nina, as they assumed her name was, had become like the Bobbsey twins, with a love/hate relationship. And Cleo was always in competition with Jojo for adult attention.

Carsie had been buying their shoes, clothes and toys from the secondhand store, so the orphans wouldn't be too much of a burden to his sister and brother-in-law. "I would be honored to be their godfather and continue to support them financially as long as I am able," he told them. Lafe offered to pitch in some money, too.

"Thank you both," Albert replied. "I'm not too proud to accept your money. After all, I'm sure it was God who put them in your path and in our care."

The adoption was finalized a year later. By that time, Nina and Jojo were solidly ensconced as members of the Walden clan. People who didn't know their story couldn't tell that they were adopted.

Chapter Twelve

LOVE AND WAR

One Friday night in early July of 1918, Alice came home from work to find Doley was not there. She had been an obedient girl all of her life, so Alice was surprised at her absence. Then she found a note on the table that read:

> Mama, don't worry; I'll be home late tonight. I'm having dinner with the Bauer's. I left you a sandwich and some soup in the ice box.
>
> Doley.

"Aha," Alice said to herself, "I think I smell romance in the air!" And she was right. Doley started spending almost all of her spare time at the Bauers' or on dates with John. Alice liked John and his whole family. They were good people-hard-working, honest and family oriented.

On October 18th. Doley and John came in the door after dinner. They were smiling. "Mama, guess what?" Doley said, trying not to be too obvious, and failing.

"Let me see," Alice said with a smirk, "Page one: you had a good time. Page two: you're madly in love with an Austrian immigrant. Page three, I'm not too sure about. Tell me about it while I fix us some tea."

"Oh, Mama, you can be such a tease. I can't wait to tell Ilda and Grace!"

They were married the following weekend. The Waldens' pastor was unavailable, due to illness in his family, but the Bauers' pastor was available.

The ceremony was a simple one at the Newman farm, with Alice, Ilda, Rose, Carl and his new bride, Lena in attendance. Everyone else stayed out of sight or was at work, at their homes, tending children or the ill. They had no honeymoon, because of the flu epidemic. They couldn't afford one, anyway. John had just purchased a moving van a few months before and signed a lease on an office space with an apartment upstairs. He had sold the bicycle repair business to his brother, Carl.

That autumn, the flu pandemic caused more deaths among the troops than the war did. Carsie, Guy, Tucker, Charles and Albert were all required to register for the draft. Carsie was exempted, because his job at the lumber mill was considered essential for the war effort. Tucker was excluded because he flunked the physical due to his bad eye and flat feet.

Charles was sent to Walter Reed hospital in Washington DC to tend to the returning, wounded soldiers.

Albert and Guy were trained on the East Coast, just as Frank and Lafe had been. They were both sent to Europe, but neither of them saw much, if any action, because the war ended while Albert was on the ship, and a few days after Guy arrived. Guy was assigned guard duty in Belgium, watching over the German prisoners, while it was being decided what to do with them.

He hoped and prayed that none of the prisoners would try to escape, because he had orders to shoot anyone who tried, and didn't think he would be able to do that. He even made friends with one of the prisoners, who spoke English. He was assigned to guard the prisoners, from just outside the fence, while they were in the yard. On the second day of his assignment, this prisoner walked up to the fence, near Guy's post, turned and leaned against it, while smoking a cigarette. He looked askance at Guy and spoke to him. "Hello, my name is Fritz. What is your name?"

Guy didn't answer. He had been told not to talk to the prisoners, and was a little surprised that the man talked to him in English. All he had heard them speak to each other was unintelligible gibberish, to him.

"If you don't want to speak to me, just say so and I'll leave you alone." Guy was intrigued and didn't see what harm it would do to talk to the man. After all, the war was over and they weren't really enemies anymore, he reasoned.

"My name is Guy," he replied while looking away from Fritz.

"It's nice to meet you, Guy. I was a teacher until I was drafted. How about you?"

"A train engineer."

"My father worked on the railroad most of his life. He wanted more for me, so he worked hard to be certain I went to college," Fritz said.

"I doubt I'll be able to help my sons much with that, Guy answered. I have a pretty big brood already, and it will most likely grow even bigger. College is expensive."

"I have only one sister and a sweetheart waiting back home for me. Do you think I'll be able to go home soon?"

"I have no idea, but I wish you the best, Fritz."

They talked like this almost every day, until Fritz was processed out of the camp. They exchanged addresses and corresponded for several years.

Albert's duties included retrieval of bodies from the battlefields in France. It was an unenviable and dangerous task-picking through the smelly, fractured corpses and loading them on wagons, while watching for unexploded ordinances. Occasionally, he would hear a grenade, landmine or shell explode, usually followed by a scream, as the soldier who had disturbed it was seriously injured or killed.

He didn't tell his family what he was doing, so as not to worry them. He knew he was in their prayers and under God's protection. He also knew that if he became a casualty, God would watch over his family.

One rainy day, right after Christmas, one of his fellow soldiers, working nearby set off a grenade, which blew off his arm and sent shrapnel flying into Albert's leg and groin. He was in pain but still in one piece-or so he thought.

The other fellow was unconscious and bleeding profusely from the stub of his severed arm, his face and side.

Albert couldn't stand. He bound his own wounds, while a medic rushed to tend to the other man. They were both placed on the partially-loaded wagon of corpses and taken to the nearest medical aid station. At the aid station, upon examination, the other fellow was found to be missing one eye and most of his ear and his nose, as well. Albert prayed for and kept tabs on him, but as long as they were both at the aid station, he never regained consciousness.

The shrapnel in Albert's leg had broken his femur and damaged the muscle, so that he would have a pronounced limp the rest of his life. The groin injury that he had thought to be just a flesh wound, the stateside surgeon informed him later, had rendered him sterile.

"Don't look so sad, Doc," Albert told him, "I have four children already. My wife and her sisters are all very fertile, just like their mother. I don't know how many more I could support with my farm, anyway!"

"You'll be sent stateside for further treatment and then home to recover," the doctor at the aid station told him. "I don't imagine that you'll miss the body retrieval process."

"It will probably haunt my dreams for quite a while, but at least I didn't have to kill anyone."

"There is that," the doctor agreed. "Many of the men I've treated are emotionally scarred by having to do that. Some, I think, may never recover totally."

"How about you, Doc, I suppose all the death and pain you've witnessed has changed you, too?"

"Yes, very much. Medicine has been my life. I was a surgeon in a Dallas hospital for fifteen years before I was drafted. Now I just want to go to a small town and treat nothing more serious than stomachaches and broken arms."

Two days before the war ended, Alice had been notified, via telegram that Lafe was missing in action. All his family could do was hope and pray that he would be found alive and returned to them in a timely manner.

As it turned out, he was alive, but injured. He had been shot while riding horseback on a detour through the woods. He was carrying a message to the front lines, when he had encountered opposing troops on either side of the road.

He had developed a strong rapport with the horse in the previous weeks. It was an intelligent animal-well trained and loyal.

Lafe was hit in the arm and the horse was hit in the neck. They were able to continue until they were out of danger, but Lafe soon realized that neither of them could continue on their mission, without first getting medical aid.

They found a small cottage in which to hide out. It was inhabited by an elderly couple and their grandson. Neither of the grandparents spoke English, and the grandson knew very little, but they welcomed this American soldier and his horse, tended to their wounds and hid them from the German soldiers. It was two weeks before Lafe and his horse were recovered enough to travel. By then, the shooting had stopped and the grandfather heard from the neighbors, that the war was over.

Lafe thanked his hosts, mounted his steed and went to the nearest road to wait for an American troop passing by, to determine which way he should go.

He traveled with the troops to an aid station, where he checked in with the officer in charge. "I don't know where my unit is-my horse and I were both injured two weeks ago and have been recovering and hiding out in a farmhouse."

"Well, by now they probably think you're dead or in a prisoner of war camp somewhere," the officer replied. "They haven't all been emptied and the prisoners processed, yet. You need to be checked out before we ship you home, in order to verify your story. Then we'll notify your unit and get you on your way home. It may take a while to get the paperwork all straightened out. We'll find a bunk for you around here, somewhere, until then."

That somewhere turned out to be a large tent. When he entered it, he saw about twenty men in the tent-some amputees, some with head wounds, some blinded, and a few with relatively minor wounds such as his own.

He found an empty bunk, stretched out on it and closed his eyes. A minute later, he heard a familiar voice. "You don't look injured to me. Are you just goofing off, or what?"

Lafe opened his eyes, to see his brother-in-law, Albert, standing over him, with a big grin on his face. "Albert, fancy meeting you here," he said as he sat up.

Albert sat next to him, being careful not to run his cast into the next bunk, in the process. "Here we are, half a world away from home, and we end up in the same tent."

"I didn't even know you were in the same country, or even alive, for that matter," Lafe smiled back at him. "I see you got your leg banged up. How long have you been here?"

"Four days now. I ship out tomorrow-probably be home, getting into mischief again within a month. I'll have to go through Walter Reed, and maybe get the shrapnel removed, first."

"I took a bullet in the arm, while the horse I was riding was shot in the neck. We barely escaped getting captured, and took refuge in a farmhouse for two weeks, while we were recovering. Looks like I'm going to be cooling my heels here, until some paperwork is straightened out."

"If you get back home before me," Albert said, "be sure to tell the family that I'm fine, and will be home soon."

"Okay. Do the same for me?"

Albert nodded. "I'll let you get some sleep now, you look tired. My bunk is at the other end."

Meanwhile, back at Walter Reed hospital, Charles was experiencing the other side of war. His patients were mostly amputees, though some had traumatic brain injuries, loss of vision and /or hearing. And many with physical injuries also were experiencing mental breakdowns, nightmares, dependence on pain medications and the like.

It took a little longer for him to return home, because his patients kept coming-most needing prolonged medical attention, amputation of injured limbs that wouldn't heal, reparative surgery and rehabilitation, before being sent home.

One patient, in particular, really impressed him; a Navy captain who had been rescued from the ocean, after his ship was sunk. He had lost his hearing, and the use of his legs, due to a spinal injury. He insisted on bunking with his men, rather than being put in a semiprivate room with another officer. He could have been bitter like some of the other men-shaking his fist at God and shouting, "Why me?" But instead, he accepted his lot and encouraged the other men to do the same-to count their blessings. He ministered the gospel to them, and led many to the Lord.

As his less severely injured shipmates recovered and were released, the nursing staff moved troubled men onto his ward, for spiritual healing, via this remarkable man. He wasn't one of Charles' regular patients, but he often visited him when he was off-duty.

Captain Bovard was lying on his bunk with his eyes closed, when Charles approached him. He touched him lightly on the shoulder and Ken's eyes opened immediately. He sat up as he greeted his visitor, "Charles, it's so good to see you. I got back from physical therapy about an hour ago. They really gave me a workout! How are you doing? Any word on when you'll be going home?"

"No, not yet," Charles mimed. "What about you?"

"I'm in no hurry," Ken replied. "There's no one waiting for me at home, that needs me, and I really feel that I'm needed here. I seem to have become a very popular fellow."

Charles had his tablet and pen ready, and wrote, "I think God put you here for His purposes."

Ken read the note and replied, "I couldn't agree more. He's impressed upon me the call to stay here and become a chaplain."

Charles wrote back, "That sounds perfect. You've done a lot of good work here already."

"No," Ken said. "He's the potter, I'm just the clay."

"Well said," Charles motioned. Then he indicated that he was hungry and had to go.

"My nose tells me that my dinner is on the way too. See you later," he said as he clasped Charles hand warmly. "You know you're in my prayers."

When Ken was released from the hospital two months later, he rented an apartment a couple of blocks from the hospital and spent all of his spare time continuing his ministry to the soldiers. He had already learned to read lips and had signed up for seminary classes.

When Charles was released from his duties there, he visited Ken at his apartment to say goodbye. They ate and prayed together.

Before leaving, Charles shook his hand warmly and teased him, "Promise me you'll stay out of trouble."

Ken teased back, "Spoilsport." Then pulled him down for a hug.

Charles and all four men from the Walden clan returned home within eight months of leaving, but while they were gone, their families were waging a war at home with the Spanish flu.

The first reported cases in Portland, were on October 5, 1918. Six days later, Mayor Baker and Dr. Parrish, Portland's Health Service's Director, made the decision to close Portland down, meaning all public meeting places, such as pool halls, churches, theaters, amusement parks and schools were locked up to try to stem the tide of infection transmission. On October 19th a hospital was opened in an auditorium to house flu victims, because the hospitals were overwhelmed.

Casualties from the flu pandemic continued to rise at an alarming rate, in spite of many cities and states implementing quarantines. Despite rosy predictions from the newspapers, hospitals were bursting at the seams with flu victims, at the rate of 350 new reported cases per day. Most people didn't take the precautions recommended by doctors, seriously.

On October 4th, the Dressler's middle child, Andrew, had come home from school with a runny nose and a fever. Elsie kept all of her children home from school and isolated Andy from the rest of the family-but too late. The next day, Heloise, the oldest, whom Alice had treated for croup when she'd first arrived in Portland, fell ill. Then two days later, the surviving twin. By that time, Andrew was critically ill, and Elsie and Pete were struggling to care for them. They succeeded in not infecting themselves or baby Elizabeth, but were heartbroken when they were unable to save the three oldest children.

Because of the closure of the city on October 11th and the fear and grief they experienced, they felt compelled to bury the children in homemade coffins in the woods behind their home. Many other people did the same. The morgues were overwhelmed.

Tucker fell ill, next, by not being careful to follow his mother's guidelines, when in town on an errand, the second week of Portland's outbreak. He survived, but only because his mother's and sister's nursing skills.

Alice was kept busier than she liked, during this time. She still had her midwife duties and was back in harness as a nurse, treating flu victims. She insisted that Doley stay home until the outbreak was over. The Newmans isolated themselves, also, living off the bounty of their farm.

Guy got sick during the first wave, Ronny and Buddy Rowley survived the final wave in January, but little Ercyline Rose perished in the middle wave of December.

There were 350 reported new cases every day in November, in Portland alone.

When the war ended, there was celebrating in the streets. Ordinance or no, in spite of the flu, everyone wanted to party-there was no holding them back. So the ordinance was lifted on the 15th. A couple of weeks later, the number of reported cases was on the rise again, then peaked in mid-December. By then, the auditorium hospital had been closed and a quarantine ordinance had been adopted for the homes of the afflicted.

The newspapers did a grave disservice by publishing positive reports about the downturn of new cases, when in fact they had decreased very little. Everyone was so happy that the war was over and the boys had returned, that caution was thrown to the wind, as Christmas and New Years were celebrated with abandon. As a result, the number of reported cases rose again, sharply, in January.

It wasn't until Valentine's Day, that the number of reported, new cases fell to zero. In Portland alone, 20,000 people fell ill-2,000 of which were casualties. The first American victims were Soldiers, serving in Europe. It was determined later, that most likely, the virus had been brought to our shores by returning, injured soldiers.

One of those soldiers who returned, without being infected, was an amputee, whose wife was a nursing acquaintance of Alice's.

Vivian confided in Alice one day, after the pandemic was over, that her husband, Zach was being released from Walter Reed Hospital and would be coming home the next week.

"I can tell from his letters and phone calls, that he isn't the same man that left here last year. He sounds bitter. But that's not all. Our home isn't equipped for a wheelchair. Do you know where I can get help to modify it? I've been looking for another house that'll work. There aren't any that we can afford, or within a reasonable distance from the hospital. I don't know what to do!" she cried. "Zach has no family and mine can't help us out. There's no money for house renovations."

After consoling her friend, Alice pulled a pen and paper from her pocket. "Here, write down your address and phone number. I'll talk to my family and our pastor, to see if there's anything they can do to help."

"I'd heard that you and your family liked to help folks in need," Vivian said. "I'll be so grateful for anything you can arrange for us." She said, wiping her eyes.

The first thing Alice did was call her pastor for prayer and any construction or materials help that he could round up from their congregation. Then she called Doley and asked her to relay the same message to all their family and friends.

When Vivian got home from work that evening, there were three men in work clothes and tool belts waiting for her.

"Alice Walden sent us. We came to take some measurements and make a plan and a list of supplies we'll need to renovate your home," the leader informed her.

"Oh, my!" Vivian was overwhelmed at the speed with which her request had been answered. "Come on in and look around. Let me know if you need me for anything."

While she was fixing her dinner, the men swarmed over her little house, taking measurements, making drawings and discussing possibilities and problems they might face. By the time her dinner was ready, they had finished with their assessment and bid her farewell, saying, "If you'll leave the key under the mat when you leave in the morning, we'll get started tomorrow. It'll probably take several days to knock this out. We'll do our best to get it done before your husband gets home. Do you know when that'll be, exactly?"

"He told me the middle of next week, probably."

"Hmm, that gives us six days from today, at best. With the Lord's help, we'll get it done!"

And they did. While she was gathering her things to go out the door the next morning, a truck full of lumber and workmen pulled up and started unloading. They were followed by a car with three women. They informed her that they were there to make sure the men didn't break anything, and to keep the mess to a minimum. They also had a basket of food to feed the men, so they wouldn't have to raid her refrigerator.

Vivian thanked them and hurried off to work. She didn't see Alice all week, to thank her for arranging the help so quickly. When she arrived home that afternoon, her house was swarming with workers carrying boards and making all kinds of sawing and hammering noises. She peeked in the house, and seeing the number of workers and how much demolition there was, she decided to go to the corner diner to eat.

They worked through the weekend and finished the work on Tuesday. The last workers were packing up when she got home. She picked Zach up at the train depot Thursday morning.

The house looked about the same as he remembered it, save for a small ramp over the front step. Vivian had decided to let the remodel be a surprise.

She held the door for him, and he wheeled inside. "I'll need some help to get to the toilet. I know the doorway is too skinny for the wheelchair," he told her.

"No it isn't," she replied with a smug smile. He looked at her like she had lost her mind. When he saw her smile, he turned into the hallway and saw that it was not only wider, but had a fresh coat of paint. Then he noticed the paint fumes and coughed a little. "We'll have to open up the house to air it out," he called back over his shoulder. Then he reached the bathroom doorway and was amazed that he could fit in easily. He turned to close the door, but didn't see one. Then he noticed that there was a railing on the wall, and the vanity had been changed, so that he could fit his wheelchair under the sink and reach the faucets.

He was so overwhelmed that he sat there with tears of wonder, as he looked around. Vivian waited in the hallway and gave him a kiss, when he came out. "Isn't it amazing? And they did it all in less than a week."

"Who did this, and how much did it cost?"

"It didn't cost us a dime. A band of unlikely-looking angels descended on the house and transformed it from top to bottom, just for you. There's more. Want to see it all?" She took the handles of his chair and took him on a tour to see the other wider doorways and the rails next to the bed in their room.

From there she took him into the kitchen, where the sink and part of the counter were accessible to him, as in the bathroom. The crew had put in extra storage shelves, to make up for the cabinets that had been removed. He found out a little later, that the bathroom door had been changed into a pocket door to save space.

"I'm overwhelmed," he said blowing his nose and wiping his eyes. "I never expected anything like this. Who were these people, Vivian?"

"I never saw them before. Alice must have arranged it all. She is a miracle worker, isn't she?"

Zach's bitterness melted under the weight of all this generosity, and he agreed to go to church with Vivian. She decided that the best place to go would be Alice's church. There she recognized a couple of the people that had worked on their house. The one in charge turned out to be the pastor.

"My father was a carpenter," the minister said, when she introduced him to Zach, and told him what role he'd played in the renovation.

"It felt good to roll up my sleeves and get my hands dirty again."

"How can we ever repay you for your kindness?" Zach asked him.

"Keep attending services, and do what you can to help someone else," was the reply.

Chapter Thirteen

THE PROPHECY

On Mother's Day, 1919, when the family sat down to lunch at Ilda and Albert's farm, Doley offered to give the blessing on the food. She and John met with his family most Sundays now that they were married, but on special occasions such as Mother's Day, alternate Christmases, Thanksgivings or a family birthday, they had lunch with the Walden clan.

It took a minute for all the children to quiet down. Then she bowed her head and cleared her throat. "Lord I thank you for all the loved ones around this table, for watching over us and blessing us through the years. Thank you for the food which you have provided and thank you especially for the children, of which there soon will be one more. Amen"

Everyone's head popped up, quickly, as they looked at Doley in surprise. She and John were both grinning from ear to ear.

"Congratulations!"

"Really!"

"Just what we need; another baby in the family."

"I'm so happy for you!"

"When?"

"The doctor says December."

"Maybe it'll be born on my birthday!"

"Maybe it'll be a Christmas baby."

"This is all well and good, but we'd better eat the food before it gets cold."

"Yeah, I'm hungry!" Tucker commented as he grabbed the meat fork and started loading his plate.

Everyone laughed and followed suit, not noticing the gleam in Grace's and Guy's eyes.

When it came time for dessert, Grace and Ilda brought out the pies and stopped two feet short of the table. They stood there silently until the room grew quiet again. Then Guy stood up and raised his water glass, "It may not be champagne, but then we don't drink it anyway."

Everyone giggled.

"Happy Mother's Day to the most wonderful and prolific mother, mother-in-law and grandmother I know," he nodded to Alice. "To Ilda, who opens her home to this rowdy mob almost every Sunday. To Doley-congratulations-may you have a happy, healthy baby. And to Grace, the mother of my children, who is *also* expecting-in November!"

The room erupted in laughter, applause and more congratulations as the pies were served.

He woke up shivering and sore all over. It was raining hard and the cardboard box he was under had soaked through and collapsed on him. There was a gnawing in the pit of his stomach. It took him a minute to remember where he was. He struggled to his feet, pulled his collar up tight around his neck and stumbled toward the church two blocks away, where he knew there was a soup kitchen.

Without warning, he found himself slogging through a foot of snow. "Where did this come from?" He asked himself, confused.

When he rounded the corner, he saw that there was already a long line of men, women and children. It seemed to stretch for miles. He hoped they wouldn't run out of food before he got to the front of the line. Then suddenly he *was* at the front of the line and it was nighttime. "Wasn't it just morning a second ago?"

He picked up a plate and spoon and stepped up to the woman holding a serving spoon, which she dipped into the pot in front of her. The hollow, scraping sound sent a chill through his whole body. The woman smiled at him as she pulled it out and ladled smoking coal onto his plate.

"What? Are you crazy? I can't eat this!"

"Beggars can't be choosers," the woman said to him cheerfully. "Now move on."

The sound of the siren finally broke through to Alice's consciousness and she awoke with a start. "Oh, what a horrible dream!" It seemed so real, yet surreal at the same time. She had the strong feeling that this dream was a premonition.

She told all the men in her family about her dream the next time they were together. Those who knew and believed in her sixth sense withdrew their money from the banks, just in case.

Two months later the stock market crashed, causing all the banks to close. Poverty, hunger and homelessness, just like in Alice's dream, were rampant in the entire country for many years.

Fortunately, most of Alice's family weren't affected that much. Carsie had seniority with the lumber company, and some lumber was still needed. Albert converted most of his crops to fruits and vegetables to feed their extended family and the needy. He still had pigs, goats, chickens and sheep, which occasionally needed to be slaughtered, but he'd had to turn that job over to someone else. After his war experiences, he could no longer stand the sight of a corpse of any kind.

Tucker was still living on the farm.

The hospital's midwife program was discontinued, in order to save money, but Alice was as busy as ever as a personal midwife. Transportation was not a problem anymore-Grace, Mattie, Henry and John all had automobiles and were at her disposal any time they were available. There were also streetcars and taxis when they weren't. Of course that meant she had to have a phone installed in her home.

People still needed doctors, so Charles retained his job.

Frank and Mary had moved to Seattle when the postal service job he'd had with the army had opened up an opportunity to work in the post office in that city.

Lafe had no family to support, so was passed over for retention by the lumber company, in lieu of a married man with children. He moved in with Alice and did whatever work he could find, so as not to burden her. Whenever he couldn't find a paying job, he volunteered at the soup kitchen or a nearby church, which had a shelter for the homeless.

The trains were still running, albeit on reduced schedules, so Guy's job was secure.

John and Doley barely managed to keep their heads above water with his moving and storage company.

The rest of the Bauer clan were in the same boat: Henry had a wrought iron business and learned creative ways to expand his repertoire to stay in business.

His brother Carl managed to make ends meet, because many people couldn't afford gasoline for their cars, and utilized bicycles more. He worked with Henry to make trailers for people to pull behind their bikes. The children competed for picking jobs and gleaning in the orchards and fields. The women helped out, by growing and canning all their own produce and spinning the wool from Albert's sheep, to knit and weave into garments and blankets.

On Thanksgiving Day, 1919, the family gathered early at the farmhouse. It was unseasonably cold and Alice thought it safer to have the meal early and try to get home before dark, especially for those with little ones.

It was almost time to eat-the turkey had come out of the oven, the gravy and the mashed potatoes were being fixed, but the Rowley clan hadn't arrived yet.

"I hope they're all right," Ilda said with concern in her voice.

"Maybe they got held up by a visit from the stork," Alice commented with a smile. "A few days ago, she stopped by on her way home from a doctor appointment and said she'd been having some false labor."

Just then, the door burst open and the Rowley boys spilled in, carrying the pies that they had volunteered to bring for dessert. They were followed by the twins and Guy. Guy stopped in the doorway and waited, while the boys put the pies on the counter and gathered everyone in the front room. They were all curious about the interruption.

Then, with a flourish, Guy stepped aside to let Grace in.

Everyone was surprised and delighted to see her carrying the new baby in her arms.

"When did this happen?"

"Why didn't you tell us?"

"Is it a boy or girl?"

"Shush, you'll wake the baby," Alice directed. "Give them a chance to speak."

"It's a boy-9 pounds and 6 ounces," Grace announced as she transferred her bundle to her mother's arms. "He was born at home two days ago. We didn't tell you then, because we know how you all like surprises."

"Well, you definitely surprised us!"

"What did you name him?"

This time it was Guy who spoke up, "We named him Merle, after my favorite uncle who passed away last year."

"Did you at least tell John and Doley before they left for his family's gathering today?" Albert asked Grace.

"Yes, and I made her promise not to tell anyone until tonight."

After dinner, when they were serving the pies, Alice asked Grace, "You didn't make these all by yourself, did you?"

"Of course not-not entirely. I had lots of help," she said as she tussled Chip's hair.

"I helped take care of the baby while Mama was busy in the kitchen," Ronny said, proudly.

"And I took care of the twins and tried to keep them quiet," Jerry volunteered, "maybe the hardest job of all."

"I'll attest to that!" Guy admitted.

It was Thursday evening, December 16th. John had been asleep for about an hour, but Doley was still up. She had been busy all day making cookies for the church Christmas party. When the last cookies came out of the oven, she set about cleaning up the kitchen. She had been experiencing a little back pain all evening, but attributed it to the weight she was carrying out front and the amount of time she had spent on her feet. She was too busy to dwell on it-there was too much to be done.

She rinsed the last cookie sheet and put it on the drain board. She massaged her sore back as she glanced at the clock, "Eleven already? I think I'll leave these to air dry and get to bed," she said aloud.

She undressed and pulled on her nightgown. While she was brushing her teeth, she felt a strange sensation-something warm running down her legs and into her slippers. She pulled up her nightgown, thinking, "Not urine-I just went ten minutes ago." Then the first contraction started. "John," she yelled, "it's time!"

John didn't stir-he was sound asleep.

Doley reached for a towel and dried herself off, then a smaller one to put between her legs. She went into the bedroom and shook her husband, "John, wake up, John!"

"Huh, vat vant you?" He mumbled as he looked at the clock on the bed stand, "Almost midnight, it is."

Just then, Doley was gripped by a stronger contraction. John was suddenly wide-awake. "Sitten ze down," he said as he bolted out of bed. "Vat you vant I should do?"

"Find someone to fetch my mother," she directed him, "then bring me the box on the shelf in the bathroom."

"Should I, your mother get?" He asked.

"No, the baby may come before you get back." She replied, "Now go, quickly!"

It was one o'clock when Alice came in, courtesy of Henry Krauss. She shooed the nervous John out of the room and took control of the situation. Two hours later, she emerged from the bedroom with the baby in her arms. "It's a girl, and a big, healthy one, at that."

She gave the baby to John and said, "I need to tend to Doley for a few minutes, then you can see her."

They named the little girl Ilda, "after my favorite sister, who practically raised me." Doley said to her sisters-in-law. "Mama was working full-time all my life. Grandma and Grace each played a role, but I remember Ilda's attention and teachings more than anyone else's."

Alice and Doley took the baby into the hospital a week later to get her checked out and show her off. They weighed her at over fourteen pounds.

Since Doley and John had spent Thanksgiving with his family, the Walden clan had the pleasure of their presence for Christmas, when everyone got to hold Little Ilda and Merle.

Because budgets were so tight, the children had to settle for homemade clothes and toys. The adults were happy just to be together and healthy. Tucker, on the other hand, wasn't very fond of crowds or crying babies. He came in from the barn for the meal, then went to his room.

The best present any of them got was seven inches of snowfall on Christmas Eve morning. The children spent the day playing in it, and the adults enjoyed watching the children make snowmen and catch flakes on their tongues. It wasn't cold enough to stick to the roads much. The clouds cleared off enough that night to make the snow that didn't melt, develop what looked like diamonds the next morning.

The Newman children were up early Christmas morning. They couldn't wait to see what Santa had brought them. The younger ones were a little disappointed at first, when they found the meager offerings in their stockings and under the tree. Then their parents showed them the "diamonds" that God had left for them outside, and reminded them that they had food, shelter, good health and each other. "That's more than a lot of people have this year," Albert said.

Twelve-year-old Fay reminded them that the baby Jesus and his parents had to sleep on a bed of hay in a stable, surrounded by cows and sheep.

The same scenario was playing out at the Rowleys and countless other homes that Christmas, and would for several Christmases to come.

Three days later, the children were delighted to wake to two feet of snow on the ground. It was still coming down and blowing into drifts. Carsie knew that the mill would not be in operation in this kind of weather and that the homeless would be in dire straits, so he bundled up and braved the storm to try to reach the shelter.

It took him three hours to travel the eight miles to his destination. He stopped and picked up three half-frozen people along the way, and arrived at nine a.m. When they got to the shelter, two men came out to help them get inside.

Carsie was pleased and surprised to find his mother and Lafe there, attending the injured and sick people.

"What are you doing here?" They asked him.

"God woke me at four this morning and told me I was needed here," was his reply. "I half expected to find Lafe here, but why you, Mama?"

"The same reason as you. We got here before the snow piled up, and have been busy since five o'clock."

"I've been out with Jimmy and Ernie twice, to round up people and bring them in," Lafe told him. "We were planning another foray in about half an hour. You wanna join us?"

"I think he's been out enough for a while," Alice broke in. "It's so rare that we get such severe weather here."

"Wasn't the last bad storm the year Grandpa died?" Carsie asked.

"The ice storm?" Alice answered. "I think you're right. That was a few years ago, wasn't it?"

"Only if you count by fives," Carsie said.

"I remember that!" Lafe chimed in. "That was just before we moved from Bridal Veil, wasn't it?"

Just then, a man burst in the door. "Is there a doctor here? My wife's in labor and I don't think we can make it to the hospital in time!"

"No, but I'm a midwife," Alice answered. "Help him bring her in, boys."

Carsie and Lafe jumped into action and followed the panicked husband outside, as their mother set up a bed in the most private area she could find. As soon as they got the tiny woman inside, she directed them to set up a screen, and other volunteers to bring supplies, as needed. She had brought her medical bag, but everything she would need could not be contained in one small valise.

She listened to the baby's heartbeat and monitored the woman's contractions while the screen was being erected. She examined the woman, who said her name was Kristina, to determine how close she was to delivering.

All this time, one of the other volunteers was keeping the husband busy, and as calm as possible. "Mrs. Walden is an excellent midwife and nurse. In fact, the best in Oregon, I'd guess. Your wife and baby are in good hands."

"Not only that, but they're in God's hands." another told him.

Kristina told Alice that she had received no prenatal care. "We have an old car and just enough food to get by on," she told her.

Her husband, Jim, told Carsie, "I have a part-time, menial job that barely pays our rent on a tiny apartment which we share with my parents."

Upon examination, Alice found that Kristina's cervix was fully dilated and the baby was in distress. "How long ago did your labor begin?" she asked her.

"Last night, at bedtime," was the reply. "Is my baby all right?"

"He hasn't descended as far as he should be. I think his cord is tangled."

She didn't say, "around his neck," as she feared it was, because the baby's heartbeat slowed dramatically with each contraction. Not only that, but the infant was most likely too large for a successful vaginal delivery.

After several more hours of exhausting labor, the baby's heartbeat ceased. Alice had anticipated this outcome and had medicated Kristina, so that she was unaware of the baby's death.

Jim had been listening in and knew, by the lack of crying, that the baby was probably dead. He was very worried about Kristina, now. She was also silent, and he thought, as did the others there, that she might be dead, also. He was afraid to ask or even look Alice in the eye when she emerged from behind the screen.

Those who had been sitting and praying with Jim, stood and left her alone with him.

"Is she...?" He couldn't bring himself to say the word.

"She's sleeping now," Alice answered, as she put her arm around his shoulder. "She lost a lot of blood and I gave her something to help her sleep."

"Does she know...?"

"No, she was too tired and weak to be aware of the outcome."

"Can I see her now?"

"Of course. You should be there when she awakens. It may be quite a while, though. We should get her to the hospital as soon as we can. She needs surgery and a blood transfusion."

The storm was winding down by then, and an hour later, a plow had cleared a path to the hospital. Kristina had not regained consciousness when the ambulance took her away. Jim thanked them all and told Alice, "I know you did all you could for them under the circumstances. God bless you."

"I wish I could have saved the baby, but I guess God had other plans," she answered. "You wait and see; he'll turn this into something good someday and somehow."

He gave her a bear hug and followed the ambulance in his jalopy.

"Are you ready to go home now?" Carsie asked her.

"Yes, as soon as I collect my gear and clean up the mess."

"The mess is already cleaned up, and I put the equipment you used in a pillow slip for later washing. I don't know just how you do that or how you like to pack your bag."

"Thank you Clara. Carsie, why don't you warm up the car while I wash up. Lafe, are you coming?"

"No, I'm going to stay here as long as they need me. I'll see you at home... whenever."

There were several people with frostbite, which the volunteers had treated before. They didn't need to bother Alice about it. She was tired and went straight to bed after eating some oatmeal that Carsie cooked for them. He figured it would be a while before all the outer roads were passable, so he stayed the night at Alice's house.

The next day was Saturday, so both Alice and Carsie slept in. Lafe called at nine o'clock and asked if Carsie could come pick him up. "I'm bushed," he said. "I've been up most of the night."

"We were just finishing breakfast," Carsie replied. "I'll be there soon. How is it going over there? Should I bring Mama along, too?"

"No, we have fresh troops here, and the really sick ones have all been taken to the hospital."

Lafe rested that day, and Carsie went to the farm to see if Albert needed any help. When he pulled up the driveway he heard construction noises at the back of the house. Ilda peeked out the door as he pulled to a stop. "I'm so glad you're here!" she called. "The roof of the addition collapsed early this morning. They're out working on it now."

"I heard the noise and wondered what was up," he called back, then went around to the back of the house.

"Hey, bro," Tucker said when he saw him. "Glad to see ya!"

"Carsie, we could sure use your help with this project," Albert chimed in. "Now that he's here, Tuck, why don't you go check on the livestock?"

As soon as Tucker was out of earshot, he said, "He's great with the animals, but a liability with almost everything else."

"You don't have to tell me. I grew up with him!"

They both knew to keep Tucker busy with fail-proof tasks when and if he returned to help. While they were working together, Albert filled Carsie in on the morning's happenings.

"I had just gotten up to milk the cows when I heard a crash. I checked it out, and found that Tucker had just missed being crushed by a ton of snow that had blown off the main roof. If I hadn't woken him when I did, he would've been asleep when it fell in. I had planned to replace this roof last summer, but..."

"Life doesn't always work out quite as we plan, does it?" Carsie broke in.

"It sure doesn't."

Chapter Fourteen

EASTER SURPRISES

January, 1920 was mild and rainy, but February brought a chill that caught most people off-guard. March was no better-there were a few warmer days in mid-month, leading some to believe that spring weather would come on time. The plum and cherry trees were blooming right on cue, as well as the crocuses and other early spring flowers, lifting people's spirits and hopes.

Easter was in late March that year. The Newman children went to bed on Easter Eve, all excited about wearing their new Easter clothes to church and finding the eggs and candy that the Easter Bunny would hide for them. When they woke up the next morning, they had a bigger surprise than they expected-four inches of fresh, fluffy snow!

Naturally, Albert was the first to discover it. It was only about two inches deep and still coming down steadily when he arose at four o'clock to do the morning chores. "Thankfully, it's not nearly as cold out there as it looks," he told Ilda as he came back in for breakfast.

"Good," she said, "as soon as I saw it, I worried about the fruit trees-thinking we might have a limited crop this year."

Just then, they heard children's shouts from upstairs.

"Look, it's snowing outside!"

"That's good. I wouldn't want it to snow inside!"

"Ha, ha, ha, very funny!"

"I want to make a snowman!"

"I hope the Easter Bunny made it okay."

"We'll have to wait until it melts to find the eggs, if he did."

By this time all of them were downstairs. They came streaming into the kitchen, as excited and noisy as on Christmas morning. Grace placed a large platter of pancakes on the table as they took their seats.

"Did you see the snow, Mama?"

"Are we going to be able to make it to church?"

"Any sign of the Easter Bunny, Daddy?"

"I want to make a snowman!"

"You'll have to wait until we get back from church."

"What if it melts by then?"

"Too bad!"

"Mama, do we have to go to church today. I'd rather stay home and play in the snow."

Ilda put the rest of the food on the table as they took each other's hands in preparation for the blessing. Ilda took her seat, and they bowed their heads. Before praying, Albert looked around to make sure no one was peeking.

"What a wonderful family I've been blessed with," he thought to himself. Then he prayed: "Dear Lord, thank you for the family gathered around this table and for the love we have for each other. Thank you for good health, this warm, dry home to shelter in, for the beauty of your creation and for the food to sustain us. Thank you for the cross that you willingly bore for our sins, and for the promise of the resurrection, which we celebrate this day. Thank you for your love and care, amen."

As they ate, they discussed the possibility of changing their plans for the day.

Ilda spoke up first. "I don't think we can make it to the morning service with this snow," she reasoned, "Besides, we don't know how much longer it'll keep coming down."

"Yes, I agree," Albert answered her, "It would be risky, and we'd probably be too late getting there, anyway. Don't they usually have an evening service, on Easter?"

"Yes, Papa, it starts at six o'clock," Faye chimed in.

"But it'll be dark by then," Elsie May pouted, crossing her arms over her chest. "I don't like the dark. Besides, my friends won't be there."

"We'll go to the evening service if the snow doesn't pile up much more," her father confirmed.

"You mean I get to stay home with Uncle Tuck and make a snowman?" Cleo nearly bounced out of his chair, "yippee!"

By the time they finished eating breakfast and got bundled up to go outside, it had stopped snowing. The Easter egg hunt was forgotten as they frolicked and formed large snowballs for a snowman.

While they were playing in the yard, Grace prepared their usual Easter lamb roast. She wondered how many other family members would brave the elements to attend. They were supposed to bring the rest of the food. She sent Albert to the cellar for a bag of potatoes, a couple of onions and some beets and green beans that she and her sisters had put up the previous summer. Since they had no telephone, she had to be prepared. She wouldn't worry about the desert. They could live without it if it didn't arrive.

Faye came in the door, knocking the snow off of her boots and removing her gloves and hat. "Papa, you better go check on Dotty. She's acting funny-like maybe she's getting ready to drop her foal."

"Well, maybe we *won't* be going to the evening service after all," Albert surmised as he pulled on his rubber boots and took his hat and coat off the hook. "Don't hold supper for us."

On his way out to the barn, he called to Tucker, having a snowball fight with the children, "Tuck, come with me. Faye says the mare needs attending."

"Can we come too, Papa," the children asked.

"No, if she's in labor, we want to keep her as calm as possible."

The spell was broken then, and the children suddenly realized that they were cold and wet, so they wandered back inside.

"Don't track snow and mud on my clean floors!" Ilda reminded them. "And don't just drop your boots and coats either. We're expecting the rest of the family, any minute."

"I think they just drove up," Buddy said as he helped Jojo get his boots off.

Ilda looked out the window and saw Doley and John pulling up in front. Carsie, Alice and Lafe were right behind them.

"It looks like we may have a full house after all," she said. "I guess we won't be needing the vegetables and onions."

"I wonder what Uncle Guy and Aunt Grace brought for dessert?" Nina said as she peered out the door.

"You and your sweet tooth!" Faye exclaimed. "You're going to get another toothache if you keep it up."

Lafe came in the door with the vegetables, followed by Doley with the baby and Alice with the mashed potatoes. They closed the door and started removing their coats and hats.

"Where's Uncle John and Uncle Carsie?" Faye asked.

"They heard some noise in the barn, and went to investigate," Alice replied.

Lafe took a deep breath as he gave his sister a hug, "The roast sure smells good."

"Were Grace, Guy, and the children at church, this morning?" Ilda asked as she embraced her mother and sister.

"Yes, but they had to go home for something. They'll be along shortly," Doley answered as she shifted Little Ilda to her other hip.

"You got a lot more snow out here than we did in town," Alice remarked. "We wondered why you weren't at church until we were halfway here. The roads are a little slippery, but I think they'll be clear, by the time we're ready to leave."

"We were talking about going to the evening service," Ilda told them, "but we may not make it, then, either."

"Why is that?" Doley asked. "By the way, what's going on in the barn?"

"Dottie decided to have her baby, today!" Nina answered, excitedly.

"Elsie May?" Buddy called; his arms loaded with plates, "Will you help me set the table, please?"

"Did you see the snowman Uncle Tucker helped us make?" Cleo asked his grandmother when she picked him up.

"Yes I did. You all did a fine job. Oh my, you're as cold as we are! Did you just come in?"

Carsie came in the door smiling. As soon as he closed the door and got his coat off, there were more hugs and greetings.

They went into the living room, where everyone wanted to hold Little Ilda. Doley relinquished possession of the baby and went into the kitchen to see how the dinner preparations were coming along.

Fifteen minutes later, the Rowley clan arrived. The children came in the door with their usual ruckus-Jerry trying to keep them under control while carrying one of the pies that they had brought to contribute to the feast. Chip was carrying a pie, also.

Grace came in next, with baby Merle. "Guy will be in shortly with the last pie. He heard voices in the barn, and had to go investigate."

Ilda spoke up next, "Dinner is almost ready. I hope they'll all be in soon. Though Albert said not to wait for him and Tucker."

"Dottie's having her baby today!" Ginny and Ginger exclaimed, repeating what they'd heard from their cousins.

"Oh, how exciting!" Grace replied.

Half an hour later, the babies were changed, fed and put down for naps. The food was on the table and the family were being seated, when John, Tucker and Guy came in from the barn. Immediately, the children began clamoring for an update on Dottie and her foal. The men did their best to ignore them, while removing their outer things and warming themselves in front of the fire. Carsie and Alice were in the kitchen carving the roast and pouring the gravy into the gravy boats.

"Sit back down and be quiet," Grace and Ilda urged them. "You'll wake the babies, and the food will get cold."

Alice said the blessing.

As the dishes were being passed around, Albert and Tucker came in the door, "Well, what's the news on Dottie?" Ilda asked.

"Everything is fine. You go ahead and start eating while we wash up," Albert directed. "I'll tell you all about it when I come back."

Most of them were almost too excited to eat, except that they were all very hungry. When Albert returned, he sat down calmly and accepted the plate that Ilda had prepared for him. He took a bite of potatoes and turkey as if nothing had happened. Most of the eating was put on hold as Albert became the center of attention.

"Well, Papa?" Ilda asked. "We're all on pins and needles. Is it a boy or a girl?"

Albert looked around at all the expectant faces, and with deliberate slowness, put his fork down, finished chewing, swallowed and dabbed his mouth with his napkin. The silence was palpable. "Both," he said, and then resumed eating.

At first, everyone looked confused, then they realized that he meant twins! The children got so excited that they wanted to go see them immediately. Alice had to take the reins in hand. She stood and waited for the tumult to die down, then turned to Albert.

"They're your horses, and you know what's best for them. You decide what to do and we'll all abide by it.

"Children, finish your dinner and wait your turn to see the foals." When she heard some groans, she added, "The first one to complain, won't get to see them at all, today!"

After dinner, Albert conferred with Guy and Alice in the kitchen to come up with a plan.

"Here's what we'll do:" he announced, when they were all assembled in the living room, "The Rowley's need to be the first to leave, so their family will go first. One parent will take the youngest children, then the other parent will take the older ones. When they come back in, the visiting adults can go out. My children can wait-they'll be able to see the foals every day. If there's no time before we leave for the evening service at church, they can wait until morning to see them."

Grace, Ginny and Ginger were the first, with Albert attending, to see the new arrivals. "Oh Mama, they're so cute."

"What're you going to name them, Uncle Albert?"

"They're so wobbly on those skinny legs."

"Look, they're knock-kneed, just like us."

"That one has spots just like his Mama."

"What are those things hanging down from their tummies?"

After a few minutes, Grace told them, "Okay girls, it's time for the boys to have a look,".

Guy, Chip, Jerry and Ronny were next, while Grace nursed Merle. Then Doley, John, Lafe and Carsie-all with many of the same comments.

Ilda and her children only had time for a quick peek before sending off their extended family and getting changed for church.

The Easter Bunny arrived while they were gone, courtesy of their uncle Tucker, who stayed behind to keep an eye on the new foals.

"The Easter Bunny must have figured the eggs would get buried under the snow, so he hid them in the barn. I almost stepped on one while cleaning up in here earlier," Tucker told them.

"I guess the Easter Bunny is smarter than we thought," Ilda remarked with a wink at Tucker.

The children were already full of candy from church, so had to save their personal stash for later.

Dottie's babies were the hit of the Newman children, their cousins and friends that whole spring and summer. Unlike their mother, they weren't needed, so had to be sold as soon as they were weaned. The children were heartbroken, but understood how it was on a farm.

Two weeks after Easter, both of their ewes gave birth; one to twins and one to triplets. As soon as they were weaned, one of the male lambs was sold to the butcher and the other was slaughtered to share with the family, but the females were kept for their wool. The money from the sale of the colts and the lamb, was used for paint and lumber, to repair the barn, the house roof and the fence. What little remained was used to purchase new shoes for the children.

Jerry and Chip had caught some rabbits the year before and bred them for their meat and pelts. Carsie and Guy helped them tan the skins, so their mother and aunts could make them into winter coats and hats, and buntings for the babies, as they were born into the clan.

The Newmans' pigs ate leftovers from everyone's tables, and their meat, along with the other animal products that they didn't need themselves, was shared or bartered with neighbors and friends or traded for goods at the store, dentist and doctor, veterinarian services and animal feed. They had six brood hens, instead of just two, as before, to increase the number of fryers and of eggs. They also kept four cows instead of two, to supply milk and veal to their extended family.

The women worked hard sewing, spinning, weaving, knitting and preserving the garden crops at harvest. The children who weren't old enough to help with the farming were enlisted, as soon as they were able, to weed and pick vegetables in the gardens, collect eggs and feed the smaller animals. Since the whole clan relied on products from the farm, they all pitched in on chores and expenses whenever they could.

Carsie had inherited his father's leather tooling kit and used it to repair shoes, make belts, wallets and other leather goods for Christmas and birthday presents. He and Lafe supplied them all with scraps and branches from the mill and the forest, for firewood. They all felt very blessed to have each other to rely on through these hard times, and shared what they could of their goods, talents and time with the less fortunate.

One of those less fortunate was a prostitute, who tried to entice Lafe as he was walking home from the soup kitchen. He had always been pleasant, but walked on past her without stopping, so as not to cause her or himself any trouble. He had noticed the last few times that he had seen her, that she was getting weak and skinny. When she called to him this time, her eyes seemed to plead, "Help me." So he talked to his mother about her.

"If you can spirit her away in the guise of a date, I'll check out her health and see what I can do to get her away from that horrible situation. Just be careful. Her employer may be watching and can probably spot a phony a mile away. You could be attacked. It would probably be a good idea to have Carsie or Guy standing by to watch your back.

"Here's the money you may need to show or give ahead of time to take her. You're a good man to do this for her," she said as she gave him a kiss and sent him off. She knew she could trust him, because he had been raised in the love and admonition of the Lord. He was morally strong and wise for his age.

The only one of Alice's children, that she wasn't sure about, was Tucker. He was so naive. He had never showed any interest in the spiritual life. He said he believed in Jesus and accepted his forgiveness, as a child of ten, but she never heard him praying or saw him reading his bible. He seldom attended church services with them, and he had always kept to himself so much, that she wondered if anyone really knew him well.

Two days later, Carsie came to the shelter after work. When the brothers had a few minutes alone, during cleanup, Lafe told him what he wanted to do, and asked if he would help.

"Of course, little brother. How could I turn down an offer like that?" He gave Lafe a punch in the arm and said, "The weather is on our side, I think. It's dark and moonless tonight. If she's there, we'll get her. What's the plan?"

"I thought you could help me with that," Lafe answered. "After all, you're much older and wiser than I am."

Carsie stooped over and mimed using a cane, like and old man. "Yes I am, Sonny. And don't you forget it."

Lafe punched him back and they laughed, drawing some grins from the other volunteers.

An hour later, the two went outside and made plans as they walked toward their destination. When they got to within half a block of her corner, Carsie went on ahead while Lafe hung back in the shadows. It had been decided that Carsie would be a better candidate for the role of the John, because he was not known to the girl or anyone else who may be watching. Lafe had given him a description of the girl so Carsie could identify her.

The poor girl looked as if she would pass out at any moment. She was pale and her eyes were sunken. When she saw him, she straightened up and, with obvious effort, called out, "Hi there, handsome, lookin' for a good time?"

"I just might be," he answered. "Depends on how much it'll cost me."

Her pimp stepped out of a doorway, nearby, and answered for her. "That'll be five bucks, mister, in advance."

Carsie looked around to make sure there was no one else watching but Lafe, and pulled out his wallet. He gave the man a crisp five-dollar bill, and the man pushed the girl over to him. "Have her back in two hours. She's got more clients to serve tonight," he said with a sneer.

Carsie didn't offer his arm to the girl; pretending not to care about her at all. "Come on," he said a little gruffly, "My room is back this way about a block."

As soon as they were out of sight of the pimp and within reach of Lafe, both men took an arm to support her and led her back toward the Shelter, where Carsie's car was waiting.

She didn't seem very alarmed. She was too sick and numb to care anymore. She had prayed that someone would put her out of her misery soon. When they walked into the light of the shelter sign, so that she could see Lafe's face, she knew she was safe. She gave into her exhaustion and fainted.

They put her in the car and drove to their mother's house. Alice was expecting them and had her bed and medical bag ready. She held the door while they carried the semi-conscious girl in and placed her on the bed. Alice took her vitals, then shooed the boys out so she could undress the girl and do a thorough exam. Besides being dehydrated, feverish and obviously malnourished, the girl had bruises all over her body. Alice found exactly what she had expected to find, when she did a check of her privates. Her heart went out to the poor girl.

Alice made her as comfortable as possible, then left her alone just long enough to report to her sons that she needed to be taken to the hospital by ambulance.

"I'll go with her," Lafe offered. "After all, it was my idea to rescue her." Carsie was already on the phone, ordering the transport.

Lafe rode along in the ambulance, while Alice called the maternity clinic. She knew that Teresa was working the night shift all that month. She filled her in on the girl's situation and asked her to make sure that she had the best and most tender care that they could supply.

When the ambulance arrived at the hospital, a nurse and an orderly were waiting at the emergency entrance, along with a woman gynecologist.

They checked her over and hooked her up to intravenous fluids, typed and cross-matched her blood and started a transfusion. Then she was taken to intensive care.

Lafe was still there, waiting when she awoke the next morning, at seven. Teresa had just left for home, but Alice had come in a few minutes before and was sitting in the waiting room with Lafe. The nurse came out and told Alice that she could come in to see her for a few minutes.

Permission was not given for Lafe to go in, so he stood, looking through the window. Her color was much better than the night before, he noted.

Shortly after Alice went in, she cranked the bed up a little, so the girl, who said her name was Sylvia, could see out the window. She waved at Lafe and smiled. He could see her lips form the words, "Thank you."

Alice talked to Sylvia a few minutes while the nurse was taking her vitals. "Wasn't there another man, too, last night?" Sylvia asked.

"Yes, that was his brother, Carsie."

"I think you must all be Angels sent by God," she said as she squeezed Alice's hand. "I had been praying to die, and thought my prayer had been answered last night."

"You almost did," Alice told her. "God must have other plans for you."

"I can't imagine what. I'm a nobody, with no talent and no value to nobody."

"Don't sell yourself short," Alice replied. "God uses the weak to conquer the strong and the simple to confound the wise. One of my best friends was found in a situation similar to yours, and she is now a wife, nurse and mother of two precious children."

The nurse Interrupted, "The doctor will be in to see you in an hour or so. He'll decide if you can be moved onto the ward and meet your rescuer. Breakfast will be served, shortly. Do you think you could eat something?"

"I'm hungry, but I don't know if I can. My mouth hurts."

"We'll bring you something soft to eat."

After the nurse left, Sylvia had some interesting and important questions to ask Alice.

"You talk like you know God personally. Are you an angel?"

"I am not, I assure you. I'm just as frail and imperfect as anyone. But I can say that I know God, as well as I can with my limited mind. So do most of my children, my closest friends and many of my colleagues here at the hospital."

Sylvia looked incredulous. "How is that possible?"

Breakfast arrived then, and Alice could tell that Sylvia was tired, so she promised to return later, to continue their conversation.

Alice was glad that the witnessing opportunity had been delayed. She was getting a nasty headache. She went home, took some aspirin and laid down. Sleep didn't come easily, but after about an hour, she dozed off. She was awakened by the telephone at three in the afternoon.

"Hello, Mr. Jones. Yes, I understand. I'll be there as soon as I can." She grabbed her coat and obstetrical bag, locked the door, then remembered that she hadn't had lunch. She went back inside and snagged an apple from the bowl on the table, relocked the door and caught the bus to her patient's house.

She was grateful that it was an uncomplicated delivery, but by the time she left their home, it was after visiting hours at the hospital. She went home, had some leftovers from the ice box and went to bed. Lafe had come home while she was gone, and was fast asleep in his room. She awoke to the smell of bacon, eggs, toast and coffee. She put on her robe, opened the door and greeted Lafe on her way to the bathroom.

"Good morning, Mama. I'll fix you a plate while you're in there."

While she ate, he told her what he'd learned from Sylvia, and how much her health had improved. "I got to visit her after she was transferred to a bed on the ward. I'm going back there after breakfast. Do you want to go with me?"

"Yes, I wanted to go back yesterday, but I got a maternity call."

"I figured as much and told her that. She wants to see you and thank you."

On the way to the hospital, Lafe told her more about the talk he'd had with Sylvia the day before. "She asked me about spiritual matters, and I was able to lead her to the Lord. She said that you'd opened that door for her earlier."

Sylvia continued to improve. By the time she was released a week later, an aunt of hers had been located. She came to take Sylvia to her home, in Idaho. They never saw her again, but she stayed in touch, via letters. She never married, but became a social worker, specializing in rehabilitating children of abuse, and former prostitutes, such as herself.

Chapter Fifteen

ORPHAN BOYS

Frank and Mary were shopping at their local market in Seattle one Saturday afternoon in February, 1920, when they heard a ruckus at the back of the store. A boy was yelling, "Let me go! Let me go!" Then a man's voice, "You thieving little brat-I'll teach you not to sneak in here and steal from me! Violet, call the police!"

All the shoppers were craning their necks in the direction of the noise, when Frank noticed a young boy; maybe four or five years old skulking about, working his way toward the front door. Frank assumed that this boy was in league with the captured lad, so reached out, scooped him up and tucked him under his arm. The boy struggled, but uttered not a word. Frank carried him to where he'd heard the confrontation.

When he got to the office, where the store owner was holding the other, older boy, he said, "I think these two are together. He was acting suspiciously." When Frank put the boy down, he ran straight into the other boy's arms.

"You're brothers, aren't you?" The store owner asked them, "Where are your parents?"

"Ain't got none," the older boy said. "We don't need nobody."

"Did you run away from an orphanage?" Frank asked.

"Never been in no orphanage," he replied. "Don't wanna be, neither. We take care of ourselves."

"Yeah, by stealing from hard-working people like me!" The proprietor growled.

"Living on the streets and stealing is no way to take care of your little brother," Frank told the boy. "What if one of you should get sick? What would happen to him then?"

The boy looked sad, hung his head and pulled his brother closer.

Mary was standing at the door listening. She came in, put her hands on the boys' shoulders and spoke to them. "How would you like to come home with us? We don't have any children, so there's plenty of room for the two of you. You'll have a warm, safe place to sleep and plenty of food."

"That sounds nice, don't it Bobby?"

The younger boy nodded his head, looked up at Mary, and smiled.

Just then, a policeman walked in. "What's the problem here? Someone call about a robbery?"

"False alarm," the owner said. "The boy was just fetching something for his mom."

The policeman looked doubtful-he'd seen the boys before. They were dirty, always in the same clothes, and never with an adult. He had tried to take them to the police station or a shelter, but they had always run away. He could see that Frank and Mary had genuine compassion for the boys and that the boys seemed to trust them. "I'll see you around," he said, "take care."

Frank and Mary continued their shopping with the brothers in tow, picking up some extra items for the boys, including some new clothes. When they got home, Mary put the groceries away and started dinner, while Frank got the boys into the bathtub and made sure they washed every crack and crevice, thoroughly. He changed the water twice during the process and shampooed their hair three times to make sure all the dirt and vermin were removed.

While the boys were drying themselves and putting on their new pajamas, he put their old clothes in the outside trashcan. Then he made up the bed in the spare bedroom.

When the boys came out of the bathroom, Mary was surprised at how handsome they were without all the dirt.

After devouring three helpings of "the best supper they'd ever had", the boys went to bed and slept twelve hours straight.

When they got up in the morning, Frank had already gone to church. He had promised to do usher duties that Sunday morning. Mary volunteered to stay home with the boys, to let them sleep as long as they needed.

She pulled a platter of pancakes, scrambled eggs and bacon out of the oven. "Sit down at the table. We've already eaten."

"Is this all for us?" Terry exclaimed.

"If you leave any, I'm sure our friend's pigs and chickens will be happy to finish it for you."

She poured them some milk and orange juice, then sat down with a cup of coffee and asked Terry, "when you're done with breakfast, would you mind telling me how you ended up homeless and alone, and why Bobby doesn't speak? We didn't want to bother you about it last night. You were so hungry and tired."

The boy mumbled, "Uhm, hm," as he chewed a large mouthful of pancakes.

"Bobby, do you know how to read?" she asked the silent boy. He looked at her and shook his head.

"No," Terry answered for him, "he ain't never been to school."

"I'll be right back," she said as she went out the door. She came back a few minutes later with some picture books and toys for Bobby to play with. "I borrowed these from our next-door neighbor," she told them.

When they finished eating, Bobby went into the living room to play, while Terry told Mary their story: "Papa got drafted and went off to the war, leaving us, Mama and our sister Penny, home alone. We got a telegram that said he was missing in action. We were all very sad-not knowing if he was dead or alive.

"A couple months later, Bobby and I got real sick. We thought we were going to die. Penny got sick, next. We were just startin' to feel better, when Mama got sick." He paused as tears welled in his eyes.

"They both died?" She asked him, gently.

He nodded and looked at Bobby, playing in the other room. After collecting himself, he continued, "We were pretty shook up, seeing 'em die. I went to the neighbors for help, but they were all too sick, or scared to come over. The ground was froze, and I was still weak. After a few days, when Bobby and I was both feelin' stronger, we wrapped 'em in blankets and drug 'em out behind the shed. He ain't spoke since that day.

"We stayed there 'bout two months, hopin' Pop would come home-till we run outta food. Then we packed a bag, left 'im a note and set out. We jumped a train and came here. I figured we could find some place to hole up, beg or scrounge through garbage cans if we had to."

"How long ago was that?" She asked him.

"About a year," he answered.

"It gets so cold at night, especially this time of year. Where do you sleep?"

"We usually sneak into a store or restaurant just before they close, and hide. When everyone was gone, we could eat whatever we wanted."

Frank stopped by the police station on his way home, to see if they could find out anything about the boys and track down any relatives. Terry had told them their last name and what town they were from the night before.

They gave the boys a week to get settled and comfortable before taking them to their doctor for a checkup, then enrolled them in school. Bobby was introduced to kindergarten, and Terry, after testing, was placed in a third grade class, though he was of fourth grade age.

The Doctor had found nothing wrong with Bobby's throat, and said that his condition was most likely trauma-induced. "We don't know that much about it. It could last weeks or years, then one day something may click in his brain and he will start talking again. In the meantime, just be patient and encourage him to do things for himself and communicate with you, as best he can, without his brother's help."

Terry adjusted well, although slower than they'd hoped. He started keeping company with another shy boy on the playground and in the cafeteria. He continued to be very protective of Bobby, who remained silent, extremely shy and aloof. His teacher reported that he seemed to be very intelligent, but had made no friends, yet. "I catch glimpses of his brother checking on him almost every day on the way to and from recess and lunch. Bobby is usually watching for him."

Frank and Mary took the brothers to church services, where both boys remained in the auditorium with them for several Sundays. Then one Sunday, a pleasant young woman approached them as they were leaving. "Hello, my name is Susan. I'm the children's church coordinator. Are you new to our congregation?"

"Yes, fairly so," Frank answered. Then he introduced them all.

"We'd love to have you boys join us in Sunday school next week," Susan told the boys.

"It's up to them," Mary said.

Bobby was hiding behind her skirt, but Terry looked thoughtful, then he said, "Would we be able to stay together?"

"Of course you can. You can stay in his class or he can stay with you."

"I'll think about it. It's probably not as boring as the big room," he replied.

The next Sunday, they arrived at church a little early and went looking for Susan. She seemed genuinely thrilled to see them again. "Did you decide to join us today?"

"We thought we'd give it a try," Terry answered.

"Aggie," Susan called to a young woman nearby, "would you take these young men to class while I get some information from their parents?"

"We're not their parents," Frank remarked. "They're orphans that we're caring for until the authorities can find some relatives to take them in."

"Oh, I'm sorry. Are you their foster parents?" She handed Frank a form to fill out.

"No," Mary answered. "We rescued them off the streets. They'd been on their own for over a year."

"Oh my goodness! They must be very resourceful to have survived on their own! Do you know what happened to their parents?"

"Terry told us that their father didn't come back from the war, and the rest of their family died from that horrible flu."

Frank finished filling out the form and handed it back to her. "We'll be sitting in the back row if you should need us for any reason."

"Thank you. I'm sure they'll be fine."

And they were. They looked forward to Sunday school every week from then on.

One day in early May, Mary got a visit from a policeman. "Mrs. Frank Walden?"

"Yes, may I help you?"

"I understand you reported finding and taking in a couple of orphaned boys. We've heard from Washington D.C, that some relatives have been located, back East. We would like you, your husband and the boys to come down to the courthouse for verification purposes, as soon as it's convenient for you."

"Of course. May I have the address, please? We haven't lived here long, and don't know our way around Seattle very well, yet."

She had mixed emotions-it would be best for the boys to be with relatives, providing they could take care of them properly. On the other hand, she and Frank had become very attached to them. They really weren't much trouble.

When the boys came home from school, she kept them busy with homework and chores until Frank came home. They sat down to dinner and said the blessing. As they were passing the dishes around, she said, nonchalantly, "I had a visitor today-a policeman."

The boys didn't pay much attention, but Frank's curiosity was piqued. "What did he want?"

"He asked if all four of us could come down to the courthouse at our first convenience."

Bobby was the only one eating at this point-now she had Terry's full attention. "All four of us?" he asked.

"Yes, it seems they've found some relatives of yours back East, somewhere."

At this announcement, Terry's focus went back to his plate, silently pushing his food around. Bobby stopped, slid off of his chair, came over to Mary and clung to her.

"What's wrong, Bobby?" She asked.

"We don't want to leave you," Terry answered without looking up.

"We're very fond of you, too," Frank said, "But it's best if you be with kin, providing they are good people. Let's give them a chance, at least, okay? Now let's finish eating. Mary went to a lot of trouble to fix this delicious meal."

Two days later, Frank got off work early enough to get to the courthouse well before closing. He stood in line while the rest of them found seats. Half an hour later they were ushered into an office, where they were greeted by a gray-haired gentleman with wire-rimmed glasses perched atop a large pointed beak.

Frank handed him the paper given to him by the clerk. He read it then said, "Have a seat while I locate the document."

He stood, turned to a large bank of file cabinets and rifled through one of them until he found what he was looking for. He sat back down and spent several minutes perusing the contents of the folder.

Then he closed it and placed it on his desk, sat back and folded his hands over his ample belly. "Do you have any positive identification of the boys' identities?"

"No, only what they told us the night we found them," Frank answered.

"You should have seen them when we first found them-It was obvious that they were homeless. Our hearts went out to them," Mary added, "We had no reason to doubt their story."

"Well, everything they told you *seems* to be true," he looked over his glasses at Terry, "A couple in South Carolina: A Mr. and Mrs. Clive Richardson have been located and contacted, who seem to be the sister and brother-in-law of your father."

Then he turned to Frank. "They have three children of their own; two girls and a boy. They said they would send train fare for the boys and one of you to come and meet them. Then if the boys agree to stay with them, they would be pleased to accept them into their family."

Frank and Mary looked at each other, then at the boys, who were very quiet and solemn. "Let us think and talk about it couple of days, then I'll get back to you," Frank said, as he stood and shook the man's hand.

The day after school let out for the summer, Mary and the boys boarded the train bound for Charleston, South Carolina. It was a long journey. The train wasn't crowded; not many people could afford train travel anymore, due to the depression, but the farther east and south they went, the hotter and stuffier the air inside the train car became.

Mary got quite ill-unable to keep any food on her stomach. By the time they arrived in Charleston, Jerry and the conductor had to help her down from the train, where their hosts were waiting on the platform. They were an attractive and pleasant couple. They greeted the boys cheerfully, but reservedly. They also seemed genuinely concerned about Mary's condition.

"Now I'm really glad we left the children at home," Jolene said. "We didn't want to overwhelm you or the boys."

"We would have had to bring both cars," Clive added.

Jolene sat in the back seat with the boys, leaving the roomy front seat for Mary. Clive drove home slowly and carefully for Mary's sake. The car ride seemed interminable to her, just as the train ride had been, though it only lasted half an hour.

During the ride to the house, Jolene talked with Terry. He unraveled their sad story, while Bobby craned his neck at the shacks, dark-skinned people, then the grand estates, stables and horses along their route.

When they turned into the long driveway, the boys couldn't believe their eyes. "Wow, this is where you live?!" Jerry exclaimed.

Mary was impressed with the neatness of the house and grounds. It was larger and nicer than any house she'd ever lived in, but not large enough to qualify as a mansion. She had expected the couple's children to come running out excitedly to greet them, but it was ominously quiet.

Jolene ushered the boys into the foyer, while Clive was assisting Mary. She asked to use the restroom first, so Jolene took over as her assistant, while Clive took the boys into the kitchen for a snack and a drink. "There's some fruit on the table, or if you would prefer, a plate of fresh, homemade cookies on the counter there," he directed as he took a pitcher of milk out of the refrigerator. "Help yourself, while I go find our children."

A black woman, dressed in a plain grey dress with a white apron and cap, entered the room just then. "Welcome home, Sir," she addressed her employer. "The children are in the back yard. I came in to fetch some lemonade for them."

"Terry, Bobby, this is our housekeeper, Julia." Then he turned to the woman and asked, "Would you like me to take the drinks out? I think these boys might like to wash their hands and faces before digging into your delicious, molasses cookies."

"That sounds like a fine idea, Sir," Julia replied. "Come with me, boys." She led them into the children's bathroom.

After she left them and closed the door, Jerry remarked, "They seem nice enough. I wonder what the kids are like."

After they finished in the restroom, they went back to the kitchen, where Julia was waiting for them with plates of cookies and cut fruit, along with full classes of milk. While the boys were enjoying their snack, Jolene came in alone. She explained that Mary was resting in the main guest room. "I came to get her a glass of cold water and some crackers to help settle her stomach."

"What's wrong with her?" Julia asked.

"It could be a number of things: The heat, the train motion, a virus, or the usual for a young married woman."

Julia smiled. "Aah, that's probably it. Whatever it is though, I hope she's better, soon."

"Me too. If she's not better in the morning, I'll call the doctor."

She dismissed Julia, then turned to the brothers. "How do you boys like it here, so far?"

Terry nodded as he washed a bite of cookie down with his milk. "We never been in such a fancy house before. We never saw nobody like her, neither, till a couple days ago. There sure are a lot of 'em in these parts."

"I've lived here all my life," Jolene said, thoughtfully. "I've never been out west. It never occurred to me that other places might not have any Negroes."

"Mr. and Mrs. Walden said they've seen a few out west, but there aren't very many."

Then he changed the subject. "Your kids sure are quiet. How come we haven't met 'em yet?"

"When you're done with your snack, I'll take you out to meet them."

A few minutes later, she led them through the house and out to the back yard. The brothers were at first taken aback, and then puzzled by what they saw: A strange-looking boy, obviously impaired, about Terry's size, in a wheelchair, and twin girls, a little smaller than Bobby, who acted and talked much like two-year-olds. There was a young woman with them.

"Children, I'd like you to meet Terry and Bobby; your cousins from Seattle." And then to the brothers: "This is Sam, Melissa, Bonnie, and their nurse, Ramona."

"Hello," Terry said, shyly.

Bobby clung to his brother-halfway hiding behind him.

Sam, sitting slumped sideways in his wheelchair, made a guttural sound and flailed his arms a bit. The girls toddled over, smiling broadly and aiming their outstretched arms at the two boys, who stepped back.

"Slow down, girls!" Jolene laughed, as she knelt down and gathered them into her arms. "They're a little shy. They need to get to know you first."

"Ahwite," they answered in tandem.

A few minutes later, after the girls' friendliness had won the boys over, Clive came out of the house, "I see that you've met the rest of the family, boys. Would you like to tour the house and grounds with me?"

They both nodded, whereupon the girls took the boys' and their father's hands, and off they went.

Mary slept until just before dinnertime. Jolene went to check on her and met her coming out of the bathroom. "Are you feeling better, dear?"

"Yes, but I think I'll feel even better after some dinner and a nice, hot bath."

"I understand. You let me know when you're ready and I'll have our housekeeper Julia get one started for you. I had her fix up something special for your dinner, just in case your stomach isn't ready for our usual fare."

"Where are all the children?" Mary asked, as Clive seated her at the dining table, set for three.

"They're eating in the kitchen tonight," Jolene answered. "We thought it best to keep things quiet and simple for you tonight. You can meet them tomorrow."

"How are Bobby and Terry doing? May I see them?"

"Of course; I'll get them," Clive said. He stood, exited the room and returned with the boys, who seemed to her to be much more relaxed than when they arrived.

"How are you boys doing?" She asked them. "How do you like it here?"

"We're fine. They've been good to us." Terry answered.

Bobby gave her a rare smile and a quick hug before running back to the kitchen.

"What was that all about?" She asked Terry.

"I think he wanted to get back to dinner. The housekeeper, Julia, is a real good cook."

"I'll let you go, then. I just wanted to check on you."

He gave her a quick kiss on the cheek, then ran after his brother.

"Well, it looks like I needn't have worried about them."

During dinner, Clive and Jolene told Mary all about their family; that they'd been unable to have children of their own, and had adopted Sam and the twins because they had compassion for them as soon as they met them.

"Their parents had rejected them, and they weren't getting the love or the care they needed at the orphanage. Sam had been there since birth, and was three years old when we first saw him. The girls were two years old, and weren't even sitting up or eating solid food, yet."

"We fell in love with them, instantly. They were so lonely and obviously craving affection."

"You are stronger than I," Mary said. "The boys were in need of help, but they aren't nearly as needy as yours must be."

"We have plenty of help," Jolene admitted. "I don't think we could have managed to take in all three without Julia and Ramona's help. Whenever one of them is sick or takes time off, I find myself overwhelmed and exhausted before they come back."

"I try to help when I can, but my work keeps me busy, and I can't lift Sam anymore, because of a war injury I received while on assignment in Europe," Clive admitted.

"That reminds me; I heard from the war Department last week, that their father's body had been found and processed. I'm having it flown here for burial. Do you know what happened to their mother and sister's bodies?"

"We looked into it, but the boys had been unable to bury them, and had to leave them where they were. It seems they had been collected and disposed of by the health department shortly after the epidemic was over."

Mary was only able to stomach chicken soup and bread and butter for dinner that first night, and only plain crackers for breakfast. It wasn't until nearly lunchtime that she got to spend any time with the children. She was surprised and pleased to see how happy and well-cared-for they all were. After a light lunch, Jolene took Mary to her doctor for examination. He confirmed that she was pregnant.

"I think I'll wait until I get home to tell Frank about the baby," she told her hostess. "I think the boys will be staying here when I leave, and this news will help ease our loneliness for them." Within two weeks, Mary was feeling well enough to return home.

And indeed, the boys were adjusting to their new surroundings and family members more quickly and easily than she had hoped. Although they were grateful to Mary and Frank and would miss them very much, they wanted to stay with their uncle, aunt and cousins.

Their father's remains arrived on the train from Washington D.C, and Mary stayed an extra two days, to attend his funeral service.

Most people don't bring their young children to funerals, but both Mary and Jolene thought that the boys needed this chance to mourn, so they could heal. The boys were somber and silent throughout the ceremony, but when the casket was taken outside, Bobby wouldn't let it out of his sight. It was raining, and the wind was blowing it sideways, so the women were concerned about the boys getting sick or chilled. When they tried to reason with Bobby, he refused to listen, but wailed and fought to stay with the coffin.

Terry told them, "I've never seen 'im like this. He got sad when Papa left for war. And then, when Mama and Penny were so sick, he cried all the time and wouldn't go in their rooms no more. When I told 'im they were dead. That's when he quit talking. I think we better let 'im go with Papa."

They all bundled up against the weather and followed the pallbearers to the gravesite. When the casket was lowered onto the support boards over the open grave, Bobby broke away from the others and threw himself onto it, sobbing, "Papa, Papa, don't go Papa!"

Many of the mourners were brought to tears by this pitiful sight, but those who knew the boy were also smiling, because he was speaking again. Jolene and Terry put their hands on Bobby's back and leaned in close to comfort him. After a few minutes, Bobby started to calm down, and Terry said, "Bobby, you talked again, you talked!"

Bobby stood back and wiped his eyes "Are they... together in... heaven... now?" He asked Jolene.

"Yes Bobby, they're all together, and they're happy. They love you, and they're watching over you."

"I heard... Daddy... tell me... to be strong... that he had... to go... be with Mama... and Penny. He told me... we had a new... family to love us... and take care of us. He also told me... that Mary and Frank... will have a baby to love... and be happy, too."

Jolene turned and looked at Mary, who had overheard what Bobby had said. "It must've been an angel from God," Mary said. "Now I feel doubly confident about leaving them behind. I know it's the right thing to do."

Clive had to work the next day, so Jolene took Mary to the train station. The boys went along to say goodbye. It was a bittersweet time for all three. Mary made them promise to write, and she promised to do the same. "Now, be as good for your new parents as you were for us." Then she gave each of them a hug and a kiss and boarded the train. They corresponded for a few years, then eventually lost touch as the boys grew up and got involved in various interests, such as girls.

In late October, Alice got a letter from Frank:

Greetings from Seattle,

I have some vacation time coming, and my supervisor said I need to take it before the end of the year, or lose it. The postal service gets too busy after December 1st, so we're planning to come to Portland the end of November. Our doctor thinks it would be safe for Mary to travel now. She's over her morning sickness, and feeling strong.

We've purchased train tickets to Portland, and will be arriving at three pm, November 22nd. Mary's parents will pick us up, but we would love to see any of you there, too.

We'll be staying with them and then celebrating the holiday with her family the Saturday after Thanksgiving before returning home.

I hope you can find room for 2 1/2 more people at Ilda's Thanksgiving table!

Love, Frank

When Frank and Mary's train arrived at the Portland depot, there was a sizable crowd waiting for them: Mary's mother, aunt and sister-in-law, Alice, Lafe, Doley, Grace and her little ones, Ilda and Cleo. The other men and children were at work or school.

"They all wished they could be here, but there probably wouldn't be room for all of us here-not with all these other people," Alice told them. "You're both looking hale and chipper."

"It was a lovely ride down here, with the sun shining on all the autumn leaves, and the flocks of geese flying south, the snowcapped mountains on either side of us, and the blue sky above," Mary sighed.

"The train was quite comfortable, and the meals were tasty, as well," Frank added. "It was very relaxing. Our table mates were a delightful, retired couple from British Columbia. They're on their way to Tigard for their granddaughter's wedding, next month."

On Thanksgiving Day, the Newman's farmhouse was bursting at the seams. The entire Walden clan was there-Alice, Ilda, Albert and their six children, Grace, Guy and their six children, Doley, John and Little Ilda, Carsie, Tucker, Lafe, Frank and Mary.

One large turkey would not have fed that many people, so Albert had to sacrifice three of them that year.

John's sisters had taught Doley how to make their sour cabbage rolls. She had spent most of the previous day cooking up a large pot of it for their contribution to the feast.

Ronny, Ginny and Ginger helped Grace make four pies to bring along.

Lafe and Alice brought a large bag of potatoes and homemade cranberry sauce.

Carsie provided firewood, transportation for Alice and Lafe, and helped keep the children entertained while the women were busy in the kitchen. He also carved the first and third turkeys. Lafe carved the other one.

Tucker spent most of the day out in the barn. Frank spent a couple of hours out there with him, catching up on the events of their lives since Frank had moved to Seattle.

At dinner, Doley and John announced that they were expecting another baby the following summer. "That's wonderful news," said some. "Congratulations," said others.

Tucker groaned, "When will it stop!"

Some of them laughed at his reaction, others just shrugged their shoulders.

Saturday's meal with Mary's family, was a much smaller and quieter one for Frank and Mary. There were only seven adults and two children in attendance.

They had wonderful visits with both families, making it difficult for them to leave. The weather didn't improve their mood either: It was cold, rainy and windy. Their return trip seemed much longer than the previous, southbound one. They could hardly wait to reclaim their little dog from the neighbor's care upon their return.

Chapter Sixteen

TORTURED SOUL

In late February, 1921, Alice received a letter from Frank, announcing the birth of their new daughter, whom they named Dolores, after his favorite sister.

In May, Doley presented John with a boy child, whom they named Carson. He was born a month premature, weak and pale. The doctor didn't know why he didn't improve. He was a cranky baby without much of an appetite. Although he grew in length, he remained thin, with little strength or physical energy his whole life. (When he reached his early thirties, technology would allow doctors to diagnose a hole in the membrane between the right and left sides of his heart.)

Shortly after Carson Bauer's birth, Lafe and Carsie were approaching their favorite fishing hole on the Clackamas River one Saturday morning, when they spied a makeshift shelter in the woods nearby.

"What do you make of that?" Lafe asked his big brother.

"Probably just some kid's hideout."

"I don't know about that. It's a long way from any homes. Let's go check it out."

As they approached the shelter, they noticed a number of items nearby that indicated that someone was living there: A permanent campfire area with a saucepan sitting on a makeshift stovetop, homemade animal traps and other items not usually found around a child's play area.

Then they heard a moan from inside the shelter. Lafe, being the first to arrive, and the younger and more agile of the two, crouched down and peered inside.

What he saw moved him to compassion. Carsie saw the look on his brother's face and asked, "What is it?"

Lafe stood up and said, "Take a look."

After Carsie had peered inside, he sat back on his heels and looked up at Lafe. "We just can't leave him here. He'll die, for sure."

"So much for a relaxing day of fishing, huh?"

"God works in mysterious ways," Carsie stated, matter-of-factly. "We need to assess him, and then figure out the best way to get him out of here."

"Where should we take him?" Lafe asked.

"Let's cross that bridge when we get to it. It might be better to disassemble the shelter. We don't know if he's hurt or just sick."

So they slowly and painstakingly, took down the man's covering until they had access to him and could see him clearly to evaluate his condition. The man made animal-like noises and feeble attempts to prevent them from doing their task, but he was far too weak to stop them.

After looking him over, amid some resistance on the man's part, they determined that he wasn't seriously hurt, but malnourished and very sick. He seemed unable to speak, and would or could not open his mouth. His joints seemed to be a bit stiff, also.

"I wonder if it's lockjaw." Carsie said.

"If it is, we need to get him to the hospital right away. Ma wouldn't be able to fix that, would she?"

"No, I think he needs medicine and twenty-four-hour support. Even then, he may not survive."

They fashioned a litter and strapped the hapless man onto it so he wouldn't fall or wiggle off. They carried him the two miles back to the car, then loaded him into the back seat.

After they carried him into the hospital, and he was taken to a treatment room, Carsie and Lafe spent the next two hours answering questions and waiting for an update on his condition. Eventually, a doctor came looking for them.

"I understand that you found the man in the woods, camping out in a crude shelter?"

"Yes, we couldn't leave him there. He was obviously in dire straits."

"Once we got him cleaned up, one of the nurses recognized him as her friend's long-lost brother. He has tetanus, but I think you found him early enough for us to cure him. We'll be transferring him to the psych ward as soon as he's stabilized. His sister works here and would like you to stay here a little longer, until she gets off work. She wants to talk to you."

Forty-five minutes later, a pretty blond nurse came looking for them.

"My name is Nettie Dawson. Are you the men who found my brother?"

Carsie introduced himself and Lafe.

She gave them both hugs and thanked them. "His name is Cooper."

They went outside while she explained Cooper's situation.

"He's been suffering from depression and nightmares ever since returning from the war. He was living with me, and I was trying to help him, but he was tortured by the memories of all the horrible things he experienced in Europe. Neither the doctors, nor I, were able to get through to him. He couldn't keep a job. I was supporting both of us with some help from our father.

"I came home from work several months ago, to find him gone, along with some of his clothes and a few household supplies. The police, park rangers and all our friends and family have been looking for him ever since. Where did you find him?"

"We were following a deer path to the Clackamas River when we spied his camp through the trees," Carsie answered.

Lafe hadn't spoken; he was mesmerized by Nettie's face and voice. She wondered if he was mute, until Carsie asked him a direct question. Then he finally snapped out of his trance. Nettie looked him over while he was looking at his brother. When he looked back at her, she averted her eyes, reddened a bit and smiled, coyly. She had liked what she'd seen: A kind face, not too rugged or too soft. He was tall, but not too tall, lean and muscular, but not brawny. And his eyes: They were like... like liquid love, she thought.

Carsie couldn't help but notice the chemistry between them. He pulled a tablet and pen from his pocket and wrote their names, addresses and phone numbers on it. Then he gave it to her, saying, "Let us know how Cooper's doing, and if there's anything else we can do to help."

After they parted, Carsie remarked, "It looks like you may have just found your match."

Lafe still looked star-struck, but squared his shoulders and said, with resolve, "That's the girl I'm going to marry!"

"I get the feeling she is thinking the same thing," Carsie answered as he grinned and put the car in gear.

The next Sunday afternoon, just as they walked in Alice's door from the family dinner, the phone started ringing, and Lafe ran to answer it.

"Hello... Oh, hi, Nettie... Oh, that's good news... This Saturday? Sure, we'll come see him. Will you be there?... Maybe we can go out to dinner afterward?... All right, see you then."

"Did you forget about the fishing trip?" Carsie asked, when Lafe hung up the phone. "We were going to try that spot again."

Lafe looked like a deer in the headlights.

"Lafe!" Carsie said, a little louder this time.

"What? Oh, who cares about some dumb ol' fish. I'm gonna catch me a mermaid!"

Carsie sighed, "Oh boy, is this how you're gonna be from now on?"

Lafe didn't answer. He ran to the closet to pick out his wardrobe for Saturday, while Carsie sat on the couch.

Alice wasn't there; she was delivering a baby that day.

Lafe called from the bedroom, "You think I should wear the blue shirt? No, wait, it has a frayed collar. Maybe the black one. No, it has a torn pocket. I'll have to go shopping tomorrow."

"She's not going to notice your clothes!" Carsie announced.

"I want to make a good impression, if she does," Lafe called back.

On Saturday afternoon, the brothers went to the hospital, and asked for Nettie at the front desk. The receptionist handed Carsie a note that Nettie had left with her, directing them to the psych ward.

When they arrived at the ward doors, they found them locked. Lafe found a red call button to push. After a couple of minutes, a nurse came out. Carsie handed her the note from Nettie. She read it and ushered them toward Cooper's room, where Nettie was waiting for them.

"Come on in," she said. "He's not dangerous."

"But the security," Lafe said, with trepidation.

"That's to keep the patients from leaving before the doctor says they're ready," the nurse answered. Then she turned and left.

Nettie made the introductions. "Cooper, this is Carsie and Lafe. They're the brothers who found you and brought you in."

"Nice to meet you," he said as he shook their hands. "The doctor said I wouldn't have lasted another day out there. I want to thank you."

Carsie spoke up next. "I believe it was God who put us in the right place at the right time.

"Why were you out there all alone, if you don't mind my asking?"

"He got it in his head that he was a burden to me," Nettie answered for him.

"My mind got messed up in battle. After I came home, I couldn't hold down a job," Cooper told them. "The shrink I'm working with will be seeing me on an outpatient basis once I'm discharged."

"They say he should be well enough to come home in a month or two," Nettie said, as she tousled his hair.

"I shouldn't have gotten tetanus from the scratch on my leg, but I'm allergic to the vaccine."

"It would still have gotten infected," Nettie told him. "You didn't have a first-aid kit with you."

When Cooper's dinner arrived, his visitors said goodbye and went out into the corridor. They talked about dinner and transportation, then decided that Lafe and Nettie would walk the four blocks to the cafe that she frequented, and Carsie would go have dinner with Alice.

The sweethearts took their leave after promising to be back before visiting hours were over at eight O'clock. As they walked out the hospital door into the sunlight, Nettie noticed a stain on her uniform and suggested that they stop by her house so she could change.

"It's only a block out of the way," she said.

"That's okay with me," Lafe answered.

She led him around the corner to a small, neat bungalow with pretty flowers, bird houses and feeders in the yard. She pulled her keys out of her purse as she walked up the path to the door.

Lafe stayed on the sidewalk with his hands in his pockets. "I'll wait out here," he said.

She opened her mouth to protest that it would be fine, but thought better of it, smiled and went inside, not bothering to lock the door.

"What a gentleman," she thought. "Now I know he's a keeper."

She changed into a flirty pink dress with white polka dots and took her hair pins out, letting her blond curls fall loose. She brushed her hair until it shined and put on a pair of pearl earrings that her father had given her for her eighteenth birthday. Then she transferred her wallet and other necessities to her white beaded clutch. She threw her white sweater over her shoulder and went back outside, where Lafe stood, still on the sidewalk, admiring her flowers and watching the birds.

When he saw her, his jaw dropped, involuntarily. He'd never seen such a ravishing beauty in his life. "Wow!" he remarked, breathlessly. "I thought you were beautiful in your uniform, but...wow!"

On the walk to the cafe, he asked her, "How is it that no handsome prince has snatched you up, yet?"

"Most of the men I know are already married or want something from me that I'm not willing to give to just anyone," she answered. "I was taught that a woman's virtue is a precious thing that the right man would be willing to respect and wait for. Have I found that man?"

"Yes, I believe you have. I would be willing to wait ten lifetimes to make you my own."

Nettie smiled at the thought. The feeling was mutual.

They walked another block in silence, then she spoke again.

"Did you say your mother lives nearby?"

"Yes, just about four miles west of here.

"I told her about you last Sunday. She seems to think that she's met you at the hospital at one time or another."

"Does she work at the same hospital?" Nettie asked.

"No, but sometimes a patient or a friend of hers ends up there, and she goes to see them."

"Maybe if you describe her, I can remember seeing her there."

"Well, she's rather tall for a woman. She hasn't much gray in her hair, yet. It's black, as are her eyes. She's slender and distinguished, without being uppity."

"With thin lips and a Roman-ish nose?" Nettie asked.

"Yes, I guess you could describe her that way. Have you met her?"

"Alice Walden, of course! I never put two and two together until now! Everyone knows who she is. I never thought I'd have a chance to get to know her personally! You must take me to meet her soon."

"Would you be willing to come to our church tomorrow, to meet her and some others of our family?"

"I think that would be okay. I don't remember anything special going on at ours."

They enjoyed each other's company so much that they lost track of time. Lafe returned to the hospital at eight-thirty to find Carsie waiting in his car. "You *do* know that I have to drive home and then come back in the morning for church?"

"Sorry. I had to walk her home first. I couldn't tear myself away."

"I hope you didn't do anything you'd regret later."

"No; not that the thought didn't cross my mind. But I respect her too much. I don't want to ruin my chance to marry her when the time is right."

"When might that be, do you think?"

"After I get a better paying job and her brother can get out on his own."

The next Sunday, Nettie attended the Waldens' church and met about half of the Walden clan. "If that's only half of your family, it will probably take me years to get to know all their names," she told Lafe afterward.

Lafe grinned, and replied, "I sure hope you stick around long enough to do that."

Two weeks later, she went with Lafe and Carsie to Troutdale, to visit her father. After a barrage of questions that they'd expected, and answered honestly, they enjoyed a pleasant meal together.

"That was delicious!" Lafe commented. "I've never tasted better beef stroganoff! And our mother and sisters are wonderful cooks."

"Nettie fixed it," her father beamed.

"You helped, Papa," Nettie added.

"Not much; I tend to burn water if I'm not supervised. How about you boys, can you cook?"

"I'm like you, Mr. Dawson," Lafe admitted. "I moved from my sister's home, to live with Carsie. After I lost my job, I moved in with our mother. Carsie's much older than I, and had to learn to cook, because he's still a bachelor."

"You seem like such a nice man. I've been wondering about that," Nettie directed to Carsie. "Surely, you've had some girlfriends, at least."

"Yes, I was married for a very short time to a lovely girl named Gretchen that I met at a logging camp just after the war started. She caught the flu and died soon after we were married."

"That's so sad. I suppose you're a little gun-shy after that experience. Are you two the only holdouts in your family?" his host asked.

"No, we have another brother, Tucker, who is a little odd. I don't expect he'll ever marry."

"Nettie says most of your family live in Portland?"

"Yes, and they want you both to come to one of our family dinners soon."

"Sounds good to me," Nettie said. "How about you, Daddy?"

"I don't know. Just how big *is* your family, boys?"

"Very, but they're seldom all there. That would be far more than you could handle all at once, probably. The kids can get pretty rowdy when they're all together."

"Well, I like to be prepared for things like this," Mr. Dawson replied. "Tell me something about each of them so I won't feel like a complete stranger." Then he reached for a pen and a tablet.

"Okay, let me see, now. Nettie has probably told you all about Mama, already," Lafe offered.

"Ilda is next in line after me, Carsie said. She and her husband Albert have six children, between the ages of 14 and 4. We usually gather at their farmhouse."

"They have the biggest house, but no car," Nettie interjected, repeating what Lafe and Alice had told her.

Carsie continued, while Lafe studied Nettie's every feature.

"She's quite the mother hen; very nurturing and patient.

"The next in line is Grace. Her husband is Guy. They have seven children between 14 and 1. The oldest three, all boys, are his from a previous marriage. I believe we'll be meeting at their house next time."

"Would you describe them for me, please?" Mr. Dawson asked.

Lafe jumped in next. "Ilda is rather dark, like Mama. Grace has lighter coloring, but still darker than Carsie's. Ilda and Grace are both tall like Mama, Carsie, Frank and I.

"Tucker is next in line. He's dark like Mama, but much shorter and, some might some might say, homely," Carsie admitted. "Then there's Frank, who lives in Seattle with his wife. They had their first child last winter."

"I'm next in line," Lafe continued, "then Doley, who is the youngest. She's married to an Austrian immigrant named John. They don't attend very often. John's family is gathering for some special occasion or another next week. I can't keep track of our family *and* his."

"Does he have a large family living locally, too?"

"Yes, though not quite as large as ours."

"You didn't mention your father. It sounds like you are all very different..." He let his question go unsaid.

"Oh, we all had the same father. He was the polar opposite of Mama, except for being tall. He passed away about fifteen years ago."

"How old were you all at that time?" Nettie asked.

Lafe did the mental math. "Doley, Frank and I were all pretty small, yet. I'm sure Doley doesn't remember him at all. She was only five when he died. I was seven and Frank was nine."

"There was a seven-year gap between Frank and Tucker," Carsie said, "so Tucker would have been...sixteen. That would mean that Grace, Ilda and I were seventeen, nineteen and twenty."

"Nettie's mother and I were only blessed with two, but I'm looking forward to grandchildren, someday." Mr. Dawson said, winking at Nettie, who blushed and changed the subject.

Chapter Seventeen

THE FISHERS

One hot day in August, 1921, the Rowley boys; fourteen-year-old Jerry, twelve-year-old Chip and ten-year-old Ronny, hatched the idea of a fishing trip, along with their eleven-year-old cousin, Buddy, while visiting with their mother and three younger siblings at the Newman farm.

"We're bored and hot." Jerry, the spokesman for the group approached Grace. "Can we go down to the river for a swim, and catch some fish for dinner."

"That sounds like a fine idea," Ilda said.

"Are you sure you can control this rowdy gang all by yourself?" Grace asked Jerry.

"If they get out of line, I'll box their ears," he grinned as he shadow-boxed all three of them.

"Oh, go on, the bunch of you before you wake the baby. Just be careful."

"Don't lose track of time. I'm counting on those fish for dinner!" Ilda called, as they ran out the door.

"Whew! Now, with most of the others napping or playing upstairs, maybe we can get some peace and quiet for a change." Grace said. "Ever since school let out, I've been counting the days till it starts back up."

"I have the opposite problem," Ilda told her sister, "During the summer, Faye and Nina are here to help me with the younger ones. When they're at school, I have to keep an eye on Cleo and Jojo by myself while trying to do chores. Those boys can get into more mischief in five minutes than any of the others ever did."

A few minutes later, baby Merle started to fuss and Grace sighed, "It won't be long and I'll have another toddler to chase after. The girls were a handful when they were two to three years old, but they've been a big help since he was born." She picked up the baby, changed his diaper and put him to her breast. Meanwhile, the four boys went to the barn to collect Buddy's and Tucker's fishing poles and the tackle box from the tack room and set off for the river, half a mile away.

By the time they got to the river, they were more than ready to strip down and jump in. They played and splashed for a while, until Jerry remembered that they had promised to catch some fish for dinner. He coaxed the others out of the river and started looking for worms to bait their hooks.

Once they were dressed they moved on to another spot, where Buddy knew the fish liked to feed, because he and Tucker had caught many fish there before. It was a sunny, marshy eddy with lots of insects buzzing around.

While Ronny was chasing tadpoles and frogs, and Jerry baited the hooks and strung up the fish, the other two used the poles and bait, with much success.

Two hours later, they had caught enough fish for dinner and noticed that it was time to head home. Jerry finished stringing up the last fish, while Buddy and Chip collected their gear. Suddenly, they realized that Ronny was gone.

"Why weren't you watching him?"

"He's your brother, too. Didn't you notice him wandering off?"

"I only took my eyes off of him for a few minutes!"

"Did anybody notice which way he went?

"Last time I saw him he was over there!"

"Ronny!!! Where are you, Ronny?"

There was no answer. They agreed that Buddy should go upstream to search, just in case, while the brothers went downriver.

Half an hour later, Jerry and Chip found Ronny in the woods about ten feet from the river; wet and crying. "What happened?" Jerry asked him. Then he noticed that his leg was caught in an animal trap. It took some doing, but they managed to get the trap off of his leg.

Buddy had joined them by then. He had watched his father bandage animal wounds, so he bound up his cousin's leg. Jerry and Chip supported him on either side until they got back to the farm. By then Ronny was weak from blood loss and pain, and the other three were exhausted.

Ilda tended to Ronny's wounds, while Grace questioned the other boys. "Jerry, you said you would watch them. I trusted you. How did this happen?"

With tears in his eyes, the normally stoic teenager replied, "I got busy with the other two; collecting the fish and the gear. He was chasing tadpoles and frogs last time I looked. I don't know how he got so far downstream. I'm so sorry, Ma!"

"Buddy said he didn't know there were any trappers in these parts," Chip added. "I'm sorry too, you think he's gonna be okay, Mama?"

"I'm sure he will." She gave them both hugs and told them, "I forgive you-accidents happen. You'll have to answer to your father, though."

Once Ilda got a good look at the leg and saw how much pain the boy was in, she had Albert take him and Grace to the hospital in the Rowley's car, while Ilda kept the other children with her. She kept the boys busy cleaning the fish and putting the gear away in the barn.

They were uncharacteristically quiet while she and Faye fried the fish and prepared the rest of the evening meal. Jerry and Buddy didn't have much of an appetite, but Chip's seemed unaffected.

"May I be excused from the table?" Jerry asked, "I think I'll go check on the new puppies out in the barn."

"All right," Ilda said, "I'll keep your plate warm in the oven with the others, for later."

After Ronny was treated at the hospital, Albert took him and Grace to their home. Guy had come home from work a few minutes before, so he volunteered to take Albert home.

It was already late when they got back to the farm. Everyone but Ilda was already asleep.

"I saw Chip on the sofa. Where are the rest of them?" Guy asked her.

"The younger ones are doubled up with ours and Jerry's out in the barn, sleeping with the pups," Ilda said with a smile. "He looked so peaceful, I didn't have the heart to wake him-he had a pretty rough day."

"I think they all learned a valuable lesson," Albert remarked, as he watched Ilda take the plates out of the oven.

"How is Ronny doing?" She asked as she put the plates in front of the two men.

"You tell her-I have to be up with the rooster," Albert said before wolfing down his food.

"Grace said that he had to get a couple of shots for tetanus and bacterial infections that he might have gotten from the trap, but he should be fine in time for school in September. We think the constant reminder of his brother's bandaged leg will be enough punishment for Jerry."

Albert finished his dinner, stood, complemented the cook and gave her a kiss. Then he put a hand on Guy's shoulder. "Take care of that boy, and good luck keeping him down. Thanks for the ride home," he told Guy as he shook his hand. Then he was off to bed.

Two days later, Ronny woke up with a fever and more pain than the day before. Grace removed the bandage and saw that his leg was swollen and red.

Guy had already gone to work. The twins and the baby had developed bad colds, so she didn't want to take them to the hospital with her or leave the whole brood in Jerry's care.

She called Alice. "Mama, I need your help! Ronny and the youngest three are sick. I don't know what to do!"

"I'll call Teresa to cover for me at the hospital and be right over," she told her. "It'll be all right-mother is on the way!"

Alice called Doley and charged her with the task finding someone to give her a ride to Grace's house. She looked at the clock and knew that Teresa wouldn't be in yet. She started the coffee pot, got dressed and packed a valise with the items she thought she'd need. She called the hospital to leave a message for Teresa, and was just finishing her coffee when John drove up in his truck.

She grabbed her bag and flew out the door. "I hope I didn't inconvenience you too much," she told John as she got in the truck and closed the heavy door. "Grace sounded so desperate on the phone."

"No problem it iss," John answered. "Yust heading out de door I vas, ven you calt."

Chip opened the door to Alice's knock.

She could hear the baby crying in the background and one of the twins coughing. It was an odd cough; one that Alice had heard before. She didn't have time to dwell on it, but followed Chip into the boy's bedroom, where Grace was just removing a bed pan from under Ronny's bottom.

"Mama, I'm so glad you're here. I was at my wit's end with so many sick children. The colds I can handle, but this," she pulled back the covers to expose Ronny's leg, "I think may need a doctor's care. They gave him antibiotic and tetanus shots at the hospital, so I wasn't expecting this."

Alice examined the leg. "I think you're right. This isn't a normal infection. What's his temperature?"

"It's 102.6° last I checked. It was 101° when I first took it an hour and a half ago. What do you think it could be?"

"It could be some foreign matter that the doctor missed, or it could be that whatever the other children have has gotten into the wound somehow. I don't think we should move him unless we have to. I'll call the hospital to see if there's someone on call who can come here."

Grace wrung her hands. "We're going to have a hard time paying for the last hospital visit. We can't afford another one!"

"Well, perhaps we can keep him stable until Charles can get here after work. He may be willing to take care of this in exchange for a couple of blueberry pies. I know how he loves them. Mattie never could make them the way he likes them."

Alice went to the kitchen and called the hospital. She filled the teakettle to brew some herbal tea, all the while listening to the children's coughing. Suddenly she remembered-whooping cough! She opened her valise and took out a mask and surgical gloves.

When she went back to the boys' bedroom, Grace's eyes and mouth popped open in surprise. "Oh no!" She exclaimed, "I know what *that* means! You suspect something highly contagious here!"

"I suppose you've been too busy with Ronny to notice just how sick the other children are. I've been listening to their coughs. I hate to be the bearer of more bad tidings, but it sounds like whooping cough."

Grace started to weep, ran to her bedroom and closed the door.

Jerry came in a moment later and asked, "What's wrong with Grace?" (Chip and Ronny called her mom, but Jerry, as the oldest boy, didn't feel comfortable with the title.) "Why are you wearing those things?"

"She's feeling a bit overwhelmed right now," Alice answered him. "I had to give her some bad news."

"Bad news about Ronny?"

"No, about the little ones. I'm sure you've noticed their strange-sounding coughing?"

"Yeah, is it from something serious?"

"Yes, it is-whooping cough-a very serious and infectious virus. I'm going to have to quarantine your house. I'll stay here to keep things under control. You're going to have to be very brave and work diligently with Grace and me until the crisis is past. Do you understand?"

"Yes, ma'am. What do you want me to do first?"

"Do you know where Grace keeps the bleach and if she has a pair of rubber gloves?"

"Yes. What do you want me to do with them?"

"Scrub out your Mama's mop bucket, thoroughly. Boil about a quart of water, then put the water in the bucket and add a pint of bleach. Then you'll have to put on the gloves and use a clean cloth, soaked in the hot bleach water, to wipe down every hard surface you can find in the house that might have been touched by germ-laden fingers. Other things, such as toys and blankets will have to be washed with hot bleach water, also."

He went out and returned a few minutes later. "The water's heating and the bucket's clean."

"Are you the only one who's been helping to care for the little ones?" She asked.

"Yes ma'am. Whenever even one of them gets sick, I'm the only one, other than Grace, who's allowed in their bedrooms to feed and change them."

"Good boy-I bet you do a fine job of that, too."

"Not good enough to save our little sister from the flu a couple of years ago," he said, hanging his head.

"That wasn't your fault," she said compassionately, "A lot of people died from that virus. It was a mean one."

When Guy came home that afternoon, he was shocked to find quarantine notices in the window and on the door. He knocked and backed away two paces. After a couple of minutes, the door opened slowly, just enough for Grace to peek out. "I'm sorry dear, but Mama says the children have whooping cough. Perhaps you could stay at my sister's farm for a while? Mama says it would be best if you stayed in the barn for a few nights-to see if you come down with any symptoms first."

"I'm pretty sure I had whooping cough already, when I was about six. Let me in, please?"

"If you come in, you'll have to stay for the duration," she warned. "It would be better for all concerned if you stayed away and continued working. We need the money, and you could lose your job. A lot of people are out of work. We can't afford for you to be one of them."

"I suppose you're right," he conceded. "I just wish there was something I could do to help."

"Stay right there and I'll make up a shopping list for you." She closed the door, and he could hear his family's voices from inside. His heart ached-he wanted so badly to help and comfort them.

A few minutes later, Jerry opened the door and handed him a list with instructions on the back. Just then, Charles drove up and exited his car carrying a large doctor's bag. He pulled a surgical mask out of his bag, put it on and went into the house. Jerry looked so sad as he closed the door behind Charles, that Guy's heart nearly broke.

His mind went back to the war and the flu pandemic, which sickened Ronny and Chip so severely and claimed their first daughter's life. The entire family had been devastated. They'd scarcely recovered emotionally and physically from that awful winter-and here was another *double* threat: The depression and whooping cough. He wasn't too worried about the boys, Grace and himself; but the little ones-they were the most vulnerable. He was grateful that Alice was here to take care of them. Her diligence and expertise would probably double their chances of survival.

He was careful to follow the instructions on the back of the list; shopping at a grocer across town, in case their usual grocery store was the point of infection. When he returned, Charles was just about to pull away. Guy stopped him and asked, "How are they doing?"

"The three youngest definitely have whooping cough, but they're strong and are getting the best care. I had to do some minor surgery on Ronny's leg to remove a tiny bit of metal left behind from the trap. I gave him another shot of penicillin. He'll be a little longer recovering, but should bounce back just fine.

"If you, Grace and the boys don't come down with Whooping cough, you should be able to return home in about ten days. Don't worry about their needs-the nursing staff at the hospital are eager to help. They volunteered to do the grocery shopping and relieve Alice, if need be."

Guy delivered the groceries to his family, then went to the Newman farm: sleeping in the barn for a few days. When he didn't get sick, he moved into their house until his children were on the mend.

The twins and the baby came through just fine, due to their caretakers' diligence and Alice's talents with herbal remedies. No one else in the family got sick. It was a busy two weeks of medicating, changing, disinfecting and washing before Alice and Albert could both return to their homes.

Grace had charged Chip with the job of keeping Ronny entertained until the doctor said he could use the leg. He was getting around in time for school in September.

That was the summer they would never forget, but wished they could.

Chapter Eighteen

GIRLS' WEEKEND

One day in April, 1922, Alice was at the hospital with one of her clients who had required an emergency C-section. Once the woman was in surgery, Alice went up to the maternity ward to check in with her cousin Teresa. Even though the midwife program at the hospital had officially been disbanded, most of the midwives in the Portland area got their supplies, referrals, accreditation, etc. from the hospital's maternity ward.

Teresa was in her office, poring over some papers when Alice walked in. "Alice, you're not due for more supplies for another week at least. What brings you here today?"

"I had a tough case that I couldn't handle on my own-she needed a surgeon. I came in with her, to keep her calm and stable on the ride and during check-in. I thought while I was here I might as well save myself the trip later, besides, the last time I was here, you weren't."

"I'm glad you stopped by. I was going to call you soon. I got a letter from my sister yesterday. She's coming for a visit next month and would love to meet you. I'm going to arrange to have a week off while she's here, to show her around the Portland area. I'll be planning an agenda, and wondered if you had any ideas-interesting places or attractions that you've been to."

"I can think of one or two off the top of my head. Let me think about it, and I'll write them down, along with any others I might think of later."

"Thank you; of course you're invited to come along on any of our outings. Now, what supplies do you need today?"

Alice opened the obstetrical bag that she had brought with her and did a quick inventory, writing down the things she would need to tide her over for a month or so.

"I'll have my assistant round these up for you while you check on your patient," Teresa told her. "Hopefully, I'll get a chance to finish this paperwork before something else comes up."

"I'll let you get back to work, and return in half an hour or so," Alice replied as she exited the office. She went back to the surgical wing and asked the nurse at the desk how her client was doing. "You got her here in the nick of time," she said. "She owes you her life and her baby's life, as well. You must have the best track record of any midwife in our program. How do you do it?"

"I have God's help, and I've been doing it, and general nursing, most of my life."

"I was just wondering," The nurse asked, "have you been in Portland all your life?"

"No, I started out in Illinois, and moved to Oregon in '86, where I worked in the logging camps and Bridal Veil. I moved to Portland about fifteen years ago-after my husband and father died."

"You didn't come here all by yourself, did you?"

"No, I had five children and my mother living with me. My two eldest children were already in the area, and Mattie Brown-you know her, don't you? She's an old friend, who got me a job in the midwife program."

"Oh yes, you worked with Teresa."

"Yes, she turned out to be a second cousin of mine, from Illinois."

"Wow! It's a small world, isn't it?"

"God works in mysterious ways, his wonders to perform," Alice quoted. "I was barely keeping our heads above water, in Bridal Veil. I don't know if we could have survived there, in this economy."

Lafe got a part-time job, with a cabinet maker, near the Portland Lumber mill, and moved back in with Carsie. Alice had her little house to herself again, for the time being.

Teresa's sister Margaret arrived at the perfect time for a trip to the Klager Lilac Garden. Alice had enjoyed going there with her family several years earlier, but it was nice not to have to worry about babies and their needs. It was a girls-only outing, with Alice, Teresa, her mother-in-law Gladys, and sister Margaret.

The owner of the garden, Hulda Klager, didn't remember Alice at first, but when Alice told her that she had come with her family, including some German in-laws, it all came back to her. "Ya, I remember now. You had two babies with you."

"I didn't see your son here, today," Alice commented. "Did he move away?"

"No, he passed away, from pneumonia, last year."

"I'm so sorry. *Your* health seems to be holding up well, though."

"Ya, but we have found it difficult, like everyone else, since the depression started. I hope it turns around soon." The other four women nodded their assent.

Each of them took a lilac start from the bucket by the gate and dropped generous offerings in the coin jar upon their departure. Alice directed them to the same diner that her children had taken her to the first time they'd visited the garden, but it was boarded up–another victim of the depression. It was still early in the day.

Teresa suggested that they go on a real adventure: She knew of a nice hotel and restaurant in Long Beach. None of them had to be back to Portland for another day or two, so they all agreed to go. Knowing they had a long trip ahead of them, they stopped at the first town along the way to buy some drinks and snacks and top off the gas tank.

Teresa and her mother-in-law were the only ones who had seen the Pacific Ocean before. Teresa and her husband had been there visiting friends just two years earlier. They arrived at the coast just in time to witness the most glorious sunset that they'd ever seen. They checked into the hotel and freshened up before going to the restaurant for a delicious salmon salad and clam chowder dinner.

"Now, wasn't that worth the trip?" Teresa asked as she finished her ice cream sundae.

They all agreed, and looked forward to another adventure on the beach the next day. After dinner, Teresa called her husband to let him know that they were staying the night, and asked him to notify Alice's family, so they wouldn't worry.

In the morning, the weather was a little foggy and drizzly, so they ventured out to the quaint shops in the town and picked up a few souvenirs while they waited for the fog to clear.

Most of the fog burned off before lunch, and they bought some sandwiches at a deli to eat on the beach. It was a bit cooler than they had expected, but they spied a group of clam diggers packing up to leave. The diggers had built a fire to keep themselves warm in the predawn hours and to prepare breakfast. They were about to douse it when the women arrived. They talked with them for a few minutes, and when they found out that Margaret and Alice had never eaten geoducks or Pacific crab before, they threw another log on the fire and cooked some up for them.

Because the diggers had cooked them lunch, Alice and her group shared their sandwiches with them. After lunch the diggers packed up, put out the fire and bid the ladies goodbye.

The foursome spent a couple of hours beachcombing before returning to the car. Their pockets were stuffed with sea glass, shells and starfish and their arms were loaded down with driftwood. They had a hard time fitting all their loot in the car.

They were almost half way home-laughing and singing silly songs, when the left front tire blew out. Teresa almost lost control of the car-barely missing an oncoming truck. After a terrifying and bumpy ride, the car came to rest fifty feet from the opposite side of the road and about twenty feet downhill, on the edge of a copse of large fir trees.

They all sat completely still for a few moments, holding their collective breaths. Margaret's eyes were still tightly closed, but she found her voice first. "Are we there yet?"

Then the other three finally breathed and started laughing, almost hysterically. They laughed until their sides hurt and tears ran down their faces. They were starting to dry their tears when the driver of the truck that they had nearly hit rushed to their aid. "Are you ladies okay?" he asked.

They took one glance at his worried look and burst out laughing again. The man's expression immediately changed to one of confusion. Alice finally managed, with difficulty, to reply, "I'm all right; just a little shaken up. Teresa, Margaret, Gladys, are you three all right?"

"I think so," Margaret choked out.

"I think I broke my ankle!" Teresa squeaked.

"My cheeks hurt and I'm wet at both ends!" Gladys replied. Whereupon they all burst out laughing again.

The truck driver shook his head as he went to check the damage to the car. "I'll never understand dames."

A few minutes later he came back. "This car won't be leaving here under its own power," he reported. "I'll give one of you a ride into the next town, if you'd like. You can call for help from there."

By this time the women had stopped laughing. "Do you have room for two?" Alice asked the man. "I'd like to take Teresa to see a doctor as soon as possible."

"It'll be a tight squeeze, but I think you're both skinny enough," the man replied.

As Margaret and the truck driver helped Teresa out of the car, Alice told the other two, "I'll send assistance for you and the car as soon as I can." Then they helped Teresa climb up the hill and into the truck. By this time Teresa's leg was swollen and very painful.

"My name is Ted," the man said as he started the engine. "Where were you ladies heading before your accident?"

"We were on our way home from a holiday at the beach. I'm Alice, and as I'm sure you already surmised, her name is Teresa."

"Pleased to meet you. I don't see many women driving cars or traveling without escorts," he said.

"We're not most women," Teresa replied. "Our menfolk know we can take care of ourselves. Besides which, there is safety in numbers."

Doley answered the phone, "Hello?... Mama, where are you? I hear people talking in the background.... Are you all okay?... Let me get a pencil and tablet so I can write this down." She wrote the information that her mother gave her and said, "I'll send John for you as soon as he can get away. Is there anything you need him to bring you?... All right, I'll call him, too. What's his number?"

The sun was setting by the time John arrived at the wreck site. He used his truck and a cable to pull the car up the hill and onto a trailer. He took Margaret, Gladys and the car to Teresa's house.

Meanwhile, Teresa's husband had gone to pick up his wife and Alice at the doctor's office in Cathlamet, where a cast was being put on Teresa's leg. After the doctor was finished and had been paid, the three checked into the town's only motel for the night, and then called home to let their families know that they would be home in the morning.

Alice was awakened by a call from the front desk, soon after she fell asleep, "Mrs. Walden?" The man asked, "I'm sorry to wake you, but I remember you telling me that you're a midwife. One of our guests is in labor, and we can't find a doctor to come here right now. Are you available to help?"

"Of course, which room is she in?... I'll be there in ten minutes."

Alice put on her dressing gown and slippers, grabbed her medical bag, which she had with her always for emergencies such as this, and mounted the stairs to the floor above. She proceeded along the hallway until she found the room number, and knocked on the door. A young man answered and ushered her in. "She's not due for another two months," the man said, "so we thought it would be safe to come out for a little fun weekend before the baby came. I blame myself for letting her overdo it out there on the beach today."

"How long ago did you start having contractions?" Alice asked the young woman as she opened her bag and pulled out a stethoscope.

"About an hour. I didn't know what it was at first. It started out as a backache. Ooh! Here comes another one!"

"The baby's heartbeat is strong. Did your water break, yet?"

"No. Is my baby going to be all right?"

"Have you timed the contractions?" She asked the worried young husband.

"No, I didn't know about that. Is it important?"

"It would have saved me time in determining how close she is to delivering, so I can judge the likelihood of stopping the contractions to give the baby more time to develop."

"You can do that?" The woman asked.

"Sometimes. I have an herbal tea here in my bag that usually works if the labor hasn't progressed too far.

"Here it is." She gave it to the husband. "See if you can get a teaspoon of it brewed up while I wash up and examine her."

Then she handed her watch to the young woman. "While I'm gone, time the contractions."

The husband put on his robe and slippers and went out the door.

While Alice was drying her hands she asked what their names were. "I hate to just point at people or try to get their attention when they're not looking at me."

"I'm Jane and my husband is Donald."

Alice examined Jane and determined by the amount of dilation and infrequency and strength of the contractions, that there was a good chance that the herbs would work, providing Donald was successful in getting it brewed for her soon enough.

While they were waiting for Donald and the tea, Alice got a briefing on Jane's medical history, and continued to monitor the baby's heartbeat.

Donald returned, out of breath, with the tea. "I hope this works," he said. "It sure doesn't smell very good."

"Most medicinal herbs don't smell or taste very nice," Alice replied as she passed the cup to Jane. "Now drink this down as quickly as possible."

She rose from the chair, and pulled Donald aside. "Any word on when a doctor might be here?"

"The hotel manager sent someone out to track one down. They haven't heard back from him yet. I hope he finds one soon. Do you really think the herb tea will help?"

"There are no guarantees, but I think there's a good chance. I'm glad you didn't wait too long to call for help."

"Her first pregnancy ended at four months, so we're desperate for this one to result in a healthy baby."

"Would either of you mind if I prayed for you while we wait for the doctor?"

"Uh, I suppose that would be all right. Let me ask Jane."

By this time, Jane had finished the tea and was lying back down. "I think I feel a little better already," she told them as they turned back to her. When Donald asked her about the prayer, her eyes filled with tears.

"What's wrong, honey?" Donald asked, worried that she was in distress.

"Nothing. It's just that no one has prayed for me since my Granny died ten years ago.

"Daddy left us and Mama was bitter. She blamed God for her lot in life, and I was mad at God for letting Granny die, leaving me without someone to love me and pray with me. Alice, I would love it if you prayed for me and our baby."

Alice got down on her knees and motioned for Donald to join her. Then she took Jane's hand, bowed her head and closed her eyes.

"Lord, I lift up this family to you in prayer-asking that you would intervene on their behalf. If it is your will, let this baby stay in the safety of his mother's womb until he's fully developed, and then let his delivery be uncomplicated. Help Jane and Donald look to you for guidance and strength-raising this precious child in your way and under your direction. Gather them under your wings-showing them, clearly, how much you love them and want what is best for them.

"Thank you for the events you brought about that caused me to be here to help them in their time of need. Help them to trust you and to realize, like I do, that even bad things can lead to good outcomes, because you are in control. Amen."

When Alice and Donald opened their eyes, Jane was lying perfectly still with her eyes still closed. Donald looked a little worried, until Alice checked her pulse and whispered, "She's gone to sleep. The contractions must have stopped. I'll stay here until the doctor arrives."

Alice changed positions in order to monitor any contractions that Jane might have. After 15 minutes with no signs of further labor and a check on the baby's strong heartbeat, she took a break to stretch and use the bathroom.

She had just finished drying her hands when there was a knock on the door. She opened it, to see a young doctor in the hallway. "Hello," he said, "are you the midwife?"

"Yes," she answered as she stepped aside to let him in. "Alice Walden, from Portland."

"I'm Doctor Alan Smith. How is our patient doing?"

At the sound of his voice, Jane opened her eyes and Donald rose from his seat. "Mrs. Walden gave her some herb tea, and the contractions stopped," he told the doctor.

"She is a miracle worker-an angel sent from heaven," Jane added as the doctor pulled up a chair and examined her.

"I don't believe in angels or miracles. You were either misdiagnosed or they stopped on their own," he said as he pulled out his stethoscope and placed it on Jane's abdomen.

"You're wrong. You weren't here!" Donald protested.

The young doctor glared at Donald, so Alice pulled him aside. "He needs quiet to hear the baby's heartbeat," she whispered. "Besides, I don't think he'll listen to us. I've met his type before."

When the young doctor had finished his examination, he stood, packed his bag and stated with an air of superiority, "There is nothing wrong with this young woman. Why did you bother me in the middle of the night?" Then he left, leaving the young couple dumbstruck and Alice shaking her head.

"Pride-it's the downfall of many educated people," she remarked. "I think you'll be all right now. Take it easy and visit your doctor as soon as you get home. I need to get some rest myself, before heading back home in a few hours."

They both thanked her profusely and offered to pay her for her time and trouble. She refused, saying, "I can't accept money for doing the Lord's work. I ask, only that you thank him and take good care of that baby."

They exchanged addresses so they could keep in touch. Alice left them, feeling tired but happy.

Two months later, Alice got a card and letter announcing the birth of their healthy, seven-and-a-half-pound son, William Francis McDonough.

> Dear Alice,
>
> We are so grateful for everything you did for us. You saved our baby's life, and saved us the grief and disappointment of losing another child.
>
> I thought you would like to know that, through your influence, Jane rededicated her life to Jesus shortly after our return home. The change in her and the miracle of our son's birth caused me to open my heart to him, as well. I became a father and a Christian on the same day.
>
> We thank God every day for sending you to our rescue that night at the hotel. May he continue to bless you and use you for his glory.
>
> Love, Donald and Jane

One day, after not hearing from his German friend, Fritz, for quite a while, Guy received a letter from his wife, written in German.

The next time he saw John, he asked him to translate it for him.

> Dear Guy,
>
> I am writing this letter to tell you that Fritz died in a construction accident a few months ago. He had talked about wanting to visit America someday. I think I would like to move there to raise our children. I know Fritz had written to you about them, so you know their ages and names already.
>
> Would you and your wife consider sponsoring us? We have money for travel, and to get established, so we would not be a burden to you.

I know some English, and if you agree, will study hard in order to communicate with you and get a job soon after our arrival.

Yours truly,
Anja Schmidt

Guy talked the matter over with Grace and the whole family, including the Bauers. They all thought it was a great idea to help this family out. They all volunteered to help them, however they were able. So Guy wrote back to Anja, telling her about their decision, and started the paperwork at the courthouse. It would be another two years before the Schmidt family's paperwork was completed and approved.

Chapter Nineteen

LOOKING UP

On July second, 1922, when the Waldens' church gathered for their usual Independence Day Saturday potluck, Doley announced that she was expecting again.

"You're starting out like I did; a baby every year and a half," Alice observed. "How are you going to manage that, financially I mean."

"John's business is starting to pick up a little. Besides, you did it, and Grace and Guy, too."

"Yes, we have number seven on the way in a few months, Mama, and we're managing," Grace commented. "Things will work out for them, just as it did for you and for us."

Carsie jumped in with his usual upbeat view. "The economy is starting to recover already, and the President is talking about implementing programs to put people back to work, and get our country back on its feet again, like it was before."

"I've seen evidence of that, too," Guy added.

"I've got a good chance at a job opening, with the lumber company, in Skamania, Washington," Lafe announced.

"How wonderful!"

"I sure hope you get it."

"I'm certain he will!"

"Chester Danielson, his foreman here, now works at that mill, and says he'll put in a good word for him," Carsie said.

"Sounds like a sure thing to me!"

"If it's God's will. He may have other plans for Lafe," was Alice's opinion.

Everyone nodded agreement.

"How are things going with Nettie and her brother?" their pastor, who was sitting nearby and listening in, asked. "Any chance he'll be able to make it on his own, soon, so you two can get hitched?"

"He's doing better since he started on that new mental health program, and has been doing volunteer work through his church, lately. If I get this new job, Nettie and I might be able to get married as early as next year."

"That's good news. We'll be praying that it works out for you."

"Thank you Pastor."

In mid-September, when Doley was four months into her pregnancy, she fell ill with the flu. She was far too sick to care for Little Ilda and Bud, and John had to work whenever he got the chance, just to keep them from starving, so Alice, Grace and John's sisters stepped up to the plate. Doley was sicker than she'd been since she was a small child, and Alice was worried that she hadn't been getting enough to eat before she got sick. She was very weak, and her mother and sisters-in-law had a difficult time trying to keep her fever down.

At two O'clock in the morning, four days after getting sick, she started having seizures. This time it was Alice who had fallen asleep on the job and allowed Doley's temperature to rise dangerously high. She woke John, sleeping on the couch, to assist her. She sent him to her house and Grace's for more ice. When he came back, Alice had bad news for him. "She lost the baby."

It was another two weeks before Doley was strong enough to be left alone to care for herself and her children. Even then, Alice, Grace, and John's sisters visited her as often as they could, when John was at work, to keep her from getting too depressed, and to make sure she was eating properly.

In mid-October, Grace and Guy welcomed another little boy, named Leon, into their tribe. He was a pudgy redhead, just like his twin sisters.

At this time, Alice had fourteen grandchildren; four from Ilda, seven from Grace, two from Doley, and one from Frank.

Carsie and Lafe came to visit Alice one Saturday evening in mid-November to give her, "some good news and some bad news."

"All right, give me the bad news first," she said.

Carsie looked at Lafe, who nodded, looked at his feet and crossed his arms, obviously trying to suppress a grin.

Alice, her curiosity piqued, looked for Carsie's eyebrow to betray him. "Go ahead, Son."

Carsie rubbed his forehead, as if to scratch an itch, "We won't be able to make it for Thanksgiving dinner this year."

"And this is because...?" Alice turned to Lafe, also trying to look stern and disappointed by Carsie's announcement.

Lafe took a deep breath, and the words burst out, as if they couldn't be contained any longer. "I got the job and Carsie will be helping me move!"

Alice had already figured out what they were there for. She could read them both the way she had read their father, but she pretended to be surprised. She was happy for Lafe, but also sad, because she knew they wouldn't be seeing nearly as much of Lafe after this. He would marry Nettie, have children, make new friends and not find the time to make the trek from Skamania.

He gave his mother a bear hug and then continued: "I already told Nettie and she is thrilled for us to finally be able to get married her brother has improved enough to land a part-time job and move in with a buddy of his Carsie is going to loan me the money for my first month's rent we just got back from Washington I found us an apartment there."

"Whoa, slow down and breathe!" Carsie laughed.

Lafe calmed down some, and continued. "She already picked out the fabric and pattern for her wedding dress and is going to see if there are any jobs for her there. Her present lease will be up in February, so we'll probably have the wedding around then."

He hugged Alice again and twirled her around. "Oh, Mama, I'm so happy I could burst!"

"Really? I never would have guessed."

"He's been walking on a cloud ever since he found out about the job," Carsie told her. "I don't know what it'll take to bring him down to earth. He's impossible to live with like this."

"I don't want to come back to earth. I like it here in the clouds," Lafe grinned as he hugged himself.

"I think I see what you mean," Alice said, after Lafe gave her a kiss and floated out the door. "But he'll calm down some when he and Nettie start stressing over wedding plans and furnishings for their new home."

"And he'll be moving next week. I hope I can hold out that long."

"Come on Carsie!" Lafe called. "We have other places to go and other people to tell!"

They embraced, and Carsie loped out to the car, where his little brother was waiting, not-so-patiently.

Thanksgiving was a bittersweet day for the Walden clan: They all missed Carsie and Lafe.

Lafe had managed to gather a few basic furnishings while living with Carsie, and went to the second hand stores for the larger items.

Lafe liked his new job, and made a friend, almost immediately, but it was lonely at night. He adopted a little dog to keep him company. He tried to keep his imagining to night-time, but it wasn't easy.

His new friend, Jimmy, had family living in Tigard, and dropped him off at Alice's house on the way to spend Christmas with them. Nettie's family agreed to let her spend Christmas Eve with the Waldens so they could talk over their wedding plans.

When they had finished dinner and sent the young children to play, their plans were revealed and the Walden's roles in the wedding party were chosen. It was decided that little Audie, a very mature, nearly-four-year-old would be the flower girl and Cleo would be the ring bearer. Nettie thought perhaps that Leon, being the same age as Audie, would be the perfect pairing for her, but his parents thought he was much too active and immature.

Nettie's family consisted of her father, her brother Cooper, two aunts and uncles, a couple of teenage girl cousins, who would be the bridesmaids, and one sister who lived in New Mexico and couldn't attend. Her mother and maternal grandparents had all passed and her mother had been an only child. Her father's father had passed, and his mother was an invalid.

"Don't worry, dear, there are enough Waldens and friends to fill the church," Lafe consoled.

The wedding would be held on Valentine's Day at her family's church in Troutdale, where one of her uncles, who would be presiding, was the head deacon.

The day of the wedding dawned cloudy and drizzly; typical February weather for Western Oregon.

Frank and his family couldn't come from Seattle, as they were all down with bad colds that week. Tucker was new at his job as a kennel keeper at a veterinarian's office, so couldn't get the day off. But all the rest of the Walden clan were there.

Nettie's dress was creamy white with tiny pink ribbon rosebuds sewn along the V-shaped neckline and along the hem of the long, sweeping skirt. The long-sleeved bodice and the top half of the skirt were overlaid with flowing white, rose-patterned lace, scalloped on the bottom edges. Her veil had the same scalloped edge and was held in place with a crown of pink rosebuds and snowdrops. er veilHeShe held a bouquet of pink roses and white crocuses. Her long blond hair, which was always pinned up for work, cascaded down her back in loose curls.

Her cousins' knee-length dresses were pink, of the same delicate shade as the rosebuds on Nettie's dress. Their nosegays were smaller versions of her bouquet. They wore white slippers with pink ribbon rosebuds attached to the tops. Instead of lace, they had creamy white ribbons tied at their waists and snowdrop crowns in their hair.

Lafe, Carsie, and the ushers, Guy and Cooper, wore their best dark suits. Lafe had a red cummerbund. The corsages for the ladies of the family, and the boutonnières for the men, were done in red rose buds and white snowdrops.

Nettie's aunts owned the bakery in town, so they made the cake. The ladies of their church took care of the food and decorations.

During the wedding there was a hailstorm, so that they had to talk louder than usual to be heard. After the reception and the meal, the couple was sent off into the cold wintery weather to stay at a charming inn for the night. They planned to stay there two nights then attend church services with the Waldens on Sunday morning before going to their new home in Washington.

During the night, however, there was a wind storm which knocked out the power to most of the Columbia Gorge and beyond.

Nettie awakened shivering, her shoulder having been uncovered by Lafe, hogging the blankets. She pulled hard on the bedding, rolling Lafe onto his back and waking him.

"Good morning, my beautiful bride," he purred and gave her a kiss.

"Good morning, handsome husband," she purred back. Then she changed her tone. "I found out that you have a flaw, Sir,"

He pretended to be offended. "And what might that be?"

"You are a thief." She gave him a kiss.

"Me, a thief! Whatever do you mean, Madam?"

"You stole my half of the blankets and I woke up cold as a snowman. Why *is* it so cold in here?"

Lafe reached over and flipped the switch on the lamp, but nothing happened. "Hmm, I wonder if the power is out." He pulled the blanket off of himself and swung his feet onto the floor. "You're right; it is a bit chilly."

"I seem to remember hearing the wind howling a few hours ago," she commented as she snuggled under the bedspread Lafe had just pulled over her. "I need to use the toilet, but I don't want to get out of bed to do it."

"I know what you mean, but you might as well get used to it. Our new home doesn't have central heating. I found that if I sleep soundly and let the fire go out during the night, it gets colder than this."

"Thanks for the warning," she said sarcastically as she sprang out of bed and raced him to the bathroom. "If I'd known that, I wouldn't have married you in the middle of winter."

He let her beat him to the "porcelain throne" then they climbed back into bed and did their best to keep each other warm for a couple of hours. The sun was streaming in through the gap in the drapes by then, and their stomachs started growling.

"I guess we're going to have to brave the cold again, get dressed and see if we can find some grub," Nettie sighed.

"Yep, I guess so." Then he gave her another quick kiss, sprang out of bed and pulled the covers off of her. "I bet I can get dressed faster than you!"

"Ooh, you imp!" she said as she ran to the closet.

They got dressed as quickly as possible, shivering the whole time, then bundled up and went to the office to turn in their key and inquire about the power outage.

The clerk at the desk was bundled up as much as they were, and so was another man who came in right behind them.

"How long has the power been out?" Lafe asked the clerk.

"Since three, and the telephone lines, too," came the chattering reply. "It looks like they won't be back on soon. I heard from a policeman friend of mine that many of the roads and the railroad tracks are blocked by fallen trees and utility poles. Most people are stranded. A few had to abandon their cars and walk to their destinations."

"Is the damage very widespread?" the other man asked.

"No one knows, because of the downed phone lines and road blockages. I imagine it is, though. I don't have a fireplace in my apartment. As soon as I leave here I'm going to try to make it to my friend's house until things are back to normal."

"We were going to stay here another night and then travel to Washington tomorrow," Nettie said, "but have family here in town to go to."

"We're stuck here," the other man lamented. "We came from San Francisco for my parents' 30th anniversary party in The Dalles yesterday. We stayed overnight before *expecting* to hop a train for home this morning."

"We can't just leave them out in the cold," Nettie told Lafe. "Why don't you folks come with us? I'm sure my father can find a place to put us all until the roads and tracks are cleared."

"We have two children with us," The man replied with trepidation.

"All the more reason to help you out," Lafe confirmed.

"Normally I would protest about putting you out, but under the circumstances… we accept. My name is Clarence Watters," he said as he shook their hands.

The newlyweds followed the man to his room, where his cold and worried family waited. Introductions were made.

"My name is Lafe Walden and this is my bride, Nettie."

"Nice to meet you. I'm Laura. This is Oliver, and this is Ophelia."

Carsie and Nettie couldn't help but notice that both children were definitely adopted. Clarence and Laura were both Blond and round-eyed, whereas both children, most likely twins, about six years old, were of Asian descent.

On the way out to the parking lot Clarence asked them: "If you have family here in town, why were you staying here last night?"

"We just got married yesterday,"

"Last night was our honeymoon."

"Congratulations!"

"How long have you two been married?" Nettie asked.

"We were married in Taiwan four years ago."

"We were both there, doing missionary work when we met."

"Our families were a little upset that we didn't wait, but they threw us a surprise wedding when we came back three years later."

"They were more surprised than we were because we hadn't told them about adopting the twins."

"Sounds like your family loves surprises, just like mine," Lafe said. "That we do!"

Nettie turned around. "You kids are awfully quiet back there."

"They just started learning English when we brought them over here last year," Laura told her. "I've been teaching them at home, but plan to put them into public school this fall. They're still a little shy about talking to strangers."

"I imagine they'll get over that before too long," Nettie assured her. "My mother said I was very shy when I was little, but once I started school, I came out of my shell."

"She's no turtle now!" Lafe broke in.

"We can tell." Clarence spoke for both of them.

They had to take a couple of detours around downed trees and repair crews, before they found themselves at another dead end near her father's house.

"Why don't we just leave the car here for now and walk the rest of the way?" Nettie suggested. "It might be quite a while before they get the streets cleared."

They all agreed and piled out of the car. Nettie led them the three blocks to her father's house. When she found the door unlocked, she called, "Daddy, where are you?"

Mr. Dawson emerged from the hallway, still in his bathrobe, a moment later. "Nettie and Lafe, I didn't expect to see you again so soon!"

"The roads are all blocked. We've been driving around town for an hour trying to get here. We'll have to stay until things get back to some semblance of normal again."

By this time, they were all jostling for space in front of the fire, trying to get warm.

"I'll get the coffee pot on and warm up some milk for hot cocoa," Their host said as he turned toward the kitchen.

Nettie followed close on his heels. "We're all starving, too. I hope you have some food in here."

As soon as he flipped the switch, they remembered that there was no electricity for the stove. Mr. Dawson started looking through the drawers for a pot that could be used in the fireplace, while Nettie searched the cupboards and the refrigerator for food that didn't require cooking, or that needed to be eaten before it went bad.

Carsie asked if there was a tool shed, where he might find something with which to fashion a cooking platform for the fireplace. Clarence went with him, and they came back with some metal items and tools. After conferring with their host about their availability to be used, they put their heads together, and fashioned something that would allow them to fix a rather hodgepodge, but satisfactory meal.

While they were cooking and eating, they all got to know each other better and the children started to open up and talk.

Mr. Dawson didn't have a battery-operated radio, so they planned to stay there until the power was back on. "We'll have to make do with what we have and what we can borrow from neighbors until then," Nettie said.

Suddenly, Mr. Dawson sat bolt upright. "Oh, that reminds me! Mrs. Peabody, two doors down; I should check on her. She hasn't been feeling well lately, and is most likely in need of help."

He had gotten dressed while the food was cooking, so left immediately. Nettie went with him to check on his aged neighbor.

They returned about fifteen minutes later, supporting the fragile old woman, bundled in a quilt, between them. "I feel bad that I forgot about her until you mentioned neighbors," Mr. Dawson admitted, as they put her into an easy chair by the fire.

"Nobody's perfect," Laura consoled as she helped Nettie with Mrs. Peabody's care.

"The main thing is that you did remember her, and in time, I think," Nettie added.

Mrs. Peabody was hypothermic, dehydrated and in need of personal care, so the men and children left the room for a while to give her some privacy.

Mr. Dawson went back to her house to get her medications and some clean clothes. He emptied her refrigerator of perishables. Then he went back for the shelf-stable items. "We might as well use these up," he said when he returned. "They won't last, and will help us all out, too. I don't have much food left here. I'll replace these when she goes back home, if she does. Her daughter has been trying to get her to move in with her for several years, but she stubbornly refuses to give up her independence. I think she'll agree to do it after this close call."

After getting warmed up, and eating some soup. Mrs. Peabody started to feel better and was more aware of her surroundings. That night, she was bedded down in the master bedroom with Nettie, while the rest of them slept in various places; the spare bedroom, the couch, recliner or living room rug, in the children's case.

The electrical power was restored to most of Portland before the end of the next day, and the main roads and railroad tracks were cleared in two days, so the stranded travelers were able to return home within a few days.

Storm damage along the Washington side of the Columbia Gorge took longer to clean up, so Lafe and Nettie ended up staying in Portland another week, visiting with family and friends. They enjoyed some relaxing time together before reclaiming Lafe's dog from a friend in Skamania, setting up housekeeping and returning to work.

Mrs. Peabody agreed to move in with her daughter, just as Nettie's father had predicted.

Chapter Twenty

IN DEEP

The winter of 1923-24 was mild, with no severe weather, only a couple of dustings of snow on either side of New Years.

In late February, Doley presented John with another son, whom they named John Junior. Bud was jealous of the new baby because he was used to being the center of attention: Doley and Audie had been so protective of him. Now that there was a baby in the family, Bud was feeling neglected. He started acting up in order to draw more attention to himself, and he fell into a trap of self-pity.

Now it was even more of a struggle to make ends meet, not only for John and Doley, but just about everyone in the country. The depression was still affecting Portland's economy, including peoples' need for moving and storage, wrought iron work, new bicycles, baked goods and new furniture and cabinets; all trades that the Walden and Bauer clans owned or worked.

Doley was finding it difficult to care for her children while running the office for John's business. Audie was as helpful as possible. At only four years old, she was becoming quite the little mother, just as her namesake had always been. Sometimes Doley's sisters, sisters-in-law or nieces were available to babysit. In return, John would loan them his truck to deliver goods or move household items when needed.

That summer the weather was hotter and dryer than usual so there were fewer berries and tree fruits to pick. Alice's family was more resourceful than most and knew where to go to find food in the forests and wooded areas around Portland. The men and boys fished in the summertime and hunted during the fall in order to provide meat for their families.

One summer morning Tucker, Chip and Buddy decided to go fishing on the Willamette River because the Clackamas was running so low. Ilda fixed them a picnic lunch, and they loaded the basket, poles and tackle onto the wagon and rode off, with instructions to be careful.

"The Willamette is much deeper and wider than the Clackamas," Ilda warned them.

"Oh, Ma, you worry too much," Buddy countered. "We'll be fine. Plan on fish for dinner tonight!" he called as they drove off.

Alice had an uneasy feeling, all that day. She thought it might be a warning of another headache coming on or maybe there would soon be a difficult maternity case she would have to deal with. Ilda had the same feeling after they left, but she had too much to do to dwell on it. She was helping Faye and Elsie May make their wedding and bridesmaid dresses.

The boy's trip to the river took longer than they thought it would because they took a couple of wrong turns. It had also started clouding up. By the time they found a good fishing spot, it was time for lunch. As they were unpacking everything Buddy heard thunder in the distance.

"A little rain never hurt anyone," Tucker said. "Especially when it's so warm."

"Yeah, it might even feel nice," Chip agreed.

The rain started as a light drizzle while they were eating but escalated to a downpour by the time they got their lines in the water. It never occurred to them that the riverbank where they'd parked might not be stable enough to support the weight of the wagon and horse, once it got soaked. The river started to rise from the rain coming off the mountain and flowing in from the city. They were sitting on a rock several feet above the river and didn't notice anything amiss until the horse started to snort in distress. Tucker had a fish on the line and gave his pole to Buddy while he and Chip went to investigate. They hopped down off the boulder and saw that the horse was up to his fetlocks in water, and the wagon wheels were buried halfway to the hubs, as well.

Tucker grabbed the reigns and guided the horse up the bank, away from the river, but the wheels were stuck in the sandy, saturated soil. Chip was pushing on the tailgate as Tucker was pulling and urging the horse. It was no use; his horse was old and hadn't enough strength to get the job done. Tucker, Chip and the horse were all getting bogged down, too. Tucker realized that the wagon was a lost cause, so he unhitched the horse and led him to safety.

Buddy stood up to land the fish and slipped on the wet rock.

Chip was starting to remount the rock when he heard a yell and a splash. He looked up, but Buddy wasn't there anymore. He ran to the edge of the rock and looked into the river for his cousin. He could just barely make out his head bobbing in the water. He hollered at Tucker and dove in after Buddy. He knew that Buddy couldn't swim very well. Chip swam as hard as he could, and finally caught up with Buddy about a half mile downstream. He helped him stay afloat as the river carried them along. He tried to swim to the side of the river where they might be able to grab something and get ashore, but the river was running too swift, and he was getting tired. Keeping them both afloat was all he could manage, so he prayed that Tucker would be able to come through for them and arrange for their rescue.

Tucker looked up when Chip yelled and saw him jump into the river. "Is he nuts?" he thought, then noticed that Buddy was nowhere to be seen. It occurred to him then, that Buddy must have fallen in and Chip had gone after his younger cousin.

He jumped on the horse's back and ran for help. He remembered seeing a fire station a couple blocks away and went straight there. He knocked on the door but no one answered. "Oh, shoot! It must be a volunteer station," he said aloud to himself. So he remounted and followed the river downstream, on parallel roads. He stopped and looked for them every time he had a clear view of the river. At the north end of town where the river joins up with the Columbia, he finally spied the boys hanging onto a log. They seemed unhurt.

The log and the boys were ejected into the middle of the Columbia, floating downstream toward the lumber mill where Carsie worked. Tucker thought they might be seen and rescued once they got there; But then, the mill might be closed. It was getting late and the rain wasn't letting up. What to do? He yelled to them that he was going for help and rode to the nearest house. In his panic, his own phone number was the only one he could remember. Alice answered his ring. "Tucker, where are you? You sound winded and upset."

"I'm at the Columbia river. The boys are okay, but they're stranded on a log in the river. I don't know what to do!"

"I'll call Carsie and see if he can rescue them. You come on home. I'll have some hot food and a bath waiting for you. I won't even ask what happened yet."

Tucker walked the horse home. The poor beast was hanging his head and still breathing heavy from the exertion of the rescue attempts.

Alice called Carsie's apartment, but there was no answer. She got her directory out and looked up the number for his office.

"Hello, Carson Walden here. May I help you?"

"Carsie, thank God you're still there!"

"Normally I wouldn't be, but I just got finished with a big order. What's up? Why are you calling me, here?"

"Tucker took Chip and Buddy fishing, and the boys ended up in the middle of the river somehow. They're headed your way on a log. I hope you can intercept them before they get to the ocean!"

"I'll sure try!"

He hung up the phone and grabbed a lantern. He went outside and spied a rafter who was just about to leave for home.

"Woody, I need your help for a rescue mission! Untie this boat and pull out to the middle of the river," he said as he ran and climbed in.

They pulled out to the middle of the river and looked both ways, hoping the boys weren't past them already and would arrive before it got any darker. Thankfully, the rain had let up some, but it was going to be getting dark soon because of the thick clouds.

A couple of minutes later Woody said, "Is that a log coming toward us?"

"Sure looks like one. I think I see someone hanging onto it. It must be my nephews. Thank God we intercepted them. Pull up alongside them, real easy now."

"Uncle Carsie, I'm so glad you're here. I was afraid we were going to end up in the ocean," Chip said as he grabbed the rope that was thrown to him.

He passed the rope to Buddy, hanging onto the other side of the log. He helped him get the looped rope around his chest and make it to his uncle's waiting arms. Then he climbed aboard the boat. Carsie loosed the rope from Buddy as Woody motored back toward the dock.

"How did you two end up on a log in the Columbia River?" Carsie asked Chip while he put his coat on Buddy and hugged Chip to himself to stave off the wind chill.

Buddy spoke up, shivering uncontrollably, "It was… all my… fault… I got… up too… quick and… slipped… off the… rock."

They were almost to the mill dock by this time, so Carsie didn't ask any more questions. His curiosity was at a boil after what Buddy had said, but it would have to wait. It was more important to get the boys dried off and warmed up.

Carsie carried Buddy to the office and Woody helped Chip up the hill. As soon as they closed the door behind them, the men got to work. They had plenty of experience with situations like this and knew exactly what to do.

Woody started a fire in the stove, while Carsie helped the boys get their wet clothes off and wrapped them in blankets and rubbed them all over. Then he changed the wet blankets for fresh ones that Woody had warmed on the other side of the pot-bellied stove.

Next, he cleaned out the coffee pot and filled it with water for tea, while Woody wrung out the boys' clothes and hung them up to dry.

"You can go home, Woody. I can take care of them from now on. Thanks for your help."

"Glad to help boss."

When the boys stopped shivering so violently and started to relax a little, Carsie told them, "You'd better call your mothers and your grandmother, to let them know where you are. They're probably frantic with worry."

"I'll go first," Chip said. "Where's the phone?"

"Mama, it's Chip… I'm fine…Yes Buddy, too… We fell in the river and Uncle Carsie rescued us… We're at the lumber mill… I don't know, let me ask.

"Are you gonna take us home, Unc, or should we wait for our parents to come get us?"

"I need to get some food and rest, or I'll be falling asleep at my desk, tomorrow. Hand me the phone.

"Grace? I think I'll take them home with me. Why don't you come pick them up at my place in the morning?... Okay, I'll tell him. Good night, Sis... I love you, too."

Then he handed the phone to Buddy, who, because of his smaller size, was still shivering too much to dial the phone accurately. So Carsie dialed it for him.

"Mama?... Don't cry... I'm okay... just a little cold from a swim in the river... No, not on purpose... I slipped and fell in... and Chip jumped in to save me... We're at the lumber mill... with Uncle Carsie... We made it all the way... to the Columbia River... on a log... and he was waiting... to pluck us out with a boat... I don't know... I'll let you talk to him."

"Ilda?... Yes, they'll be just fine once I get them warm, dry and fed... Grace is going to pick them up at my apartment tomorrow morning... Mama called me... I guess Tucker called her... Would you call her for me so I can get home for some dinner?... You're welcome. I'm just glad I was here to help... The same to you."

Carsie fixed the boys some tea with sugar and milk, then gathered their still-damp clothes while they drank the warming beverages. Then he ushered them out to the car and drove home. He put the boys in his bed and warmed up some leftover stew. When he brought the bowls in, they were both fast asleep.

Meanwhile, Tucker had made it home and went straight into the bathroom for a warm bath. Alice fixed him some dinner. When it was ready, she knocked on the bathroom door, "Tucker, I made you some dinner. You better get out before you turn into a prune!"

There was no answer, so she opened the door and found him asleep in the tub.

"Tucker!" she shook his shoulder. "Wake up! I fixed some dinner for you. Here's your robe."

Tucker came out of the bathroom and sat at the table, bleary-eyed and barely managing to keep from falling asleep in his plate. While he was eating, she asked him what had happened. He told her all he knew, saying that she would have to ask the boys for the rest of the story. When he finished eating, he went straight to bed.

Alice was cleaning up his mess when the phone rang.

"Hello?... Ilda, any news on the boys?... Oh, thank God... that sounds like a good plan... Yes, Tucker made it home all right... He just finished eating and went to bed... No, he couldn't tell me much... I'll tell him in the morning... We'll see you at church on Sunday... Sleep well... I love you, too, dear. Good night."

The next day, Albert hitched his wagon to both horses and loaded it with some tools. Then he, Tucker and Buddy went down to the river to see if Tucker's wagon was still there and try to retrieve it. It was still there, well, most of it, anyway. It was lying on its side, half buried in the sandy soil. The back axle was broken and one of the wheels was missing. Upon closer examination, they discovered that the damage was too extensive to try to fix.

"I don't really need it anymore, anyway," Tucker said. "Now that I'm living in town with Ma, I can get around on the buses or bum a ride off of John or Grace. Besides Pallie is getting old and won't be able to pull a wagon much longer, anyway."

So they disassembled the broken wagon and loaded up any reusable parts. Buddy found one of the fishing poles; its line snagged on a shrub nearby.

On Sunday, everyone wanted to know all the details of the boys' misadventure. They didn't want to talk about it at first, especially Chip. They all hailed him as a hero, for jumping into the river to save his cousin.

Tucker looked a little more distant and detached than usual. When Alice noticed this, she made it a point to give him credit for chasing them down and calling her, which led to their eventual rescue by Carsie.

Carsie wasn't there that Sunday, but they made sure to give him credit the next time they saw him.

The wagon parts that were salvaged came in handy the next few years as the Newmans' wagon started to wear out. Tucker's horse, Pallie was only able to work two more years before he was put out to pasture. One of his and Dottie's daughters, who had been purchased by a neighbor a few years before, was borrowed back when they needed two horses.

This same neighbor had bought the farm from the bank when the previous owner, who had leased it to the Dresslers, had died suddenly.

The new owners, Dick and Sally Fieldings, were a young couple who gleaned a lot of wisdom from Albert and Ilda and traded crops and tools with them. The Newman girls babysat for them from time to time, when the Fieldings became parents. Dick helped Albert's sons with the unpleasant task of slaughtering the larger animals. Albert still was unable to deal with corpses.

The only reason the Newmans had been able to afford a telephone, was that the Fieldings had payed to have the line brought in from the main road when they'd moved in. Ilda and Albert wondered where they'd gotten the money for everything, but figured it was none of their business, so they didn't ask.

Albert was like a father to Dick, and Ilda filled the role of second mother to Sally. When her children were sick or misbehaved, she called Ilda for advice. The women shared recipes, stories and family supplies from time to time. It wasn't unusual for Sally to bring the baby with her to the Newmans' for wool carding, sewing, weaving rugs or just chit chat while eating lunch. If one of their husbands needed assistance with any kind of an emergency or home repair, they knew they could count on each other's help.

Dick and Sally had a car and offered to take Ilda and/or Albert along when they went shopping. They also offered its use for emergencies. One of those emergencies came up in the autumn of 1924.

Cleo and Jojo were playing hide and seek with Nina and Elsie May, when the boys did something they were told not to do. They went into the tool room to hide. That room was off limits to the children because there were so many butcher knives, hoes, shovels, pitch forks and such, needed for farming and animal husbandry purposes. There was a latch far up, beyond the little one's reach, but it had been accidentally left unhooked that afternoon.

Nina was "it" for that round of play. She found Elsie May rather quickly and they both searched for the boys. When they couldn't find them after fifteen minutes of searching, they started calling out, "Ollie, ollie oxen free!" Then they heard a crash in the barn, and a scream.

They ran into the barn and were nearly knocked over by Jojo. He was running in terror from the direction of the tool room. Elsie May told Nina to go in the house with Jojo, while she checked on Cleo. Jojo started sobbing as Nina took him into the house.

Elsie May found Cleo sitting on the floor with a curved knife sticking out of his belly. His pants were soaked with his blood. He was conscious, but silent. He looked up at her and said, "This must be why we're not supposed to be in here." Elsie May was scared that her little brother was going to die, but tried to stay calm, knowing that getting upset would only make matters worse.

Then her mother came out and comforted her little boy. Leaving the knife in place, she told Elsie May to call the Fieldings. "We'll need their car to get him to the hospital."

As Elsie May exited the barn, she saw her brother Buddy coming in from the field and called him to go back out for their father. She went in the house and picked up the phone. She heard a conversation on the party line and said, "I hate to be rude, but I need to use the phone."

"What makes you think your call is more important than ours, little girl?" one of the women said, haughtily.

"My brother is bleeding to death and needs to get to the hospital," came the answer.

There was a gasp, and the line went dead. She called Mrs. Fielding and told her what had happened.

"I'll be right there with the car."

Elsie May went to comfort the other children and found herself crying with them. A few minutes later, she heard a car pull up and went out to make sure it was her neighbor. Then her father came out of the

229

barn carrying Cleo. Cleo was limp by this time and their mother was visibly shaken. They climbed into the car while Buddy came into the house and told them that he would stay with them.

They all hugged each other and cried.

"Is he going to die, like our mommy and daddy?" Nina asked Buddy.

"I don't know. I sure hope not."

When the Newmans and Sally arrived at the hospital, Cleo was in serious shape. He'd lost nearly half of his blood volume, so that they had a hard time starting an I V. They had to pump a lot of type O negative blood into him while they did the exploratory surgery to find the source of the bleeding. There was a call out to all the hospitals and clinics in the Portland area, for all the blood they could spare. Then a county-wide call for universal donors to replenish the supply.

After two hours and two dozen units of blood, the surgical team was able to close the spigot by removing the little boy's spleen and stitching holes in his intestines, as well. Cleo was treated for peritonitis, anemia and near renal failure.

His parents couldn't afford the rapidly mounting hospital and doctor bills. Their pastor put out a plea to his congregation and all the other churches in the area, for financial help and prayers for this desperate need. All the schools in the Portland area, starting with the ones attended by the children of the Walden clan, had fund-raisers and prayer meetings, also.

The whole family was grateful and humbled by the community's outpouring of love. Most of them participated in the writing of thank you letters to everyone they had addresses for or saw regularly. Included in each one was a quote from scripture or a prayer.

God opened the hearts of many people, not only in Portland but all across the Pacific Northwest and beyond to give, some out of their poverty, to help cover the bills. Some donations and well-wishes came from Seattle, and some all the way from friends and relatives in Illinois and South Carolina.

While Cleo was hospitalized, Charles, Mattie and Teresa helped care for the boy in their spare time, free of charge, as did many other doctors and nurses who knew Alice and her family.

Charles set up a special fund, and had enough clout with the hospital management to make sure that the Newmans never got a bill for any of Cleo's care.

Cleo was out of school for the whole winter and fell behind in his studies. Once he was well enough to do some work from his bed, his teacher and family made sure he had all the help he needed to catch up by the beginning of the next school year.

That same summer, the Schmidt family arrived from Germany. Anja had sent some photos of themselves, and Grace had reciprocated, so they could recognize each other at the train station.

The children of both families had written letters to each other, as did many of the adults. They were already good friends before they arrived, and the Schmidts had been studying hard to learn their new language. The only problem was that their teachers had been from Britain, so they spoke with a British accent for quite a while, and didn't know all the uniquely American words, such as apartment, gasoline, car, diaper and elevator.

After resting for a few days to recover from their long journey and the time change, Anja enrolled five-year old Rogert in kindergarten and started working in the position that had been arranged for her at the German bakery. Little Heloise stayed with Grace while her mother was at work.

An apartment had been found for them near the Rowleys' home. The Schmidt children called Grace and Guy aunt and uncle, and considered their children as cousins. They also developed a close friendship with the Bauer clan. Although Anja and Rogert had a commanding grasp on our language, it was more relaxing for them to converse in German and share traditional German foods. They also attended the Bauers' church, since both families were Lutherans.

Chapter Twenty-One

INTO THE WOODS

On a dark, rainy day in mid-March, 1925, Grace gave birth to a ten-and-a-half-pound baby boy, with Alice attending, while her older children were at school and Guy was at work. The twins were excited when they came home, except that they really wanted a little sister this time. "We're surrounded by boys!" they wailed. "But he is awfully cute," Ginny admitted. "And he doesn't have red hair," Ginger added. "Redheads get teased a lot," "especially boys," they said in tandem. He was named Ernest after his great grandpa Beebe.

In June, Faye and Jerry were the first of Alice's grandchildren to graduate high school. Jerry had a job waiting for him at the railroad, and Faye married her high school sweetheart in July. They lived with his parents, working alongside them at their dairy.

In September, Ronny and Buddy started high school and Audie and Merle started kindergarten. Chip made it onto the football team, and Elsie May, at twelve, was starting to blossom into a young lady.

Eight-year-old Cleo, Ginny and Ginger were full of mischief. They called themselves the three musketeers. Every chance they got, they went on adventures together. Sometimes those adventures put them in peril. Like the time they went on a camping trip with Carsie, Alice, Buddy, Guy and Tucker to Mt. Hood.

Guy knew from experience that Tucker and the musketeers would be underfoot while he and the others were setting up camp, so he sent them to gather firewood.

"Stay within earshot of the camp," he told them as they scampered off to explore the forest. "I hope they don't get themselves eaten by a bear," he said to Carsie as they unpacked the car.

Alice and Buddy were clearing branches, fir cones and rocks from the tent sites. Then they assisted the two men erect the tents. Tucker and the musketeers returned with armloads of twigs and small branches, then went back out for more. The men cleared a space for a fire and made a stone fire pit, and Alice set out on an herb and mushroom hunt.

Carsie arranged the firewood while the other two rolled out the sleeping bags and unpacked the food and utensils.

Tucker and his crew returned with more firewood and reported finding a small waterfall.

"I *thought* I heard a creek nearby," Ronny said.

"Yeah, me, too," Buddy spoke up.

"Why do you think I picked this spot?" Alice asked them. "I know my way around the woods." Then she went off in a different direction to gather more herbs.

"We'll go get some water for the rest of you, if you want," Cleo volunteered as he picked up the buckets.

"I'll sit this one out," Ginny said. "I got a scrape on my arm from the firewood. Maybe grandma will come back with something to make it feel better."

"I need to take a leak," Tucker said as he sprinted off into the woods.

Guy was checking out his car. It had started acting up a little on the way. Carsie had gone off to gather some dry moss to help start the fire, and some good wiener and marshmallow roasting sticks. When he and Alice returned, they were a little concerned to hear that the two children had gone off without adult supervision.

"Oh, they'll be fine," Tucker said as he sat reclined against a log. "They know the way back to camp."

"Maybe," Alice said, "but they're only eight years old."

"And they aren't familiar with the potential dangers of the forest," Carsie added. "I'd better go after them."

The children had a good ten-minute head start on him. When he got to the stream, he didn't see them anywhere. He called their names. Then he heard a scream and two splashes downstream. He raced toward them as fast as he could, but the underbrush was thick at the water's edge. The stream was running swift from snowmelt on the mountain, and too deep to safely wade through. Around the bend, he found a log that had fallen across the stream. "They probably fell off of it. The water is swift and deep here," he thought.

He scrambled over the log and continued following the stream until he found them several miles downstream. Where the stream bed was wider and shallower, they had finally managed to get ashore. They were both soaked to the skin and a little scraped up. One of Ginger's shoes was missing and she was crying. "Me and my big ideas." She sobbed.

"Trying to cross the log was your idea?" Carsie asked her.

She nodded, sadly. "How did you know?"

"I was a kid, once."

"It sounded like fun to me, too," Cleo admitted. "It's not all Ginger's fault."

He was holding his arm, so Carsie asked him, "Are you okay?"

"Yeah. I hit it on a rock when I fell in the water. I'll be okay."

"How about you Ginger?"

"I'm just cold."

Carsie took off his flannel shirt and put it on the little girl. "Now we have to get back to camp as quickly as possible. Since you only have one shoe, Ginger, I'll have to carry you. Hop on my back.

"You go on ahead, Cleo. Move as fast as you safely can, that way."
Cleo was cold, also, but was trying to act brave.

After half an hour of hiking, Cleo started to slow down. He was cradling his arm and shivering. Carsie called him to stop for a rest. "I can tell you need a break." There was a large, flat rock in a sunny clearing nearby, that they all sat on, in order to warm up and dry out. "Let me take a look at that arm," he directed Cleo. He examined him and determined that it was most likely just a bad bruise or sprain, not a break. He had the boy take off his shirt and repositioned it so that the sleeve became a sling for his sore arm.

"Is that better?"

"Yes, some, but I'm really hungry and kind of cold, too. My shirt and hair have dried out, but my pants and socks are still wet."

"The sun is going to be setting before too long. It gets dark and cold real quick in the woods, once the sun sets. We still have a way to go. We'll need to stop and make camp here for the night, then go the rest of the way tomorrow morning."

At that announcement, Ginger started to cry again. "I'm so sorry. We're going to die out here, aren't we?"

"We'll be okay," Cleo comforted her. "Uncle Carsie was born in the woods, weren't you?"

"Not exactly, but not far from it. Your grandma is quite a woods-woman, as was your granddad. I've lived and worked in the woods a big part of my life, so I know how to survive out here."

After Carsie helped the children find some berries and other wild food to pick, he got busy making them a shelter from fir branches. When the sun went low and darkness started closing in, he called the children in and, after they ate, pulled dry leaves in around them for insulation. "It may not be comfortable, but it'll get us through the night," he assured them.

Meanwhile, back at the campsite, Ginny was worried sick about her sister and cousin. "What would I do without my best friends," she sobbed.

"Carsie will find them and keep them safe, I'm sure," Alice said. "He comes from a long line of forest dwellers."

"You hear that?" Her father hugged her close. "You go to bed now and say a prayer for them, okay?"

"Okay," she sniffed.

Guy and Alice stayed up all night, tending the fire and praying.

Carsie didn't sleep either; he was watching and listening for predators.

When morning came, the wind shifted so that the smoke from the campfire blew right to where Carsie and his charges were. They followed their noses and were back at camp in time for a late breakfast. They were dirty, sore, tired and hungry, but thrilled to be reunited with the others.

Guy wanted to pack up and go back home, immediately, but Carsie asked Ginger and Cleo what they wanted to do. "I'm game to stay another day. How about you two?"

"All I want to do is eat some real food," Cleo said.

"And sleep on something padded and warm," Ginger added.

They looked at each other and said, "We'll stay!"

"Now you know why you shouldn't to go off without an adult?" Guy asked.

They both nodded as they started eating the bacon offered them by Jerry.

"I've been up all night," Carsie said. "I think I'll take a nap, too."

Guy spoke up next. "Alice and I dozed a little by the fire. I'll probably just go to bed early tonight."

"I finally went to bed just before sunup," Alice said, emerging from one of the tents. "Good to see that you're all okay."

After resting up, they all enjoyed the rest of their camping trip, being more cautious and watchful.

One September evening, the Bauers' phone rang. John picked it up. "Hello?... Frank, so nice, from you to hear... The children into bed, she's tucking... Surviving, we are. These days, enough that is... Here now, she comes."

"Frank, are you a father again, yet?... A boy this time? I'm happy for you! How's Mary doing?... Sorry to hear that. I'll pass along the information and say some extra prayers for you all."

"Thanks, Sis."

Doley called the rest of her family in the morning, to give them the news, then filled them in on their entire conversation on Sunday afternoon: "Mary had a really tough time with this one. The doctor had to do a hysterectomy, so they won't be having any more children. He asked that we pray for her. She's pretty broken up about it."

The next spring, Lafe was asked to monitor the fire lookout post on Lookout Mountain, in the Gifford Pinchot National Forrest, about twenty miles due north of their home. It was a twenty-five mile trek up the Washougal Creek and another steep, seven-mile hike up the mountain. If he accepted, he would be spending the entire summer there, watching for forest fires.

The logging company had a contract with the forest service to harvest some of the trees in the next few years, and needed to monitor their investment. A telegraph line had been run up there, and he was to send a wire if he saw any smoke, or needed assistance.

It was customary for two people to go there, just in case he got sick or injured. Lafe was told he could take anyone he wanted with him. His friend Max had taken his wife with him the year before, but now she was expecting their first child and he didn't want to go without her.

Nettie had spent many summers hiking and camping in the woods with her parents before her mother got sick. When Lafe told her about the assignment, she jumped at the chance.

"It sounds like quite an adventure. I used to love being out in the woods with Cooper, Mom and Dad. Let's do it!"

So they made arrangements with their neighbor to keep their dog, and with her employer for a hiatus, bought whatever supplies they needed with the allowance given them. They notified their families and set out on the adventure of their lives.

They hiked three to five miles a day, eating jerky and dried fruit, mostly. When they got to the point where the creek split up into rivulets and became non-existent, they camped for the night. In the morning, they continued northeast, per Max's instructions, on the steepest path they could find. After several hours of climbing, they finally broke out into a blue sky, with the lookout looming before them.

They walked over to the base of the structure and looked up. "It must be at least fifty feet to the top!" Nettie exclaimed.

"Max told me it's forty." Lafe told her.

"I don't know about you, but I need to rest a while before tackling that ladder," she said. She put her pack down and sat against a tree.

"I'm with you," Lafe agreed. "Let's have some lunch first."

Just then, they heard a low rumbling growl. They looked in the direction of the noise and saw a large bear heading in their direction. Suddenly, they found the strength to haul themselves and their packs up the ladder.

Lafe urged Nettie ahead of him, looking down after climbing about twenty feet. The bear was checking out the ladder and gave them one last roar of warning before wandering off with her cubs.

"Now that we're this far, we might as well continue," he remarked, as he turned his gaze back up. Nettie was already up the ladder and standing at the door. She sat down and peered over the edge, breathing heavily, unable to speak. She was relieved to see that Lafe had managed to get out of the bear's reach in time, also.

He rested a minute where he was, and then joined her on the platform. "I didn't know you could move that fast," he commented, sitting beside her.

"Neither did I," she smiled, "but then I've never had to run from a charging bear before!"

They laughed together, then rested a few more minutes, enjoying the view. They went into the cabin to check it out and unpack their gear. They had to evict a family of squirrels, a host of spiders and other uninvited guests and clean up after them all before eating lunch and settling in for the summer.

The lookout cabin had none of the amenities of their apartment in Skamania, but Max's predecessor had rigged up some ingenious contraptions to necessitate the climb up and down the ladder less frequent. There was a pulley system with several buckets designated for food, water, firewood and "other".

The first time Lafe ventured out, he followed his nose and Max's directions to the privy hole and the spring. The next day, he and Nettie went on a food-gathering excursion.

It was very peaceful there, and they got to know every small detail about each other. They spent a lot of time playing cards, exercising, studying the Bible and praying together.

The happy couple would do this assignment for the next three summers, until their turn came to become parents.

That October, Guy, Jerry, Chip and Carsie cooked up a plan.

"It's been a couple of years since we went deer hunting," Carsie said. So they made plans to go the next weekend.

"Only men this time," Guy said, when Ronny and Buddy asked to go along. "Besides, our car is getting old and cantankerous lately. I don't trust it to make the trip."

"I had my doubts about it getting you home the last time we took it camping," Carsie said.

"Me, too," Guy admitted. "But with prices like they are, and a large family to support, I can't afford to replace it, yet."

They cleaned their rifles, sharpened their hunting knives and checked out their camping gear during the week. Carsie arrived at the Rowley's house early on Saturday morning. They stopped for breakfast in a small café in Gresham just before ascending the mountain toward their usual hunting area near Sandy. By the time they arrived at their destination and set up camp, it was time for lunch.

"I'd rather spend the time hunting than building a fire and cooking right now," Carsie said as he put on his jacket, grabbed some jerky and two apples, then shouldered his rifle.

"I'm with you, Unc," said Chip as he followed Carsie's lead. "I'm ready to get my first trophy."

"You two go ahead," Guy told them. "Jerry and I will stay here and watch the car and the gear. We'll go out tomorrow morning while you stay here."

"Sounds good to us," they agreed, as Chip picked up his rifle and followed Carsie.

Carsie tossed one of the apples to his nephew, and In-between bites, briefed Chip on proper hunting etiquette and procedures. "Stay within sight of me, never in front or behind. No talking, no quick moves. Be sure of your target before you shoot. It's better to miss out on a deer than to shoot another hunter by mistake."

"Gotcha," Chip acknowledged. Carsie stopped as he finished his apple. "The creek is about a quarter of a mile ahead of us. The deer come there to drink, and that will be our best chance to nab one. Watch your step, move slowly and look my way every few seconds.

"Load your rifle and take the safety off now, and we'll proceed."

Carsie motioned Chip to move to his left while he moved right. Their pace seemed agonizingly slow for a teenager who was used to moving quickly. After what seemed to him to be hours, Chip heard the sound of a babbling brook ahead, and his uncle motioned him to crouch down. They ate their jerky while they watched and waited another hour.

When Chip finished his snack and looked over at Carsie, he could tell his uncle was watching something. He followed his gaze and spied a doe and her fawn approaching the water. He reached for his rifle, but Carsie signaled, "No." He put his hands up to his head to indicate antlers. Then Chip remembered that they weren't supposed to shoot does, only bucks. They watched as three more does and their young came to drink.

Suddenly, Chip sneezed, which startled the deer. They all jumped the creek and bounded up the hillside opposite them.

"Sorry," Chip said aloud.

Carsie shrugged his shoulders as if to say, it doesn't matter. They waited around there for another two hours, seeing lots of squirrels, birds, and a family of raccoons, but no more deer. Then Carsie stood, stretched and said, "Let's go back to camp. It'll be getting dark before long, and I'm hungry."

They locked their rifles, drank from the stream and hiked back to camp. Guy had dinner keeping warm for them and was ready to join Jerry in the tent when they returned. "We wanted to get an early start," he said as he got up and said goodnight.

"I hope you have better luck tomorrow than we did." Carsie said. "Did you see any deer?"

"Several does and fawns, but no bucks," Chip lamented.

"Well, at least the other critters were entertaining." Carsie reminded him, in his usual upbeat style.

"That's true. We don't see much of that in the city."

Carsie and Chip awoke at seven o'clock to the raucous call of a stellar jay. It was still fairly dark at their campsite, but the sky above was starting to lighten up, so that only the brightest stars were still visible. Guy had breakfast cooked and waiting for them. "You owe me for doing all the cooking again, Carsie."

"You have someone to cook for you at home," Carsie countered. "I'll continue buying the meals while we're on the road."

"That's okay with me." Guy lifted his pack and rifle. "Come on Jerry; let's go bag us some venison."

Guy led the way to a different spot than the one Carsie had picked. It was a woodland meadow a little further away. He had been with Carsie when he'd shot a four-pointer there three years before.

They hiked along carefully and watchfully, only whispering occasionally. When they got near the meadow, they readied their rifles, split up and moved more slowly. When they got to within sight of the meadow, they crouched down and peeked through the underbrush to see six bucks eating on the other side of the meadow about four hundred yards away. They both knew that they were too far away for a good shot, so they stayed still and waited, hoping the deer would come closer.

After fifteen or twenty minutes, some does and fawns came in from the left and moved in front of the bucks. Jerry was dismayed, thinking they probably wouldn't get the chance to nab one of the bucks now. Guy knew they had all day to wait, and if they were patient, staying still and quiet, they would most likely get another chance, even if this one passed them by.

So they watched and waited while the deer moved slowly around the meadow, munching contentedly and looking up occasionally for any signs of danger. One doe came very close to Jerry; so close that he was afraid to even breathe, for fear he'd be discovered and they would all scatter.

CRRACKK! Went the sound of a rifle, but not Guy's. The sound came from the other direction.

The deer were running right at him, so he raised his rifle and shot one of the bucks just before it jumped over the bush that he was hiding behind. He heard another rifle blast from Guy's direction, and stood as the last deer veered away and disappeared into the woods.

He looked, and saw a six-pointer at his feet and his father standing near the smaller buck that he'd shot. Two men were running across the meadow toward them. They looked pretty rough, and Jerry hoped they weren't as mean as they appeared to be.

As the men got closer, Guy could sense that they were determined to claim one of the deer for themselves. They were much too big and strong to pick a fight with.

"Hi, fellas, good shooting. I think this one is yours. My son shot that one point-blank, just before he trampled him."

"But, Dad," Jerry started to protest. Guy ignored him and smiled at the men, acting very friendly, offering his hand to them as if he'd known them all his life. Then Jerry realized what his father was up to.

The men were surprised by Guy's reaction and quickly changed their attitude. They had planned to claim the larger deer for their own, with force if need be, but decided if this guy is willing to give up one of them without a fight, they'd take it. They went along with the game and worked alongside Guy and Jerry to prepare the carcasses for transport.

They parted amicably and shouldered their prizes to hike back to their camps. As soon as he was sure they were out of earshot, Jerry let out a big sigh, "That was quick thinking, Dad. I'll try to remember that trick if I ever get into a tight situation again. Where did you learn that?"

"From the Bible, my boy. It says, in Proverbs 15, that a soft answer turneth away wrath, but harsh words stir up anger. Besides, they were so surprised that we didn't put up a fight, that we ended up with the most meat *and* no bullets in us!"

He didn't tell anyone that he had heard and felt that first shot go into the tree just above his head.

Chapter Twenty-Two

TEARS AND CHEERS

Late January and early February, 1926 were very cold and snowy, affording the children many chances to make snowmen, have snowball fights and go on sleigh rides with the church youth group. Of course, it also meant more feed and careful tending of the farm animals.

It was also more difficult for Alice to get to some of her patients when she was called to a delivery. One particularly icy night, in the wee hours, she received a call to go to a farm on the edge of town. She asked the husband who called her about the road conditions out there.

"I don't envy you the task of trekking out here," he replied. "I'd come and get you in a sleigh, if I had one. I fell down outside, earlier and got a nasty bruise on my backside."

His comment about the sleigh sparked an idea in Alice's sharp mind. She called their pastor and asked for the phone number of the family who had given the sleigh rides to the teens a couple of weeks before. When the gentleman answered the phone and she told him what she needed, he sprang to action, arriving at her house to pick her up within thirty minutes, just as the sun was starting to rise.

"Would you mind staying for a little while, Barry, in case there are complications and she needs to go to the hospital?"

"I'd be happy to, Ma'am," he replied. "I own a business and don't get many customers in this kind of weather, anyway."

They pulled up at the farmhouse and Barry helped her get safely inside. Barry was surprised to find that Chuck, the husband, didn't seem as worried or nervous as most expectant husbands tend to be, nor did his wife Rosemarie. They had been this route twice before with no serious trouble either time. The only reason they called for Alice was that there had been some minor complications during this pregnancy, and their doctor had recommended that they go to the hospital this time. The weather made that impossible.

This delivery was no different than the couples' first two, until the baby was born, that is. Rosemarie first noticed that her husband's and Alice's countenances had fallen, then that the baby's crying sounded strange. She reached for him, but Alice took him and turned away, while Chuck just sat there with his eyes closed. She could tell that he was trying to hold back tears.

"What's wrong with our baby?" She asked fearfully, tears brimming in her eyes. "I want to see my baby!"

Chuck took a deep breath and squeezed her hand. "He's going to be fine, dear. There's just a little problem with his lip."

"What kind of problem?" she insisted. She was starting to get angry now. "Give me my baby!"

"I had to suction him and cut his cord," Alice said as she turned back with the tightly swaddled baby. "Chuck is right; he seems to be healthy in every other way, but he has a cleft lip and pallet. I want you to be prepared before you take a look. It's going to be a bit of a shock."

Rosemarie reached out her trembling arms to take her baby from Alice. At first she just cuddled him and took in his scent and warmth. When she had calmed down a bit, she slowly and tentatively peeked under the blanket and nearly fainted at the sight before her.

The baby had a gaping hole in the middle of his face where his upper lip should have been. Her heart went out to her child, but she couldn't bear to look at him. How could she love him and be repulsed by him at the same time? She cried and cried, until Alice fixed her some herbal tea and Chuck finally convinced her to relinquish the child to him, so she could dry her tears and drink the tea. When she finished it, he gave the baby to Alice and held his wife close until she went to sleep.

Out in the living room, Alice told Barry that she was going to stay with the family for a day or so, and sent him home. Then she called Tucker to let him know that she didn't know when she'd be home, and to tell anyone who called for her, that she was with a special case, and unavailable until further notice.

Cora Brantner

After Rosemarie went to sleep, Chuck came out and sunk onto the sofa with Alice, "What will we do now? Is he going to look like this all his life? Everyone will treat him like a freak. How can we even look at him and not see something ugly? How will our other children react when they see him? Will we all learn to love him and accept him?"

The questions spilled out one after the other without any room for answers. Not that Alice had any to give.

They sat silently for a moment; Alice holding the sleeping child. She opened the blanket and looked at the baby closely as she spoke, "You'll have to take it one day at a time, I suppose. Do you have faith in God, Chuck?"

"How can I believe in a God who would curse us like this?" he asked, bitterly. Then he stood and paced the floor.

Just as she was about to speak, four-year-old Abbey came out of her bedroom, rubbing her eyes. Alice could hear her little sister crying softly, as she stood up in her crib, listening to the voices in the other room.

"Daddy, where's Mama?" Abbey said. Then she noticed Alice, holding the baby, and was instantly wide awake. "Ooh, the baby's here! Can I hold her?"

Chuck took his daughter in his arms and cuddled her tightly, crying into her neck. Alice put the baby down, carefully on the couch, and stood. "I'll go take care of Hannah for you," she said, and left them alone.

The whole time she was changing Hannah, Alice was trying to remember how Teresa had said to feed a baby such as this. It was obvious that he wouldn't be able to suckle normally. He wouldn't be able to seal his mouth around the nipple and pull it to the back of his mouth, as was needed. She finished dressing Hannah, then brought her out to the living room.

Abbey was holding her little brother, lovingly and tenderly. Chuck was still unable to look at his son without feeling sick, but Hannah and Abbey seemed to accept him as he was, with no reservations.

The baby started to wake up and cry. Rosemarie called from the bedroom a few minutes later and Abbey took the baby in to her, followed by her sister.

246

Chuck was sitting with his face buried in his hands. "What did we do to deserve this?" he moaned, as Alice put her arm around his shoulder to comfort him. "I don't think this is a punishment from God, but it may be a test that you'll have to pass in order for your family to survive intact," she told him. "If you pass the test, you'll be much closer and stronger for it."

Then he stood up and strode out of the house.

Alice followed the girls into the master bedroom, where she found a touching scene: Both girls were up on the bed, alongside their mother, who was holding her new son on her lap. They were all cooing at him, admiring his full head of hair and counting his fingers and toes; all the things she expected to see after any normal delivery. Rosemarie was crying, softly. She looked up at Alice with pleading eyes. "I don't know what to do. Can you help me?"

Alice participated in the baby's adoration for a few minutes, until the little boy's crying made it obvious that he was hungry and would not stop until he was satisfied.

"Abbey, can you get dressed and fix some cereal for yourselves, while your mama and I tend to the baby?"

"Okay," she said. "Come on Hannah." She helped her sister down from the bed and led her out of the room.

Alice helped Rosemarie put the baby to her breasts in several different positions, none of which worked very well. The little boy wasn't getting much colostrum milk, and swallowed a lot of air. They tried a bottle that Alice had brought with her, and got the same results. He had to be burped every few minutes, and cried with hunger the whole time. His mother and Alice grew more and more frustrated and concerned.

"What are we going to do, Alice? He'll starve to death at this rate, and we won't be able to get any sleep, either."

"I seem to remember my cousin, who works in the maternity ward, telling me that babies like this have to be fed with specially designed bottles."

"But I've always believed in breast feeding. I nursed both of the girls for at least a year."

"We'll get you a breast pump, so he'll still have the benefit of your milk, but you'll have to use the bottle for him if he's to survive. I'll give Teresa a call to see if she's available to come over here with some equipment and advice to solve this problem. She can probably recommend a pediatric team to see about getting his face fixed, also."

"They can do that?"

"Yes. He won't be as good as new, but more functional, and closer to normal-looking than he does now. I've never dealt with a case like this before, but have seen people before and after the surgery, and the improvement is remarkable, if not perfect."

"Thank you so much for telling me that. Now that you mention it, I have seen someone with a scarred lip, and wondered about it. Are they getting better at fixing this sort of thing?"

"Yes, I've heard about surgical techniques improving by leaps and bounds since I moved to Portland about twenty years ago."

The girls came back about then, and Alice excused herself. "I'll go make that phone call now."

"Alice, it's so good to hear from you!" Teresa had been thinking about and praying for her friend and cousin, since she'd arrived at the hospital and heard that all of Alice's patients were to be referred to other midwives until further notice.

"How did your case turn out? Are you available again?... Oh, I'm sorry to hear that... Yes, that's a tough one... If I can't get away, I'll send someone else as soon as possible. What's the address there?... And the phone number?... Okay, hold on; help is on the way."

Within the hour, a car pulled up in front and a pleasant-looking young woman knocked on the door. Alice let her in and introduced herself.

"My name is Becky Stevens," the woman said as she shook Alice's hand. "I was sent by the special needs coordinator for the hospital. I've heard about you from some of the hospital staff. I'm so happy to finally meet you."

"I hope you know what to do with cases like this," Alice said on the way to the bedroom. "I'm at a loss for what to do."

Alice made the introductions, then took the girls into their room to play, while Becky did her "magic" with pump and bottles.

A little while later, the baby stopped crying, and Becky met Alice in the living room. "I think they'll do just fine now. He's on formula until her milk starts flowing.

"She said she doesn't know where her husband went. I assume he was pretty shaken by this."

"Yes, he was. I think he's a good man, and will come around eventually, but they're going to need a lot of emotional and spiritual support to get through this."

"The director put the wheels in motion while I was packing the equipment." Becky told Alice as she gave her one of her business cards. "Here's my home phone number, as well as my office. Don't hesitate to call me at any time. I left a card with Rosemarie, too. Will you be staying until her husband returns?"

"Yes; him or someone else, until I'm certain they can handle the situation without me. Is Rosemarie asleep?"

"No, I'm awake, still," Rosemarie said as she came out of the bedroom. "I promised my mother a phone call as soon as the baby was born. She and Papa live in Colorado. She wanted to be here for the birth, but came down with pneumonia a couple of weeks ago."

"How do you think she'll take the news?" Becky asked her.

"She'll be upset, of course, but she'll be on the next train, I'm sure. Papa's the one I'm not too sure about. He's a crusty, judgmental sort. Mama will know what to tell him, and when. I don't know how she put up with him all these years."

"True love can overcome almost any difficulty," Alice commented, as Becky shook hands and went out the door.

She met Chuck as he was coming up to the walk. "Who are you? Is everyone all right?"

"Everyone is just fine. I'm from the hospital's special services. I came with some equipment, and to teach your wife how to take care of your son's needs. I'm sure Rosemarie will be relieved to have you back."

He entered the house to find his wife on the phone with her mother. She was crying, but smiled and welcomed him into her arms. He sat down next to her and joined in on the conversation.

Alice was in the kitchen, fixing lunch, and overheard part of the conversation: "Yes Mama, he's right here... I think we're going to be just fine, now... You listen to your doctor, then... Yes, Mama... A lady from the hospital... She says the doctors will decide as they monitor his health... He seems perfect in every other way... The girls accepted him right away... Thank you... I love you, too."

"Goodbye," Chuck said. "Take care of yourself. We'll see you in a couple of weeks."

Alice stayed until dinnertime to make sure the whole family was going to be all right. Grace came to take her home, and she went straight to bed with one of her migraine headaches. She called into the clinic the next morning to let them know she was available again.

Baby Philip continued to thrive, and had his first surgery to close his palate at two months, and the second and third for his lip, at eight and sixteen months. People still looked at him strangely, and some asked what happened to him, but they were no longer repulsed by his appearance. His parents felt it was better to be stared at occasionally than to have people look away in disgust, and avoid or exclude their son.

By the time he was a young adult, surgical procedures had further improved, and he would undergo further plastic surgery. The growing of a mustache made his scar almost imperceptible once the hair grew in all the way.

For Alice's sixtieth birthday in the spring of 1927, her family arranged a surprise party for her. She assumed they would do the usual cake and ice cream at Ilda's, but never thought they would go all-out and invite her friends and all the out-of-area family, too.

"If you don't mind, we'll wait until next Sunday for your birthday dinner," Grace told her. "It's so difficult to get together on a weeknight."

"That's fine," Alice agreed. "I don't want to put anyone out."

During the service on Sunday morning, Alice couldn't help but notice some extra noise and the smell of food emanating from the back of the church. She assumed there was going to be a wedding or some other to-do happening there that afternoon. She didn't turn to look, or ask anyone what might be going on. She was respectful and attentive to the teaching from the pulpit.

She was expecting to be driven to the farm for the day, but their pastor remounted the platform after the last hymn. "Don't rush off home, just yet. I have a special announcement to make. If you can stay, we are going to celebrate a very special birthday for a very special lady.

"Alice Walden, would you please join me up here?"

The whole building echoed with applause and a few whistles. Alice was so surprised that she was unable to stand at first. Then Frank and Lafe appeared at her sides and escorted her to the front. "What are you two doing here?" she asked.

When they turned her around to face the assembly, she saw that the pews were full and there were people standing all along the back and side walls and spilling out into the foyer. She hardly heard what was said of her as she looked out on the crowd and picked out many familiar faces not normally seen in this setting: Mattie and Charles, Teresa and her husband, Frank and Lafe's wives, most of the Bauer clan, Anja from Germany and some of the nurses and midwives. She also recognized some former patients of hers, including Rosemarie and Chuck. She heard many children's voices and crying babies downstairs, as well as the rattle and clank of dishes and silverware.

She grew weak in the knees; grateful that she had two big, strong sons to hold her up. The pastor said a blessing, and Alice and her family were escorted to the fellowship hall, where all the tables were set up and covered with tablecloths. Vases full of daffodils and hyacinths finished the décor. Four long tables were lined up with what appeared to be a potluck feast. On the near end of the first table, flanked by pies, cookies and brownies, there was a beautiful birthday cake with her name on it.

Her sons seated her at a table near the entry door, so she could greet everyone as they came and went. Then Ilda fixed her a plate, while the throng wound their way down the stairs and lined up for the feast.

Alice hardly had a chance to eat, for everyone who passed by her stopped to say hello and give her a hug.

By the time the crowd started thinning out and the ladies started cleaning up, Alice was exhausted. She hadn't had a party like this since that last Christmas in Oregon City, or was it Linnville, no that was Illinois. She was too tired to remember anything, and she had a headache, too. The room started to spin, and she asked to be taken home.

She went to bed after taking some aspirin, and slept through until the next morning. She didn't even wake up when the phone rang at two a.m. for a delivery call. Tucker slept through it, too. She didn't find out about it until she got a call from Teresa, later that morning.

"I sent someone else in your place," she told Alice. "You must have been very tired from your party yesterday."

"Tired isn't the word. I'll have to tell my family that I can't handle any more surprises like that. I love them dearly, and I appreciate all the hard work that went into it, but I'm getting too old to party like that anymore."

"I hear you loud and clear. We went back to Illinois for my father's ninetieth birthday last year, and he said the same thing. The trip was exhausting and, as much as I love my family, I'm not looking forward to doing it again."

Naturally, it was only a couple of months later, that Teresa's father died, and she was on the train back to Illinois again. After she returned, she retired from nursing. "I just don't have the stamina I used to have, and I've developed arthritis. I'll be seventy years old next month, and my husband's health isn't so good anymore. I think I've earned the right to kick back, grow some flowers and dote on my grandchildren and great-grandchildren."

Chapter Twenty-Three

THE FALL

In early May of 1927, Alice asked her family, when they were together for Sunday dinner, if someone would be willing and available to take her to visit Lafe and Nettie. "They invited me to visit, and I've never been to the Washington side of the Columbia River Gorge. I need to get away from the city for a while."

"When were you thinking?" someone asked.

"It'll have to be on a weekend," said another.

"Can I come along?" asked Elsie May. "I really like Nettie and miss Uncle Lafe, too."

"Can we go, too?" the twins said excitedly.

Audie opened her mouth to speak, but then looked at her mother and saw that she was avoiding her gaze. She knew that she needed to stay behind to watch her brothers. Business didn't slow down on weekends for their family. Her mother didn't drive, and they only made it to church services a couple of times a month, as her father had to work whenever he got the chance. The economy was still depressed.

Merle, Leon and Cleo all wanted to go, also.

Alice rose to her feet and stood still and silent. The room grew silent, out of respect for their matriarch.

"I need to relax," Alice stated, "not take a noisy, car-full along. If I take *any* of you with me, it will be *my* choice; understand?"

"Yes, Gramma," the children all said.

"I can probably take you," Carsie volunteered. "I'd like to see how they're doing.

"I propose that anyone who wants to go along with us to write down their reasons for wanting to go. Then Grandma can look them over and decide who, if anyone, may come along."

"That sounds like a good idea," Alice agreed. "How does next Saturday sound for the trip?"

Elsie May rounded up pencils and paper for everyone. The house grew quiet, as most of the family members thought, then wrote down their request. The slips of paper were collected before Alice left for home. She spent the next couple of days, thoughtfully and prayerfully reading through them.

Some of the answers were:

"I've been studying hard and getting good grades."

"I'll miss you too much when you're gone."

"I miss Uncle Lafe."

"I miss my brother."

Some were not for themselves, but for someone else. These were the ones that impressed Alice the most.

Audie asked for her mother to go, "because she works so hard and does without so much to give us what we need."

Ginger wrote that her mother should go, and Ginny wrote that Elsie May should go, because she had asked first.

Doley chose Ilda. She knew that her daughter deserved it, and figured she could manage without her for one weekend, somehow.

Most of the older children chose their mothers, and the husbands chose their wives.

It was a difficult decision, but Alice finally chose Audie because she hadn't asked for herself and because she worked so selflessly to take care of her brothers and the household while her mother was tending to John's business.

Alice okayed her choice with Doley, and then made arrangements for other family members to watch Bud and Johnny while Audie was gone.

Audie was surprised to hear that she had been chosen to go, "But Gramma, I asked for Mamma to go, not me!"

"And that's precisely why I chose you," Alice replied. "You are missing out on being a child, and always thinking of others before yourself."

"But Mamma needs my help."

"I've made arrangements for others to fill in for you while you're gone. Don't you want to spend the weekend with me?"

"Of course I do! I'll start packing after dinner tonight. I love you Gramma!" she said as she gave Alice a bear hug.

Doley helped her daughter pack her clothes in a cardboard box, and when she was found to not have the proper footwear, took her to the nearest second-hand store to find a suitable pair of hiking boots and some sturdy britches. Doley knew from experience, that her mother would be spending as much time in the forest as possible, and Audie would want to go along.

They left before dawn on Saturday, taking breakfast with them to eat on the way. As soon as they got to Lafe and Nettie's, they all went hiking together.

It was raining a little that day, making the old leaves on the forest floor a little slippery. Alice, Lafe and Carsie were seasoned forest trekkers, as was Nettie, since spending the whole last summer at the lookout with Lafe.

All this was new territory to Audie. She reveled in all the new sights, sounds and smells. Bugs didn't bother her one bit, because she had two bug-loving little brothers. She had to be reminded, repeatedly, to watch her step, as she was so enthralled by the huge trees, wildlife and vast variety of plants, that she sometimes stepped awry while soaking it all in.

"Ooh, look at that: A tree blooming in the woods! And a bush with pink flowers, just like the ones at my school! What are they called, Grandma?"

"The tree with the white flowers is a dogwood, and the pink flowered shrub is a rhododendron."

"What kind of bird is that? I've never seen one like that before."

"They seldom venture into the city, because there's more food out here in the woods. It's a pileated woodpecker."

"Oh he's so cute, gramma. What is he?"

"A chipmunk. I agree, they *are* awfully cute."

"Ouch, let go!"

"*That* is a forest blackberry."

They stepped into a clearing and Audie wanted to know about the pretty purple and white flower stalks.

255

"They're called fox gloves."

Lafe spoke up next, "There's a stream nearby where the deer like to drink after eating here. If we're real quiet, we may see some on our way back."

Audie made a zipped-lip motion and became silent as a mouse.

They went on to the creek and took a drink, then broke out their lunch. After spreading out a tarp, they sat on a fallen log to rest and eat. It was so quiet that they could hear every sound the forest and its inhabitants made, including the drip, drip, drip of the raindrops filtering down through the canopy. Then the dripping stopped, and Audie heard something new; a distant roar. "What's that noise off in the distance?" she whispered.

"That's the spillway at the Bonneville Dam," Lafe whispered back. "We'll go see it right after we're done eating."

The rest of their hike went just as smoothly as they had planned. They made it to the cliff overlooking the Columbia, to the east, where the dam was. They all agreed that it was awe-inspiring: The largest made-made structure they'd ever seen. "It must be really loud, to hear it this far away," Audie remarked. "How and why did they build something that big?"

Lafe took a brochure out of his back pocket. "I had the same questions when I saw it for the first time, so we visited it and picked up this information. You can have this one. I have more at home."

"We'd better be heading back," Nettie said. "I have something special planned for dinner, and it takes some time to fix."

"All right," Alice said. "I made mental notes of where the herbs that I need are most likely to be found. I'll come back tomorrow to get them, while I spend some alone time with God, enjoying his creation."

"While you're doing that," Lafe said, "the rest of us can go fishing." When he saw his niece's nose wrinkle up, he said, "Or Nettie could do something with Audie."

"I'm sure we could find something better to do than catching stinky ol' fish, can't we Audie?"

The little girl smiled and gave her aunt a hug. "I'm sure we can."

On the way back, they saw some deer in the clearing, just as Lafe had predicted. As soon as they got back to the cabin, Nettie set to work on dinner. It was her signature dish, beef stroganoff, with home canned green beans and chocolate cake for dessert.

Carsie slept on the sofa that night. Audie shared the guest bed with Alice.

When they awoke in the morning, they could smell bacon and coffee. They emerged from the bedroom, to find Carsie in the kitchen, wearing Nettie's apron and humming to himself. Nettie and Lafe came out of their bedroom, already dressed.

"He had the situation well in hand when we got up, so we thought we'd let him run with it," Lafe told them.

"Doesn't he look cute in my apron?" Nettie teased.

"Absolutely adorable," Alice replied.

"I hope everybody likes their eggs scrambled," Carsie announced, "because that's the only way I cook them." Then he plopped a big stack of pancakes on the table. "I didn't see the syrup anywhere, but did find a couple jars of homemade jam."

"I'll get the syrup," Nettie volunteered.

"I'll have the black raspberry jam," Lafe said, while reaching across the table.

"I'll sit next to you." Alice danced around Audie. "That's my favorite, too."

As soon as they finished breakfast and got dressed, they went to the little country church that Lafe and Nettie attended. Afterward, they split up the sandwiches that Alice and Audie had made the night before, and the brothers set off on foot for Lafe's favorite fishing hole. Alice and Audie were heading out the door, and Nettie was collecting her hat when the phone rang. She picked it up, "Hello?"

"Mrs. Walden?"

"Yes."

"This is Mrs. Clark. I hate to bother you, but the doctor asked me to call to see if you could help him care for my son. He needs to operate, and you're the only nurse available."

"I'll be right there." She hung up the phone and turned to her niece. "I'm so sorry, Audie, but I'm needed at the clinic." ·

"That's okay. I can stay here by myself, or maybe go with Grandma?" She looked hopefully at Alice.

"I think that would be fine, as long as you keep quiet and don't slow me down too much," Alice agreed.

Nettie and Audie went back inside to change clothes, while Alice leaned against a tree and watched a pair of squirrels chase each other around an alder. They jumped from one tree to another, to another, and round and round again. A nearby nest of baby birds chirped away as their parent brought them some food. It made her smile, and she thanked God for creating such entertaining and happy creatures as these.

The other two came out, and Nettie climbed into the car. "Normally, I'd walk, as it's only a few blocks, but it sounds like an emergency. Have fun!" she called as she drove off.

Audie fell in step with her grandmother, who had to slow down very little to accommodate her granddaughter's shorter, seven-year-old legs. She was pleasantly surprised at the girl's speed and endurance as they proceeded along the trail.

They retraced their previous day's path more easily, because it wasn't raining, as it had been for the last three days. Alice knew that their path would still be slippery, but neglected to point that out to Audie. She was focused on finding her medicinal herbs and favorite mushrooms.

"Can we pick some berries for a pie, Gramma?"

"There aren't any to pick this time of year. They don't ripen until mid to late summer."

"But I saw some nice red ones yesterday," came the reply.

"I saw them, too. Those are red elderberries left over from last fall. They aren't safe for us to eat." Then she spied some mushrooms, and went to investigate. "Stay right there," she directed.

She came back a few minutes later. "False alarm," she said. "They looked right from a distance, but we'll have to try somewhere else."

"Aren't all mushrooms the same, Gramma?"

"Oh, no; there are countless types, most of which are poisonous. There are many types of edible ones, though, each having their own flavor and texture. Did I ever tell you the story about your Uncle Tucker's mushroom experience?"

"No. Did he eat a poison mushroom?"

"He sure did, and he almost died from it."

"I bet you saved him!"

"No, God used Carsie's watchfulness and my knowledge to save him."

"You give God credit for everything, don't you?"

"He's the source for all good things, my dear. Do you want to see the deer again? We're approaching the spot where we saw them yesterday."

"I'll be very quiet," Audie whispered.

They proceeded cautiously, and saw a doe with newborn twin fawns. They stood still for several minutes, watching them. When the deer had finished drinking, the doe led her babies back into the forest, away from the trail and the meadow.

Alice led the way off the path and along the creek, knowing that she would be more likely to find one of the herbs she needed along the water's edge. She picked her way along carefully; so intent on her search that she nearly forgot about Audie. The child was being so quiet.

Then she heard Audie call out, "Whoa!" and then a splash. Alice turned around so quickly that she lost her balance, twisted her ankle and fell into the creek herself. She put her hand out to try to stop her descent, and felt her arm crack under her weight.

Alice opened her eyes, and the room slowly came into focus. "Where am I? Who are you? My head hurts and so does my arm. What happened? Why am I here?"

Nettie came into her view. "I see you're back with us. Do you know who I am?"

"Yes, you're Rebecca, Carsie's girlfriend. My head hurts. Why can't I move my arm?"

"Give her some aspirin for the pain." the doctor told Nettie. "She needs to stay awake for a while. So much for my quiet Sunday with the family!"

He went out to the waiting room, where Audie was waiting. "She's awake, but in pain and out of sorts. You can see her a little later, when she's feeling better. Nettie sent for your uncles. They should be here shortly."

Half an hour later, Carsie and Lafe burst through the door, out of breath.

"Where is she? Is she going to be all right?" Lafe asked Nettie, as she came out of the surgery.

"She's going to be fine. She got a nasty bump on her head and a broken wrist. She's going to be sore and out of commission for a while."

"Carsie, is that you?" Alice called.

"Go on in,' Nettie said. "Audie is with her now."

"Mama, what happened?"

"You'll have to ask Audie. It's still a little fuzzy to me."

"What do you remember," the doctor asked.

"I had just found some Saint john's wort, when I heard something behind me and… the rest is a blur. Audie says I was rescued by an Indian."

"He said his name was Crouching Panther," Audie interrupted. "I didn't know what to do. I was holding her face out of the water. He came along and bandaged her up and carried her here."

"He and his wife are good friends of ours," Lafe said. "You'd like them, Mama. They're good people, with a penchant for rescuing people and animals, just like you and Ilda."

"And his father is a medicine man," Nettie added. "He took your list of herbs, and said he'd be back with them as soon as he could."

"When will she be able to go home?" Carsie asked the doctor.

"I'd like to keep her here overnight, at least, because of her head injury. She'll not be able to travel without strong pain medication, for about a week, at least."

"Isn't that what she was planning, anyway?" Lafe asked.

"I can take care of her while you're at work," Audie volunteered.

"You need to get back to school, young lady," Alice said. "I can take care of myself."

"I don't doubt it one bit," Carsie spoke up. "I've seen her do some things that would tax a strong man. I need to get back to work, myself. Say goodbye to your Grandma, Audie. Then we'll collect our things and hit the road."

"We'll bring her home when she's up to it," Lafe volunteered as they stepped outside.

Not too long after they left, Crouching Panther arrived with Alice's herbs.

"I'm glad to see you are better," he told Alice.

"I'm glad you came along to rescue me," Alice replied. "Thank you."

"No problem. I was in the neighborhood." He shrugged his shoulders and waved to Nettie as he walked out.

Doctor Chervey allowed Nettie to take Alice home with her after work the next day. Alice's memory was slow to recover, and she had a horrible headache. In addition to a bruised hip and badly broken wrist, Alice had sprained an ankle. She stayed with Lafe and Nettie for three weeks before returning home.

She had a goose egg on her head for another week after that, and her wrist was never quite the same again. The migraine headaches she'd been having the last few years grew more frequent and severe, as well.

Audie had quite a story to tell when she returned home. She started thinking about becoming a nurse, herself. She'd had a chance to get to know her grandmother much better that weekend, and grew to love and admire her more and more.

Chapter Twenty-Four

REUNION AND ROMANCE

In late April of 1929, Alice got a phone call from Lafe, letting her know that he was the proud papa of a bouncing baby boy, whom they had named Ernest. "I know we already have an Ernest in the family, but there are enough Franks already," he told her. "Besides, one of Nettie's grandfathers was also an Ernest, and she wanted to name the baby after him. I get to choose the name for the next one."

Nettie quit her job and became a full-time mother and homemaker. She was still available for emergencies and to fill in for the other nurse, but wanted most of all to be a good and present mother. She thought she might return to nursing full-time after her children were out on their own, so kept her nursing credentials up-to-date by taking refresher courses and recertification tests.

One sunny Saturday in June, Carsie took Alice to Bridal Veil to attend a funeral. Their old friend and supervisor, John Harney, had experienced a sudden, fatal heart attack a few days before. They looked forward to seeing some of their old friends and co-workers while there, many of whom were still residents. They planned to spend the weekend reconnecting with as many as possible.

When they arrived at the hotel, they found it already booked solid.

"This has never happened to me before," the clerk informed them. "I've been here two years, but never heard of this Harney fellow before. Most of our guests are here for his funeral. I hope you have some friends here that you can stay with tonight."

"We used to live here. My husband and my son worked with Mr. Harney back then. I'm sure we'll find someone we can stay with. Good day, sir."

The funeral wasn't scheduled to start for another two hours, so they went for a walk and reminisced, stopping in at their old haunts and noting how the town had changed and grown since they had last been there.

The first place they entered was the general store, where they found an old classmate of Carsie's behind the counter. The two men started talking about "the good old days", so Alice excused herself-telling Carsie that she would be at the medical clinic, "providing it hasn't moved?" She directed this last part to Carsie's friend.

"No, just improved," the man answered.

She walked briskly to stretch her legs. When she rounded the corner and saw the clinic, she didn't recognize it. Just like the rest of the town, it had been enlarged and updated with larger windows, a new lobby and a fresh coat of paint.

She went inside and stood, looking around, admiring the Native American artwork on the walls, when a woman's voice interrupted her reverie. "May I help you?"

Alice turned toward the voice behind the counter to find her old friend and patient, Ka-teen-ha looking back at her.

"Alice, is that you?!" She quickly put down the papers she was holding and hurried out from behind the counter to give her friend a long hug. "I have missed you so much! I just sent a letter off to you yesterday; and here you are today!"

"What are you doing in the Bridal Veil clinic?" Alice stepped back to look her friend over. "Ka-Teen-ha, why are you wearing your hair like that, and those clothes and shoes?"

"I left the reservation a long time ago. I'm married to the Presbyterian minister in town. I'm working here as a receptionist. After six months here, I finally met someone who knew your address.

"I know you didn't get my letter, yet. So what brings you to Bridal Veil? Is it for the big funeral I heard about this afternoon?"

"Yes, the deceased was a good friend of ours and Frank's and my supervisor. He's the one who hired me as the company nurse when we first arrived here as newlyweds. Will you be attending the service?"

"No, I have to stay here. The funeral is being held at the other church. We aren't involved with it. Would you be available to come for dinner tonight? I'd love to have you meet my family."

"Family? Does that mean you have children, too?"

"We have two girls. Are you staying in the hotel tonight?"

"No, they're booked solid. I'm here with my oldest son, Carsie. We thought we might have to go home tonight."

"Nonsense! You can stay with us for tonight."

"You talked me into it. When will you be done here?"

They agreed on a time and place to meet, then Alice went back to the store. She had to pry Carsie away from his friend to get to the Baptist Church in time.

"It's not that I don't want to honor Mr. Harney or see some more old friends there," he told his mother, "I just don't like going to funerals. Most that I have attended have been for family members: Papa, Grandpa, Grandma, Gretchen..."

"I understand, but I have some good news for you," she said on the walk to the church. "You'll never guess who I ran into at the clinic."

"We have a lot of old friends here, so I could guess until tomorrow, if I could remember all their names."

"Okay, first hint: She was a patient of mine when we lived near here before."

"You'll have to do better than that."

"Second hint: I went to her grandmother's funeral."

"You're getting warmer."

"Third hint: She lived with us for a year."

"Oh, the Indian woman. I don't remember her name."

"Ka-teen-ha. She married a preacher, of all people. She invited us to stay with her tonight."

"My friend Bob also invited us to stay with him. I suppose we could split up."

By that time they were at the church. They broke off their conversation to mingle and look for familiar faces in the crowd. The church was crowded, so they signed the guestbook, picked up programs and found seats.

They were looking over the programs while they waited for the service to start, when Alice felt a hand on her shoulder. She turned to see Becky and Jim Ingeborg sitting behind them.

"I saw you two come in, but the foyer was crowded and noisy, so we followed you," Becky said. "It's been a long time. How have you been?"

"I'm just fine," Alice answered. "Most of the children are married and still living near me, in Portland. I have seventeen grandchildren and two great-grandchildren, now. How are you doing?"

"We're doing okay-could be better-could be worse. Our daughter Meredith passed away a few years ago, from cancer. Jim had to retire from the mill last year because of back problems."

"I haven't found my new career, yet." Jim added. "I've tried several things, but none of them has worked out."

Becky resumed, "We have seven grandchildren and three great-grandchildren. How do you like living in Portland?"

"I prefer the woods, but the amenities of the city are nice, too. It's always fun to get back out to the country for a visit. We'd hoped to go on an herb and mushroom collecting foray tomorrow, before we head home."

"Who is your handsome cohort-one of your sons?"

"Oh, I'm sorry. Where are my manners? This is my oldest, Carsie.

"Carsie, do you remember Becky and Jim Ingeborg?"

"I think so," Carsie replied as he stood to shake their hands. "You worked at the mill in Oregon City, didn't you?" He asked Jim.

"Yes, and you did some sweeping and other small stuff there when you were about twelve, didn't you?"

"Yep."

The organ stopped playing just then, and a hush came over the room as the minister mounted the platform and addressed the congregation.

"My friends, we are here on this solemn occasion to honor the life and accomplishments of Mr. John Harney, whose body lies here in this casket, but whose spirit departed from us recently to be with our Lord. John was an honorable man, and well-liked.

"He worked for the lumber company from the age of nineteen until his health declined four years ago. Then he retired and moved back to Bridal Veil. He is survived by his wife, Clara, two step-sons: Patrick and Phillip, one step-daughter, Mary Ellen, and two sisters: Marianne and Katherine, who were unable to come here today, several grandchildren, nieces and nephews.

"Some of you worked with or under John, and others may be acquainted with him in some other way, but you wouldn't be here if you didn't respect him.

"John was a good man, and worth respecting, but not one to attend church services until seventeen years ago, when he met Clara at the Post Office where she worked. She was a widow and he was a confirmed bachelor.

"Mary Ellen had already married and moved away. Patrick and Phillip were wary of John, at first. They were protective of their mother, as all sons should be. It wasn't long before they became his friends, and gave him permission to court their mother.

"When John proposed to Clara, she told him that she wouldn't marry an unbeliever. He had attended services with her a few times, but had never taken religion seriously until then. After meeting with her pastor a few times, he accepted the Lord, and they were married a few days later. They just celebrated their sixteenth anniversary a couple of weeks ago.

"They joined our congregation soon after moving here, and have been valuable to us, as servants and friends, ever since. We will miss him very much."

Many people took the floor to share their memories of John. Some were comical. It was definitely a celebration of his life; an uplifting and positive experience for all. After the service, Alice introduced herself to Pastor Brennan.

"Oh, I was hoping you would be here! John spoke very highly of you and your husband. Is this your son, Carson? He spoke highly of you, too. He said your family's influence was pivotal toward his becoming a Christian. He said if it hadn't been for you, he wouldn't have been open to the idea of becoming a follower. We owe you a debt of gratitude. Will you be staying the night? We'd love to see you here tomorrow morning."

"We'll be staying over. I just found out that an old friend of mine is the wife of the other minister in town. She has asked me to stay with her tonight. How about you, Carsie; do you have any plans for tomorrow morning, yet?"

"My friend, Bob didn't mention anything about it when we talked, earlier. I don't even know if he's a Christian. If he doesn't have plans, I'll probably go with my mother."

"Maybe you could come for lunch? Long before we knew there would be a memorial service, we'd planned a potluck after tomorrow's service. Being from out-of-town, we wouldn't expect you to bring anything."

"We'll see. Perhaps we can manage to stay for that?" she asked Carsie.

"Yes, I'd like that. We might run into some more old friends here tomorrow afternoon."

"Here comes Clara," Pastor Brennan said as he motioned her to join them. "I'm sure she'll want to talk to you."

After introductions were made, Pastor Brennan excused himself, while Clara gave Alice and Carsie warm hugs.

"I owe you a debt of gratitude for being such good friends to John, and demonstrating Christ-like behavior to him. He spoke highly of your family. I'm so happy to meet you after all these years. May we sit and visit a while?"

She led them to a quiet corner, away from the clamor of the crowd. They talked for over an hour, sharing stories of their husbands and the happenings of the intervening years.

Clara's children and grandchildren stopped by to meet Alice and Carsie, and a few old acquaintances also stopped by to say a quick hello as they were there talking. Then, as the building started to empty, Carsie looked at his watch.

"Mama, I think we'd better go, too. Our hosts will be expecting us before long."

They said their goodbyes to Clara and Pastor Brennan. Then they went outside to talk over possible scenarios for the remainder of their stay in town.

Carsie went with Alice to meet up with Ka-teen-ha and find out where she lived. Then he went back to the store to see Bob. His friend was making preparations to go home when Carsie arrived. They talked while he closed up the store and walked to his home a few blocks away. As it turned out, he lived only a few doors past Ka-teen-ha's house. When Carsie mentioned that, Bob looked shocked. "You mean your mother is friends with that Injun?"

Carsie stopped in his tracks and looked at his friend with new eyes. "Yes," he stated firmly, "In fact, she lived with us for a year when we lived here about thirty years ago. I guess you moved here a couple of years after that, so you wouldn't know."

"What was she doing living with you?" Bob said with a sneer.

"Never mind. I'm sorry, but I can't stay with you after all. Give my regrets to your wife."

He turned and walked back to Ka-teen-ha's house as Bob looked after him, dumbstruck.

Pastor Ken answered Carsie's knock. "Are you Alice's son? I thought you were staying with a friend."

"So did I," Carsie answered as he shook his host's hand. "The arrangement went sour as soon as he found out where my mother was."

"Your old friend wouldn't happen to be Robert Green, would he?"

"Yes. I take it you've had run-ins with him before?"

"Ka-teen-ha avoids the store when he's there. I end up doing most of the grocery shopping. He doesn't like me, either, but I can handle it."

"Carsie, what are you doing back here so soon?" His mother asked, peeking out of the kitchen. "Why aren't you at Bob's house?"

"It didn't work out. I'll tell you about it later."

Carsie was introduced to their daughter, Rebecca, a red-haired beauty with dimples in her cheeks and a fire in her large, green eyes.

"You don't look a thing like either one of your parents," he remarked, as his eyebrow shot up nearly to his hairline. "So, I surmise that you are an Irish princess who ran away from an evil stepmother," he teased.

"Aye, me mudder died, and me grandmudder hid me in de forest, to save me from de witch. I was fount and raised by leprechauns," she teased back.

"Oh, you two!" Kenneth mock-scolded. Then he turned to Alice. "She's always been like this."

"So has he," Alice replied, with a grin. "Did you notice the eyebrow? He got that and his sense of humor from his father."

"Do you play an instrument?" Rebecca asked Carsie.

"I fiddle with a fiddle once in a while."

"And he has a lovely singing voice, too," Alice added.

"Father insisted that Ruth and I learn to play the piano, but I prefer the Indian flute that Teeny brought from the reservation when she married Papa."

They had a wonderful dinner while Alice and Ka-teen-ha caught up on the events of the last thirty-odd years. Alice told them about Frank's illness and death, her parents' passing and the marriages and births that had occurred in her family.

Ka-teen-ha and Kenneth related how they'd met twelve years after her grandmother's funeral, when he was doing missionary work on the reservation. He was married, with two girls: Rebecca, who was eight years old and her four-year old sister, Ruth. His wife died of cancer, just a year after they'd moved to the reservation.

Because Ka-teen-ha was friends with them, and still single, she volunteered to help Kenneth with the children and the household duties. Over time, her heart opened to the Gospel and she accepted the Lord. She and Ken grew to love each other. They were married a couple of years after the girls' mother died.

"We will celebrate our eighteenth anniversary this September," Ka-teen ha said.

"And a wonderful eighteen years, at that," Kenneth added as he lifted his wife's hand and kissed it tenderly.

After dinner, Alice helped Ka-teen-ha with the dishes, while Ken went to his study and Carsie and Rebecca went to the parlor to play music and sing.

"They seemed to hit it off right away," Alice whispered to her friend.

"I noticed-and do you hear them making music together and laughing?"

"Do you mind my asking why she's still single? She's a beautiful girl with a wonderful sense of humor."

"She was engaged twice: The first gentleman went off to war and didn't come back. The second one went to college back east, and fell for another woman. It took her a while to get over them, but her faith sustained her."

"And Ruth, where is she now? Is she married?"

"Yes, but to a nonbeliever, I'm afraid. They live in California, and we don't hear much from her. She's not living for the Lord, but we pray for her and her family every day."

"What about Carsie? I didn't see a ring on his finger. How old is he now?"

"He's forty-two. He was married to a lovely girl for a very short time, before she died from the Spanish flu."

"We lost our son then, and Ken almost died, as well. It seemed like half of the folks we knew were down with it, and almost every family in town lost someone."

"Grace lost a daughter to that horrible disease. That was a very sad time for everyone-between the war, the flu and the depression."

"Things are getting better all the time, and we have so many blessings to be thankful for," Ka-teen-ha sighed. Then she smiled and closed her eyes. "Just listen to them singing the old hymns together. I feel like God is right here in this room, wrapping his arms around me."

Alice listened to their children singing for a moment. "You don't suppose..."

Ka-teen-ha grinned at Alice. "I was thinking the same thing."

"But we mustn't meddle," Alice said. "It's their business, not ours."

"And God's will, I hope."

The two held hands and giggled like schoolgirls.

Kenneth walked in, just then. "What's going on in here?"

"Oh, nothing!" They both said, and started giggling again.

"All right, if you don't want to tell me. It looks like you're just about done here. Shall we join the singing in the parlor?"

"Not me," Alice answered. "I can't carry a tune in a bucket. My children got that talent from their father. He used to sing them to sleep when they were little."

"How about sitting with some lemonade in the backyard? It's a lovely evening," he suggested.

"Perhaps the children would like to join us," Ka-teen-ha said. "Rebecca made a fresh peach pie for dessert."

"Sounds delicious—I haven't had peach pie in a long time," Alice said.

Ka-teen-ha cut and divided the pie, then took it out to the patio, while Alice got the glasses and the lemonade. Ken rounded up their children. They stayed there, chatting, until the mosquitos drove them inside. Then they retired to the parlor, while Rebecca and Carsie serenaded them.

When the clock in the hall struck ten, they decided to retire for the night. "I don't know about the rest of you, but I can't afford to fall asleep during the sermon tomorrow," Ken said, while yawning.

"I don't think it would look too good for the preacher's wife to nod off, either," Ka-teen-ha affirmed. "I'll show you to your rooms."

She kissed her husband and led her guests down the hallway. "We have a guest room that Carsie can use, and Alice can use the spare bed in Rebecca's room, that Ruth used before she married and moved away."

"I'll clear it off while you're in the bathroom," Rebecca told Alice. "We did laundry yesterday, and I didn't get all my things put away, yet."

Ka-teen-ha showed Carsie to the guestroom and told him what time the service started in the morning. "We serve breakfast at eight o'clock sharp, here. If you aren't there, you'll go hungry," she teased him.

"Oh, I'll be on time," he replied, with a slightly raised eyebrow. "I wouldn't want to embarrass myself by drowning out Ken's sermon with a growling stomach."

"Ken has to be in the shower at seven o'clock, because he's the first out the door for final sermon review and prayer with the deacons. Rebecca leaves at nine o'clock for choir warmups. The service starts at ten. Here's an extra blanket, if you need it. Sleep well. We'll see you in the morning."

At the service the next morning, they met some more old friends that they'd lost contact with over the years. Most of them had, like the Waldens, moved away, and were there for John's funeral the day before. Some, that they had kept in touch with, were permanent residents of Bridal Veil, or were, like Carsie, still working for the lumber company.

They had a wonderful time at the Baptist Church potluck, where they met some more old friends. Rebecca went with them, presumably to visit with some friends who attended there. When she told her mother and Alice that, they smiled at each other, mischievously.

"Are you two plotting something?" She asked them.

"No, just noticing a little spark glowing behind those green eyes of yours," Ka-teen-ha replied.

"And something akin to it in Carsie," Alice added.

Rebecca blushed, then went to find Carsie, who was talking with someone at the other end of the foyer.

Carsie and Rebecca corresponded regularly after that, while she was on a four-year missionary assignment to an Indian village in North Dakota. Their romance continued to grow deeper the whole time.

Ka-teen-ha and Ken came to Portland to visit Alice a year later. She led them to her favorite restaurant, and gave them a tour of some interesting, but lesser known attractions in and around Portland. She told them about the Klager Lilac Gardens, and Ka-teen-ha said that she'd like to go there sometime.

"It sounds heavenly," she sighed, while gripping Ken's arm and smiling at him.

"You'll have to wait until Rebecca comes back, or get someone in our congregation to take you," he replied.

"Oh, that's right, I forgot that you're allergic to lilacs. Maybe I can arrange an outing for our ladies, with Tom's bus."

Then she turned to see a curious look on Alice's face. "Tom is one of our deacons. He has a bus that he uses to shuttle groups all over the state for revival meetings, mission trips, and once or twice for patient transport. He and his bus are such a godsend to our church and our town."

"Wasn't he the one who introduced Rebecca to Larry?" Ken asked her.

"Yes, but she doesn't blame him for that." Then she turned to Alice. "He was the one who went off to school and fell for someone else."

"I remember you telling me about that. I hope she doesn't do that to Carsie."

"So do I," Ken said. "Nothing would make us happier than to have our daughter marry your son, even though he is quite a bit older than she."

Ken had some business to tend to in the capitol, but returned for the Walden family gathering on Sunday, as he had arranged for a substitute to preach for their congregation. "Even preachers need vacations," he told them.

Chapter Twenty-Five

THE PATIENT BRAT

In early 1930, Alice found herself caring for a very special and unusual patient. A member of her church referred her to his family.

"They are clients of mine. I'm their housekeeper and nanny. The husband is the problem that I think you may be able to help with," she told Alice. "He's handicapped, and bitter about his recent cancer diagnosis.

"His wife supports the family, so she needs a caregiver to tend to him when she's at work. She's hired four people for the job, and none has stayed more than a few days. We're both at our wit's end with him. He's become abusive, and makes her and the children cry nearly every day.

"I'd quit, but jobs are hard to come by, and I feel sorry for them. I've heard that you're a nurse as well as a midwife, and that you've done miracles with some of your patients."

"I'm no miracle worker," Alice replied. "God sometimes works miracles through me, but I'm nothing by myself."

"I beg to differ with you. I think you're a very special lady, Alice. And I think you're exactly what he needs to crack his shell and get through to him. Would you consider it at least?"

"I'll pray about it, and get back to you, Joy."

The following Sunday, she sought her friend out and told her that she would be willing to meet the family. "I only have three maternity clients right now. Four others delivered this week and one is moving soon. I'll be down to two then, and neither is a high risk case. They aren't due to deliver for several months, and I don't foresee any problems with either one."

"I just knew you were the right person for the job!" Joy gushed.

"I haven't said yes, yet," Alice insisted. "When do you want me to come over?"

"How about Wednesday evening? Shirley usually gets home a little earlier on Wednesdays. I'll have an extra place set for you at the dinner table."

Alice pulled a pad and pencil out of her purse. "Tell me the address and their names... What time should I be there?"

Alice took the bus to the Kennedy's on Wednesday afternoon. She rang the doorbell of the once-impressive house at precisely four thirty. She wondered while she waited, about how she would be received by the man of the house. She would have to muster all her strength and determination to deal with him, but still be loving and compassionate toward the wife and children. What if I get one of my migraines? she thought.

The door opened a crack, and she saw the eyes of a small child peeking out at her.

"Hello, my name is Alice. Joy is expecting me."

The door opened the rest of the way, and Alice entered.

"Follow me," the little girl said. She led her to the kitchen, where Joy was just taking a roast out of the oven.

"Alice, I'm so glad you're here. Shirley is getting Mark ready for dinner. Would you bring that other dish out for me?"

Alice picked up the dish and followed Joy to the dining room. It was large and neat with a table big enough for a dozen people. The china was elegant, as were the chandelier and the furnishings, with the exception of several broken panes of glass in the hutch.

The little girl who had let Alice in reappeared with two younger children in tow.

As they sat at the table, Joy introduced them, "Children, this is my friend, Mrs. Walden. Alice, this is Miriam, Leland and Liam."

Alice guessed their ages to be about eight, six and four.

"Hello children. It's nice to meet you."

"Are you going to be Daddy's new nurse?" Liam asked.

"I'm not sure, yet. I'll let you know when I decide, okay?"

"Okay."

A few second later, Shirley wheeled Mark into the room. Alice noted immediately, by the scowl on his face, just what Joy meant when she said he was bitter. She could tell by his posture that he was full of self-pity as well.

The children looked almost disappointed to see that he had joined them.

"You must be Alice," Shirley said as she locked the wheelchair and turned to shake her guest's hand. "Joy tells me that you have quite a reputation in Portland and beyond for rescuing and saving otherwise hopeless cases."

"Humph," Mark grunted. "So that's what I am now; a hopeless case?"

"Of course not, dear," Shirley consoled him. "Joy has told me so many good things about her that I just had to meet her. She's here to meet us, and decide if she wants to take on the job as your nurse."

"I don't need no damn nurse!" he roared, scaring the children. Liam started to cry and ran to Joy for comfort. Leland and Miriam were visibly shaken, but still and tight-lipped.

"I made your favorite pork roast, with sweet potatoes and pearl onions," Joy told Mark, trying to break the spell.

"And banana pudding for dessert?" Liam sniffed.

"Yes. That's your favorite, too, isn't it?"

"It all sounds and smells delicious," Alice added cheerily.

"Would you do us the honor of saying grace over the food?" Shirley asked Alice.

"Humph," went Mark again. Alice ignored him and took the hands of the boys, seated on either side of her. Liam pulled away at first, but Leland smiled at her before taking his mother's hand and bowing his head.

When Alice finished the blessing, she noted that Miriam had been holding her father's hand, and that his expression had softened a bit. That was when she felt that there was hope for this family, and that she was supposed to take the job, no matter how difficult it might be. This family needed God in their midst, and she would be the door through which he would enter.

After dinner, Mark went to his room and closed the door, while Joy washed the dishes.

Alice and Shirley went into the parlor to talk. "I get a good feeling about you and what you might be able to accomplish for us. Will you take the job?"

"I'm seriously considering it. I need to know a little more first."

"Anything," Shirley said, "I'm desperate. Did Joy tell you that we've had four nurses quit on us already?"

"Yes, she did, but I don't scare easily. I birthed five of my seven children without help, and then raised the last four after I was widowed. I think I can handle your husband. I'd like to hear about what happened to him."

Shirley told Alice that Mark had been a policeman, and how he was crippled by a gunshot to the spine. "I was pregnant with Liam at the time. He seemed to be dealing with that setback, considering he knew he would never walk again, or play ball with his sons like most fathers do. But when he was diagnosed with liver cancer a few months ago, he became a different man. He blames God for everything bad that's happened to him. He says he won't believe in a God who would take away his manhood, his independence, and then his life, too."

"Has he cried yet, that you know of, or is he expressing all of his grief through anger?" Alice asked.

"His father was a Navy Captain who taught him that only babies and women cry."

When Joy finished with the dishes, she went upstairs to get the children ready for bed.

"Did he ever have faith in God?" was Alice's next question.

"I thought so when I married him. He had grown up attending church with his parents. But now I think they just went for appearances sake, and that Mark did the same when he was on the Police Force."

"Is that when he stopped attending; after he was shot?"

Shirley lowered her head and nodded. She started to weep softly. Alice held her and prayed with her.

Then the children came downstairs to say goodnight. They each gave their mother a hug and a kiss. Then Joy took the boys back upstairs. Miriam stayed behind, and climbed into her mother's lap. She dried her tears and said, "It'll be all right Mama; I just know it."

Then she stood and took Alice's hands. "I sure hope you stay, Mrs. Walden. You're different than the others." Then she gave her a hug and ran after her little brothers.

"Well, how could I turn *that* down? Do you want me to start tomorrow?"

Alice knew that she had a hard task ahead; one that would require a lot of prayer and stubborn determination. She prayed that she had what it took to do this job, then remembered what the Apostle Paul wrote in Philippians 4:13 and 4:19, and knew she wouldn't be doing this job with her own intelligence or through her own strength, but God would supply what she needed.

Joy answered her knock at seven o'clock the next morning. "He's being difficult this morning, just like usual, when he knows there's a nurse coming. Shirley is trying to get him to eat and get dressed, but he refuses to get out of bed. His bedroom is the first door on the right, down the hallway. Good luck!"

Alice knocked on the door. A few moments later, Shirley opened it. She came out of the room and closed the door behind her. "I have to get to work. He's being impossible this morning. I hope you have better luck than I've been having so far. Here's his medication list and schedule. Joy can answer any questions you may have."

She reopened the door and quickly closed it again, as something hit it and clattered to the floor. "Oh, yes," she said, "don't turn your back on him when he's like this. I'll be back around five."

Then she called through the door, "Mark, please don't kill her while I'm gone."

Then she smiled at Alice and hurried off.

Alice said a quick prayer before opening the door, slowly and cautiously, half expecting a barrage of anything that might be within Mark's reach. Instead, he had his face turned away from her. His arms were crossed over his chest and he had the same scowl on his face, as when she first saw him the night before.

"My name is Alice. We met last night, remember?"

He ignored her.

"I understand you're being a brat today."

His eyebrows knit together. He looked askance at her, then away again. She could tell that she'd hit a nerve, and braced herself for a possible assault. Instead, his scowl softened and she could see the gears turning in his mind.

"I'm going to examine you, thoroughly, to see if there are any issues I need to address right away." she told him. Then she opened her valise, pulled out her stethoscope and put on her surgical gloves.

His scowl deepened and his arms tightened. "Shirley and Joy take care of me; I don't need no damned nurse," he grumbled.

"They say you do. It's getting to be too much for them to handle, along with the children and the housework."

She started at his head; combing through his scalp for signs of lice or the need for a shampoo. He resisted her efforts, saying, "What are you looking for?"

"Oh, vermin, bed sores, ingrown toenails, fluid on your lungs…"
She had him at "vermin," and he stopped squirming.

It took an hour to do the complete examination. Mark was glad that he had no feeling below his waist; he was embarrassed enough, just knowing that she was poking around "down there".

When her examination was done, she told him, "I didn't find anything unexpected. You have the beginnings of some bed sores on your back, and you could use a shower and shampoo. Have you been taking your medicines?" She asked this, to see if he would tell her the truth. It was evident to her that he hadn't been.

"Yes," he said, looking away. He glanced back, and could tell by her stern look that she knew he was lying. "Okay, most of the time."

"Uh, huh," Alice muttered. "Let's try that again. Have you been taking your medicines?" She held out a handful of pills that she had found under his mattress.

Alice knew she was making progress when he got a guilty look on his face. He looked away, crossed his arms again, and quit talking.

She treated his sores, cleaned him up and changed his catheter. By this time, she was ready for a break. She heard Miriam and Leland leave for school.

"I'll be back in a while," she said as she took off her exam gloves, put her things out of his reach and pulled the blanket back over his legs.

She told Joy what had transpired, and what she had found during her examination. She talked over Mark's and the family's schedule and reviewed Mark's prescription regimen again. She went back to Mark's room and emptied his urine bag "Do you want to join us for lunch?" she asked him.

"I'm not hungry," he said as his stomach growled.

"All right, I'll see you after lunch," she said merrily as she exited the room.

Joy was surprised to see Alice smiling when she entered the kitchen. "I don't believe it, I didn't hear any crashing or yelling, and you don't seem upset at all. Are you all right? Is Mark all right? Is he taking lunch in his room?"

"He's not eating lunch today. Everything is just fine."

"Are you sure? I can take him a tray."

"No, he said he's not hungry. He has to learn, just like any disobedient child, not to lie, and to respect others."

"Daddy's not a child," Liam said, looking confused.

"I know that," Alice replied, "but sometimes, when a grownup acts like a naughty child, they have to be treated like one."

Liam smiled at her, but Joy looked dumbstruck.

"But he gets mean when he's hungry," she replied.

"So what? Isn't he always?"

"Yes, but he gets even worse, and he has pills that he needs to take with lunch."

"Are these the pills?" Alice asked, holding out what she had put in her pocket.

"Where did you get those?" Joy asked.

"He'd hidden them under his mattress," Alice replied. "Leave him alone to think for a while."

"He's all yours," Joy declared, holding her hands up in surrender. "I'm not going near him until he's eaten again!"

Alice continued to treat Mark exactly the same all that day and the next. Mark grew furious; raging like a lion in musk. The children wouldn't go in his room, and cried when he bellowed. He refused to let Alice bring him out, and she insisted that no one else offer to do it. "He has to learn who's the boss. You can't break a wild mustang until you establish dominance over him," she told them. "You'll just have to trust me. It'll work."

She advised Shirley to take the children away for the weekend, while she stayed there alone with Mark. They were hesitant to oblige, but knew from experience, that kindness and pampering didn't work.

Early Sunday morning, Shirley came in the front door. "I couldn't stand it anymore," she whispered, "and figured you could use a break. I sent the children to church with my sister and came to check on you two."

"We're just fine," Alice told her. "I think he's on the verge of cracking. Why don't you give me your sister's phone number. I'll call you when it's safe to come home. Joy will be back tomorrow to help me with the cooking and cleaning. I'll take a three-day weekend once he simmers down and starts acting like a human being again."

On the phone that weekend, she told Ilda, "I think this arrangement is going to work out quite well. I'm confident that he'll be tamed within a week."

And she was right. When his pastor came to visit on Tuesday, it was ominously quiet during his stay in Mark's room. When he emerged, he reported that Mark had experienced an epiphany. He'd finally wept, and had surrendered his life to Jesus.

The spell had been broken. Mark asked her, politely, to see his family. He apologized to her and to them when they came home the next day. He was a completely different person.

Not only that, but the children's and Shirley's attitudes changed, as well. They weren't walking around as if on egg shells anymore. They started smiling and laughing. She even caught Mark smiling a little, though he tried to hide it at first. Alice stayed the rest of the week to retrain Mark's family not to spoil him so much, and to initiate a family prayer and Bible study time every day. Then she took that three-day weekend that she'd promised Shirley and herself.

Saturday was a blur; she spent the whole day with a horrible headache, but recovered in time to attend the family dinner the next day. For the very first time, she went to the Sunday evening service that had been instituted the previous year.

She spent Monday catching up on housework and gardening, then packed her bag for one day at a time, instead of the whole week, as she'd done at first.

There was some time to relax and get to know the whole family better, now that Mark wasn't isolating himself and causing discord all the time.

Alice found out that Shirley was a criminal defense lawyer who had been born and raised in Portland. She and Mark had met at the courthouse right after she had started working there as a legal assistant.

Joy had been born in Nevada and moved to Bend, Oregon, with her family when she was ten. She was the oldest of six children, so had no trouble getting a job as a nanny when she was ready to leave home at twenty.

After a couple of months, Mark's cancer started to cause him quite a bit of pain and digestive issues, so that Alice had to monitor his medications and diet even more closely. She returned to packing her bag for a week at a time, and taught Joy and Shirley exactly what to do on weekends.

Her garden suffered that summer. Tucker didn't have her green thumb. He only did what he was told to do, and sometimes he forgot. Alice didn't know about problems that came up until the weekend, after the damage had been done. Her son-in-law, John, was a consummate gardener, but his business and family were growing. She knew he didn't have time to monitor it for her.

Now Mark was isolated to his room by necessity, not choice. Shirley took a leave of absence from work when his condition deteriorated to the point that he could pass any day.

The children didn't want to go back to school in September, fearing their daddy would be gone when they returned.

The Saturday morning before Halloween, the phone rang. Before Alice picked it up, she knew it was Joy, saying that Mark had passed.

"I stayed with them last night for moral support. Mark went to be with Jesus at ten p.m. His whole family was at his side, including his sister-in law and his pastor.

"Shirley asked me to thank you. She says you can pick up your last paycheck and say goodbye on Monday. She's keeping the children out of school until after the funeral."

Alice rang the doorbell at four pm on Monday. Miriam answered and immediately gave her a big hug, and cried. Then the boys came and joined in the hug.

"Let her come in the house now, children," Shirley directed. They let go of Alice, reluctantly, and wandered off while their mother embraced her. "I don't know how to thank you for saving our family and for making it possible for Mark to open his heart to Jesus."

"I was just doing my job the way the Bible says to; using common sense and my experience as a mother," Alice replied.

"You are an angel sent from heaven, as far as we're concerned," Shirley told her, with tears and a smile. "Will you stay for dinner, please? Our pastor is coming over to help me iron out the final details of the funeral. He wants to meet you."

Alice agreed. They went into the kitchen, where Joy was putting a turkey back in the oven. She took off her oven mitts and came over to give Alice a hug.

"Alice will be staying for dinner," Shirley told her. Then she left them alone and went to get the children bathed before dinner.

She was still upstairs half an hour later, when Reverend Schumacher rang the doorbell.

As it turned out, Alice had met him once before, when she'd attended Teresa's daughter's wedding.

They had a pleasant dinner. Then Alice helped Joy wash the dishes while Shirley and the reverend talked in the parlor.

Alice attended the funeral on Saturday. There were a few people there that she recognized as government officials. Because Mark was a decorated veteran, there was an army contingent, as well, to perform the flag ceremony and a twenty-one-gun salute at the gravesite.

Chapter Twenty-Six

SPOT OFF

One week in late June of 1930, the Rowley family took a trip to Seattle to visit Frank and Mary. Grace and the children loaded the suitcases in the car. They were waiting at the depot when the Seattle-bound train pulled into place to unload its passengers on Saturday morning.

Guy finished his last task and turned in his time card. He joined Grace, twelve-year-old Ginny and Ginger, ten-year-old Merle, eight-year-old Leon and five-year-old Ernie on the platform as the conductor called out, "All aboard for Vancouver, Washington, Longview, Centralia, Olympia, Tacoma and Seattle, Washington!"

Ronny, who had just graduated from high school the year before, had to stay behind for his new job. Jerry and Chip were sharing an apartment in Salem, where they both were employed with the same company.

Guy and the porter loaded the baggage onto the train, while Grace assisted the children up the steps. They found their seats, but the children spent most of the first hour on their feet, craning their necks out the window. They chatting away, excitedly, and asking questions about the train. Guy had spent most of his life working around and traveling in trains, and thus was able to answer most of the children's questions.

This was Grace's second train trip to Seattle. The first time had been to attend Mattie's wedding. There had been others, as well. When she was about ten years old she had taken the east-bound train, with her family, all the way to Pendleton, and then on to Milton-Freewater on the narrow-gauge, when they had moved to the cabin her father had built on the Umatilla Indian reservation. Then of course, there was the return trip from Milton-Freewater to Bridal Veil after the fire.

It was nearly four o'clock when the tall buildings of Seattle came into view. The children had been fairly quiet as they'd travelled through the farmlands and wetlands south of Tacoma. Ernie and Guy had napped, while the others had played card games to fight off boredom. They were on their feet again now, watching the sea birds and the boats on Puget sound.

The train pulled into the station and all the passengers disembarked. As Grace stepped onto the top step, she paused and spied her brother's head above the crowd. She waved to him and he waved back. They collected their luggage and joined Frank inside the station.

"It's so good to see you, Sis!" Frank gushed as he embraced Grace. "Welcome to Seattle!" he said to them all. He shook Guy's hand and led them out to the parking area.

They crowded into Frank's automobile and meandered through the streets to his home on Queen Anne Hill, where Mary had lemonade waiting, dinner almost ready, and the table set with her best china, and fresh flowers from their garden.

The twins and Dolores became instant friends, and so did Ernie and J.R, as Frank Junior had been dubbed. Merle and Leon spent most of their free time playing with their hosts' dog, Spot; a beagle/terrier mix with lots of energy.

After dinner, Frank and Mary took Grace, Dolores and the twins to see a play, while Guy went to the park with the boys and Spot.

Frank had to make two trips to get everyone to their church the next morning. Their minister and his wife invited them for lunch at their favorite dock-side seafood restaurant. The girls rode with them. After lunch, they all went for a sailboat ride around Lake Washington.

It was an exhilarating, but exhausting day, so they stayed home to rest on Monday. Mary and a good friend of hers had two-days-worth of shopping planned for Grace and the girls. Frank, who was on vacation, had gathered all the gear necessary for an overnight hike on Mt. Si, for Himself, Guy and the boys.

Frank woke Guy at dawn on Tuesday morning. "Let's let the girls sleep in," he whispered. "We'll stop for breakfast on the way."

He hadn't planned to take Spot along, but neither the dog, nor the boys were for leaving him behind. Try as they might, to be quiet, Grace awoke and saw them off. "Be careful," she told her husband. "I had a disturbing dream last night about falling off a cliff."

"All right; I'll keep a close eye on the boys," he assured her. "It's still early. Why don't you try to get back to sleep?" She didn't tell him, but doubted she would get any rest until they were all back safely.

It was a beautiful drive to the mountain, taking them only two hours, minus the breakfast stop in Issaquah. The boys were fascinated by the eagles and other birds of prey, soaring and swooping overhead.

Before they knew it, they were at their destination near the base of Mt. Si. Frank parked in a wide spot at the trail head, alongside another car. They got out and stretched their legs a bit, while breathing in the moist, woodsy air. Then they unloaded the gear from the trunk and divvied it up. The men toted the heavy items, such as the tent, food and cooking utensils, in backpacks, while the boys carried lighter items, including fishing poles and tackle box.

It was a rather steep climb, requiring a slow pace for the youngest two boys and Guy, who found out he wasn't as fit as he'd thought. Frank was used to navigating the hills of Seattle every day on his mail route, so had no problem managing this climb. Two-thirds of the way up the mountain, at a picnic area next to a stream, they stopped for lunch and a much-needed rest.

Frank and Merle took the canteens that they'd drained on the way up, and refilled them with the stream water. Guy took one gulp and made a face. "What's wrong," Frank asked. "Did you swallow a bug or something?"

"No," came the reply. Guy took another long drink, then held the canteen up. "I'm permanently spoiled, now. It's going to be hard to go back to drinking city water after this."

"I know just what you mean," Frank laughed, "but after a cup of bad coffee at work..."

Guy nodded. "You're probably right. The fellows at the station make some pretty awful coffee sometimes." Then he poured the rest over his head to cool himself, and went to the creek for a refill.

While Frank started getting lunch out of his pack, Spot started barking. They all looked in the direction that the dog was facing, to see a troop of Boy Scouts coming up the trail. Their leader was a tall, slender, white-haired gentleman. The man at the rear of the line was a younger, slightly shorter and heavier copy of the first. They stopped for a rest there, also. The leader greeted Frank.

"Hello, Mr. Postman, fancy meeting you way out here!"

"Likewise," Frank replied as they shook hands. "I didn't know you were a scout leader, Jim."

"Have been for many years. I started out as an assistant when my son Jeremy, here, joined. Now he's a Cub Scout leader."

The two men shook hands.

"Two of those scouts over there are my sons," Jeremy told Frank. "Are all four of the other boys yours?"

"No, just the small, dark-haired one. The other three are my nephews."

"Frank, here has been our postman for the last few years," he told Jeremy, as two other men and the last of the boys flooded past them.

Guy finished filling his canteen and waded through the flood of scouts swarming the creek around him. "Hello, my name's Guy Rowley," he said as he joined the other men and shook their hands. "And these are my boys: Merle, Leon and Ernie. I'm Frank's brother-in-law, from Portland."

"Nice to meet you, Guy. Name's Jimmy Bell, and this is my son, Jeremy."

Some of the scouts came jostling around them, chatting like magpies.

"I'm sorry, the boys are hungry. Maybe we can talk again later," Jimmy said as he turned his attention to his troop.

After lunch, they all hiked together, with Frank and Jimmy leading and Guy and Jeremy pulling up the rear with the younger boys. The two groups remained together until dinnertime, then camped a short distance apart for the night.

They went off on different trails in the morning-the troops to practice scouting skills, and the Rowleys and Waldens to reach a popular lookout point, and then to fish for their lunch before returning to the base of the lone peak.

It took them only a few minutes to reach the lookout point, where the entire Cascade Range was visible: from Mt. Baker to the north, Mt. Rainier, Mt. St Helens, and even a glimpse of Mt. Hood to the south. They went around to another vantage point a short hike away, where they hoped to see the Olympic Mountain range, but most of the higher peaks were obscured by clouds.

They had no sooner turned away from the view to go look for a fishing spot, when they heard the chirping of a chipmunk. Spot was instantly on high alert. The tiny animal darted across the edge of the precipice, and Spot darted after it. Frank, Merle and Leon all grabbed for him, but he slipped through their grasps and immediately disappeared over the edge. They all gasped in horror as they heard a yelp. Then there was silence. Ernie screamed, J.R. grabbed his father's leg and started crying. The other two boys headed for the edge. Frank and Guy held them back and comforted their sons. They were all convinced that Spot had fallen to his death.

Guy managed to turn Ernie over to Merle, then went to peer carefully over the edge, where the dog had gone. About fifty feet below him lay Spot, as still as death, on a rock ledge. He watched the dog carefully for a minute, to see if he showed any signs of life. He was rewarded by the twitch of an ear and a hind leg.

"He's alive!" Guy yelled back to the others. "He fell onto a ledge a little way down!"

Frank and the boys all came over and peered down, as Spot lifted his head and looked up at them, then put it back down again.

"He's hurt!" one said.

"That's a long way down!" said another.

"How will we get him back up?" Guy asked.

Frank thought for a moment, then suddenly sprinted off. "I'm going to find the scouts!" he called back. "I bet they'll know what to do!"

While Frank was gone, J.R. tried to comfort his pet. "Hang on, Spot. Papa's going for help," he cried. "We'll get you out of there and fix you up. You'll be home, playing catch before you know it." He sat back and looked at his uncle, with pleading, tear-filled eyes. "Do you think he heard me? Do you think he'll be okay?"

"Only God knows for sure. Why don't we all pray for him while we wait?"

Frank found some of the scout troop after a frantic, half-hour search. The younger boys were fishing or swimming in the small, icy-cold lake, attended by Jimmy and one of the other men. When Frank told him what had happened, he sent two of the boys to tell Jeremy, who was with the older boys, a short distance away, practicing mountaineering skills for their next rung on the Boy Scout ladder.

Frank cooled down and caught his breath while he waited. Fifteen minutes after the boys left, Jeremy and some of the older boys arrived.

"Show us where the dog fell, and we'll see if we can rescue him."

Jimmy stayed at the lake with the younger boys, while Frank led Jeremy and the fledgling mountaineers back to the lookout.

They examined the cliff and the area above it to determine the best way to safely retrieve Spot. Jeremy stayed topside to supervise, while the boy with the most mountaineering skills and the one who aspired to be a veterinarian went down the rope to see to the dog.

"He has a broken leg and some other minor injuries," the second boy called back up. "But I can't tell if there's any internal damage."

He strapped Spot to his partner's back and watched them ascend the cliff. Spot found the strength to wag his tail and lick some faces, in thanks. The scouts returned to their comrades and finished out the week on the mountain. Frank carried Spot to the car, while Guy and the boys split his load between them.

As soon as they reached the town of North Bend, at the mountain's base, Frank looked up the phone number of the town veterinarian, and gave him a call. The clinic was busy when the phone rang. The receptionist listened to Frank's story and gave him directions. Then she arranged for their arrival.

Doctor Walsh was just finishing an operation on another dog, when Frank and his worried son came through the door with their beloved hound. The vet examined Spot, while Frank filled out some paperwork. After a few minutes, an assistant came to the waiting room to get Frank and J.R.

"He has a simple fracture of the right, front leg and a badly bruised chin and chest. I hear a little rattle in his breathing, which means he has some fluid in his lungs," the doctor told them. "His leg is too swollen for a cast, yet. I'll have to splint the leg until it returns to normal size. I'd like to keep him overnight for observation and medication."

"Could you give him something for the pain, and let us take him to our vet in Seattle?" Frank asked.

The doctor's eyebrows met in the middle. "Oh, that's different," he said, rubbing the dog's ears. "I thought you lived nearby. I wouldn't recommend any trips over a mile or two for at least a week."

So they said goodbye to Spot and left him in Doctor Walsh's capable hands until he would be well enough for the trip home.

The Rowleys had gone to a nearby diner while they were waiting, and had returned with some sandwiches for the other two. Guy could tell that they had gotten not-too terrible news about their dog, so he offered them the sandwiches. "Here, eat something; it'll make you feel better."

Frank took the offering gratefully, but had to coax his son to eat. On the way home he told them what the vet had said. "I hadn't planned another trip out here or a large vet bill in the near future, but that's the way life goes sometimes."

"You'll manage somehow." Guy assured him. "God always gets us through."

J. R. sniffled just then, and Frank gave him a little hug. "The doc says Spot's going to be as good as new in a couple of months. We'll have to be gentle with him, and give him extra love and attention until then. Do you think you can manage that?"

J. R. looked up at his father, smiled a little and nodded. Then he found his appetite and finished the sandwich that he'd been nibbling for the last fifteen minutes.

When they got back to the house they found it empty. Further inspection revealed some gift and shopping bags from the Pike Place Market and other nearby shops.

"It looks like the ladies have been having a better time than we have," Frank remarked. "I just hope Mary hasn't spent all the money we'll need for the vet bill."

"Maybe he'll let you pay it off in monthly installments," Guy suggested. Then smiling, he said, "If my ladies did the same thing today, we may not be able to afford to go home!"

After they showered and changed, Frank went to the refrigerator looking for dinner fixings. He found a large bag full of Chinese takeout boxes. Mary had left a note inside the bag:

> We'll be out late tonight taking in a show at the Paramount. I hope you don't mind leftovers!
>
> Love, Mary

The sandwiches Guy had bought had been only a snack for the men and oldest two boys. J. R. and Ernie were perfectly happy sharing a small bowl of grapes before getting ready for bed.

J.R. and Dolores missed Spot, but having their cousins there while he was absent helped keep their spirits up. They all went to the Independence Day fireworks display over Lake Union before the Rowleys packed up and boarded the train on the fifth.

Doctor Walsh said that Spot was well enough to come home, so the whole Frank Walden family went directly from the train station to North Bend, to pick him up.

When Frank returned to his mail route, he found Jimmy waiting at his mailbox to reconnect with him. "How's your dog doing, Frank?"

"He's still pretty sore, but he's home again, being spoiled rotten. His leg was broken, and he had some minor internal damage, but the vet says he'll be back to normal by the end of summer. I want to thank you all for your help. I don't know what we would have done if your troop hadn't been there to rescue him off that ledge."

"I'm glad we were there and able to help," Jimmy replied.

"Why don't you and your wife come over for dinner tomorrow?" Frank said "I know the children and Spot would like to thank you."

Frank's and Jimmy's families became close friends after that. When J.R. joined the Cub Scouts, Frank became the assistant leader, under Jeremy.

Shortly after returning to Portland, Merle and Leon asked their parents if they could join the Boy Scouts. They had been so impressed with the skills and helpfulness of Jimmy's troop, that they aspired to be like them.

Chapter Twenty-Seven

CAUGHT!

It was Saturday, September 9th, 1931. Cleo, Ginny and Ginger, all age 14, went for a fruit picking hike in an abandoned orchard near the Newman farm while their mothers, seventeen-year-old Elsie May, eleven-year-old Merle, nine-year-old Leon and six-year-old Ernest worked or played together. The women were canning fruits and vegetables for the winter.

The three musketeers stopped at the local corner store for a soda after picking several baskets of apples and pears. They were sitting on the grass on the shady side of the store, quietly sipping their drinks when they heard a commotion inside the store. Ginny leaned over and peeked around the wall, to see two young men with guns in their hands and bandannas over their faces emerging. One of them was holding a bag, which she could only assume contained the money from the cash register.

"Get down," she whispered to the others, "so the robbers won't see us."

The robbers took off on foot, toward the woods across the street. As soon as they were out of sight, the children rose to their feet. Ginger went into the store to check on the proprietor. Cleo grabbed Ginny by the hand and said, "Let's follow them, so they don't get away with it."

"Do you really think we should?" Ginny asked him. "They have guns-it could be very dangerous."

"We'll keep our distance and stay quiet," he answered. "We'll find out where their hideout is, then come back and tell the cops." They were across the street by this time, and stealthily watching for the robbers as they progressed.

"I don't think this is such a good idea," Ginny said. Cleo put his finger to his lips, then whispered, "It's our duty as citizens and good Christians to make sure they get caught."

Meanwhile, Ginger was tending to the storekeeper. He had been knocked unconscious by one of the robbers. She went to the frozen food case and grabbed a bag of frozen vegetables to put on his head. Then she called the police. She didn't see her cousin and sister go after the crooks, and wondered where they were and what they were doing.

Cleo lost sight of the robbers for a minute, but then heard their voices. He crouched down, and pulling Ginny down with him. When he peeked around a tree, he saw them exit the woods and cross a lane. He could see that they had removed their bandannas and stowed their guns. They stopped to light cigarettes while looking around for any sign that the police were in pursuit. Then they congratulated each other on their apparent success. They entered a long driveway leading to a house that was barely visible through some thick trees and brush.

As soon as they were out of sight again, Cleo and Ginny followed them, staying in the woods alongside the drive and out of sight. The robbers went inside the house, where the children could hear voices. There was a large, old pickup truck in the driveway, loaded down with what l looked to be household appliances and furniture, covered with a tarp.

"You look under the tarp, and memorize the license plate. I'll take a peek inside the house," Cleo instructed. "I have a feeling that these guys are behind the local rash of burglaries I heard about this week."

"Okay, but be careful," Ginny said. "These guys are bad news. There's no telling what they might do to us if they catch us."

While Ginny sneaked over to the truck and confirmed Cleo's suspicions, he went around to the back of the house, where he thought he could spy on them without being noticed. The back yard sloped away from the house, so that the living area was above his head. He was going to look in the basement windows, but suddenly found himself face to face with a very large, growling dog. The dog barked once, but didn't attack. Cleo turned to run, but the dog knocked him down and kept him pinned, until a bearded, middle-aged man came out of the basement door. He ordered the dog off of Cleo, then pulled the teenager to his feet.

One of the robbers had come out onto the back deck. "Looks like your mutt found us a peeper, Pop."

"You boys better check out front, in case he ain't alone," the older man ordered as he pushed his captive inside. He made him sit on an old dog-hair-covered sofa. A few minutes later came a homely, scrawny woman, pushing Ginny ahead of her down the stairs. "What're we gonna do with these two, Pete?" she asked.

"I don' know, just yet," he answered. "We'll let Fred and the boys keep an eye on 'em tonight, an' I'll decide before we leave in the mornin'."

The cousins kept silent when their captors were close by. When they were left alone with the dog to guard them, they whispered to each other.

"You think one of us could escape through the bathroom window?" Ginny asked.

"Maybe, but as soon as they found us gone, they'd send the dog after us. We better just sit tight and pray they don't kill us."

Ginny began to cry softly. Cleo held her and started praying, "God, please keep us safe so our families won't be sad." Then he peeked to make sure no one was listening, and continued, "Help us remember what we need to remember, to help the cops catch these guys. Amen."

As it turned out, there *was* no window in the basement bathroom. The older of the robber boys came downstairs carrying a hammer and nails. They heard him driving the nails in the other downstairs rooms. Then he came out and announced, "Now you can have the run of the basement while Fred guards you and we sleep upstairs. There's a blocked door at the top of the stairs, so you can't get out." Then he ran up the stairs, and they heard some furniture-moving noises.

Both cousins jumped up immediately and went to check on all the possible avenues of escape, only to find themselves trapped. The young man had nailed all of the windows shut. The only possible way out, other than breaking one of the windows, was the patio door, guarded by Fred. The only time he left his post was when Pete came down later to feed the dog and let him out for his toilet.

While Fred was in the yard taking care of business, Pete asked them, "Are you two sweethearts or brother and sister?"

"We're cousins," Cleo answered.

"My twin sister was with us and will probably have the cops here any minute," Ginny declared.

"Thanks for the tip," the man growled, "I'll keep that in mind, when deciding what to do with the two of you."

When Fred came back inside, Pete went back upstairs and reblocked the door behind him. The two looked around the sparse contents of the basement, and concluded that most of the goods in the pickup truck had probably come from this house. They found a pencil, a tablet and a deck of cards while rifling through some drawers, and made use of them to pass the time.

By dinnertime, their stomachs started to growl, so they started looking around more thoroughly for any food they might find.

"Here's some cough drops I found on the floor in the small room," Ginny reported.

"I found some jelly beans in the cracks of the couch," reported Cleo, "but they're covered in dog hair, and hard as rocks."

They heard the robbers talking and moving about upstairs for several hours, but didn't see another soul until morning, when the woman came downstairs with a bakery box half full of stale doughnuts. "Found these in the dumpster behind the bakery this mornin'," she told them. "They're too old for us, but I thought you might be hungry enough not to care.

"I talked Pete into locking you up in the bathroom before we leave. Someone'll find you after we've had time to get away. I'll see about leaving you some food before we pull out."

An hour later, the younger of the two boys brought them a bag of food that his mother had taken from the refrigerator, then he led them into the bathroom and shut the door. There were some undefinable noises and banging in the hallway and on the door. Then he called to Fred and went upstairs.

Ginny put her ear to the door and heard the pickup truck's engine start. "Well, I guess they're gone, now. All we can do is wait for someone to find us," she sighed, sitting on the commode lid.

"I'm going to try to get out of here," Cleo replied. "This food he brought us is nearly spoiled already. It won't last us very long. Who knows how long it'll take the cops to find us."

"Is there anything I can do to help?' Ginny asked.

"I don't know just yet," he said as he looked through the medicine cabinet and the drawers. "If I can find something to take off the doorknob, maybe we can look out to see how he blocked the door."

He found a pair of fingernail clippers with a file attachment, and started working on the screws. He worked half the day, until the clippers broke and the file was so twisted as to be useless. He figured he had enough screws out to try muscling the doorknob off.

He yanked on it with all his might. It broke free and he went careening over Ginny, sitting on the floor and into the bathtub, hitting his head on the back wall. Ginny screamed.

Cleo was a little dazed and had a bump on his head. Ginny's hand was sore and starting to swell where he'd stepped on it.

The escape attempt was temporarily forgotten while they nursed their wounds. Then Cleo got up and found the door open. The blockade had been a piece of metal with holes, nailed to the wall on either side of the doorway and wedged under the doorknob. They merely had to duck under the metal to exit. Then they walked back to the farm.

When they got there, they found both of their mothers in the kitchen, keeping busy, so they wouldn't fret so much.

"Thank God! Are you two all right?"

"We were so worried!"

They welcomed their offspring into loving arms.

"We're okay," Cleo affirmed "Just a little banged up from our escape."

Grace called the police, while Ilda found something cold to put on their wounds. Then both mothers brought them some aspirin and milk while they waited for the police to get there.

When the policeman arrived a little while later, they gave him a detailed description of the robbers and their truck. While he was calling in the information, Albert came in for dinner.

"Well, I see our wandering children have returned. What kind of mischief have you two been up to while you were gone?"

The policeman finished his call, then told Grace and Ginny they could go home, but to be available for further questioning. Then he left.

"Would you like to stay for dinner?" Ilda asked Grace.

"No, thank you. I think we should be getting home. Guy will be home soon, and Ginger will be working on dinner. She's been so worried about her sister, that she hardly slept last night."

"And I need a shower," Ginny interjected. "It's going to be so nice to get home and sleep in my bed tonight."

Hugs were exchanged, and mother and daughter left, arm in arm.

"Where did you sleep last night? Grace asked her daughter as they were going out the door. "You're covered in dog hair, and smell like one, too!"

"We spent the night on an old sofa that was covered in the stuff. We were guarded by a big dog, in the basement of a house. The owners of the house must've been away on vacation or something."

"Maybe they saw them pack up and leave," Grace replied. "I'll wait until we get home to hear your story, so you won't have to tell it twice. But be sure that you will have to answer to your father."

"Yeah, I know. Our motives were right, but we acted foolishly."

During dinner, Cleo told his parents what had transpired over the last twenty-four hours.

"It was all my fault," he told them. "I should've gone alone and called the police as soon I knew where they were hiding out. Now, because of me, they got away."

"I'm glad to know that your actions were honorable, if not wise," Albert told him, "But you'll still have to be punished. I'll let you know what my decision is on that tomorrow. I know you're tired after your escapade, so go on up to your room now and ask God's forgiveness before you go to sleep."

After going home for a shower and dinner, Grace took Ginny over to her mother's house to have her look at her hand. "Do you think it's broken, Mama? I don't want to spend the time or money to go to the hospital if we don't have to."

Alice examined Ginny's hand and felt the bones move in a way that was normal, but some of her probing caused more pain than she liked to see. "I don't feel any obvious breaks, but I think there's a possible crushing fracture, right here. I recommend a trip to your doctor tomorrow. I'll bandage it to protect it until then. You should keep an ice bag on it, fifteen minutes on and fifteen minutes off, until bedtime. Keep it elevated as much as possible, also."

"It was all Cleo's idea to follow the robbers, but I could have tried to stop him, or not gone along," Ginny told her parents. "It was the thrill of the chase that drew me in, I suppose. My life *is* kind of boring."

The next day, both families got a call from the police, saying that the robber family had been caught, thanks to Ginny and Cleo's keen observations and quick escape.

Cleo was punished for his carelessness and his cousin's endangerment by being restricted to school and home for the rest of the month. He also had a nasty headache and a goose egg that he wore like a badge of honor.

Ginny's punishment was finding out that her hand was indeed fractured. She had to have a cast put on, which was definitely not something an active and lovely girl of fourteen wishes for. Of course, it also meant that she and Ginger couldn't pull the ol' twin switcheroo for quite a while.

All three were considered heroes by their classmates and family members, but Cleo had to be reminded that he had also put himself and Ginny in danger unnecessarily.

Lafe and Nettie had a little girl in early October, whom the named Marion; his father's middle name. When Alice asked to visit them, Carsie spoke up first, "That's prime deer hunting territory, and I haven't been hunting with Lafe in years. Let me give him a call and see what I can arrange.

That Friday, Carsie got off work early. His gear was already in his car. He went directly to pick up his mother. She came out of the garden with a bagful of vegetables, while Tucker carried her suitcase and valise out. "I knew that Tucker wouldn't pick these, and I checked with Nettie first to make sure she could use them. That's just about the last of my garden for this year. You're such a good son to take me to see Lafe, Nettie and the babies," she said as she kissed Carsie on the cheek.

"I miss Lafe, too, especially after living and working with him for a few years. Besides, it's about time I bagged a deer for Grace and Ilda's freezers. I can almost taste your venison stew now. Time's a wastin'!" he said as he pushed down on the throttle.

They arrived at Lafe and Nettie's after dark. She had held supper for them, and they were grateful, as they were famished by that time. In the middle of dinner, the baby started to cry. Nettie excused herself, and returned with the infant at her breast, covered with a blanket. "You needn't have bothered with that," Alice told her. "With all the babies in our close-knit family…"

"Nettie's family is not as open and sharing as ours," Lafe explained.

"Oh, I'm sorry. What was I thinking?" Alice smiled. "I guess the trip and my hunger muddled my brain."

"It's okay," Nettie replied. "I understand that you're anxious to see her. I'll let you burp her before I switch her to the other side, if you want."

A few minutes later, when Carsie saw that she was ready to do that, he got up from the table and went to the stove for something. When he turned back, Alice was holding the baby and Nettie was buttoned back up.

Nettie finished eating, before taking the infant back to the bedroom to finish nursing her. Alice took Ernie from his high chair and went along, while the brothers washed the dishes and made plans for the next day.

When Alice rose the next morning, the men were already gone, and Nettie and Ernie were eating breakfast.

"I thought you were an early riser," Nettie remarked. "Did the baby keep you awake?"

"I suppose that's what happens when you live without them for a while," Alice answered. "When I was living with Ilda and Albert, I could sleep through the crying, once I realized they weren't mine to deal with."

"I suppose that's a survival tactic that God gives us for the sake of our sanity?"

"You're probably right."

They had a wonderful day together. Alice was in hog heaven, playing with and caring for her grandchildren, while Nettie took an afternoon nap.

Doctor Chervey and his wife came for a visit, late that afternoon. He gave Marion an exam, and accepted Nettie's invitation to stay for dinner. After dinner, Alice was just starting to cut into the apple pie she had made, when her sons came in the door.

"We bagged our limit already!" Carsie grinned. "We hung them up in the shed for the night."

Then Lafe saw their guests, and greeted them. "Please excuse us while we wash up and change clothes. Nettie, can you rustle us up some grub? We're starved!"

No sooner had they gone into the hallway than the phone rang. Nettie answered, then handed the phone over to the doctor.

"Keep pressure on it. I'll be right there." He hung up the phone and turned to his wife," Why don't you stay here. Ralph cut himself with his butcher knife again. I'll be back in a little while." He gave her a kiss, and asked Alice to hold his pie until he returned.

Nettie went to the kitchen, and started reheating the leftovers, while she made some biscuits.

Alice and Loretta offered to help, but she turned them down. Then the baby started crying, and she stopped and sighed. Both women came to take over while she was gone.

Carsie came out first. "Is that apple pie I see over there?"

"Yes, but you can't have any until after dinner," Alice mock-scolded, as she took the leftovers out of the oven, and Loretta put the biscuits in.

Lafe emerged just then. "Where did Doctor Chervey go?" he asked, as he sat at the table.

"You know Ralph White don't you?" Loretta asked him.

"Nettie told me about him. I think I met him once. Isn't he the big guy with a couple of fingers missing?"

"Yes, and there may be more of them gone the next time you see him."

They all went to church together the next morning, before butchering the carcasses and getting them ready for the freezers. Carsie and Alice packed up, said goodbye, and went home.

Chapter Twenty-Eight

COUNTERFIT

One summer day in 1932, one of Ilda's neighbors was arrested for suspicion of murder.

Josie and Billy Worth had always been devoted to each other and their community. They were hobby farmers; having bought the farm with the money they had saved while he was serving as a General in the Army. They had been in the neighborhood over ten years and were considered as a second grandma and grandpa to many of the local children.

Billy had been rushed to the hospital a couple of days before, gasping for air and having seizures, but passed away before reaching the hospital. He was seventy-two years old, but still very slender and fit for his age.

The doctor, not knowing the couple, and being an amateur sleuth, suspected foul play and reported the case to the police, who ordered an autopsy.

Cleo and Jojo were walking home from the store, when the police car passed them, with Josie in the back seat. Her daughter-in law was following in her car.

They ran home to tell their mother what they'd seen. She dropped what she was doing and rushed over to their house, where she figured their son Will would be arriving soon. He drove up a minute later, to find policemen swarming the house looking for evidence.

He was visibly shaken and angry, so she tried to calm him down and prevent him from doing anything rash.

"You can't stop them, and it would only upset your mother and your wife even more if you get arrested, too."

"I suppose you're right, but how could they suspect my mother of murder?"

"They don't know her like we do, and have to act on the evidence they have, so far, I suppose."

"That's right," said a policeman standing guard at the door. "You might as well leave. You won't be allowed back in, until the investigation is over."

Ilda walked him to his car and told him, "Go be with your family, now. We'll keep an eye on the farm for you."

"I'll come back for the mail, and to check in with you, whenever I can."

"Please keep us apprised of the situation with your mother, too," she said.

"I will. Thank you for being such good neighbors. Oh, you might as well keep the fruits and vegetables, when they're ready; Mom and Dad would want that."

"We'll keep all of you in our prayers." Ilda assured him.

He closed his eyes, obviously holding back tears, nodded, then gave her a quick hug before getting in his car and leaving.

Ilda walked back to the policeman guarding the front door, and told him she would be sending her boys over to check on the animals and the garden every day.

"He said we could take the garden produce, and we may have to take the dog and some of her livestock home with us temporarily, in order to keep a closer eye on them."

"Let me take down your name and address for the chief," he replied. "I'm sure someone will be over to talk with you and your husband tonight or tomorrow."

As soon as she walked through the door, the boys wanted to know what was going on at the neighbors.

"I need to get started on dinner now. Why don't you go take care of her animals, then I'll tell you all about it at dinner?"

"But," the boys started to protest.

Ilda gave them a stern look that stopped them short. "Oh, and bring their dog home, too," she called, as they slumped out the door. "He's going crazy in the barn, barking at the policemen."

Albert came in from the back field an hour later. "Where are the boys? They were supposed to help me with something this afternoon."

"Oh, I'm sorry dear," Ilda replied. "After they got back from the store, I sent them over to Josie's to check on the horses and feed the chickens."

"Haven't her son and daughter-in-law been helping her with that?" he countered as he washed his hands and face at the kitchen sink.

"They're all down at the police station."

"The police station! Whatever for?"

The boys could be heard talking as they stepped onto the porch.

"I'll fill you in at dinner," she replied. "Will you take these out to the table for me?" She was carrying a large pot, and nodded toward a couple of bowls of food sitting on the counter.

"Where's Nina?" Albert asked, as the boys came out of the bathroom.

"She's babysitting for the neighbors." Ilda answered. "Sit down and say grace, then I'll tell you about Josie's predicament."

While the biscuits and butter were being passed around, and the stew ladled out, she told them what she had gathered from her exchange with Josie's son and the policeman.

"It seems that the doctor who received Billy's body at the hospital, got suspicious about his death, and ordered an autopsy. Then they arrested Josie on suspicion of murder."

"That's preposterous!" Albert exclaimed.

"That sweet old lady?" Cleo added.

"She wouldn't hurt a fly!" Jojo insisted, "Why?"

"I agree, and I don't know for sure. She and Billy were devoted to each other. I was there when Will arrived at their house, and told him we'd take care of the farm as long as he needed."

"Is that why you boys didn't come out back to help me?" Albert asked his sons.

"It's my fault," Ilda interrupted. "I sent them to the store and then over there, not knowing that you needed them."

"We saw the cops take her away," Cleo said. "She looked real scared."

Albert had already retired for the evening, and the boys were getting ready for bed, when a police car drove up. Ilda let the officer in and ushered him into the living room, where she sat opposite him.

"Where is your husband, Mrs. Walden? I'd like to talk to him, too."

"He's asleep, already," she replied. "You'll have to come back around midday tomorrow to see him."

The boys heard the discussion, and came downstairs.

"Hello officer," they said in tandem.

"Do you want statements from them before they go to bed?" Ilda asked.

"Will you be available tomorrow?" He asked.

"I don't have any plans."

"Me neither."

"I may have a question or two for you, then."

"Off to bed now," Ilda instructed. "You need your sleep, too."

After they left, the officer pulled a pad and pen out of his pocket and started asking her questions.

"How long have you known the Worths?"

"About ten years."

"What is your general opinion of them, individually, and as a couple? Do you know if they had any disagreements?"

"They were obviously very much in love. She was devastated when he died."

"What do you know about their health?"

"Josie has some arthritis and the beginnings of cataracts, and Billy's hearing was diminished quite a bit. He was under a doctor's care for colitis, but they were about as healthy as could be hoped for, at their age. Is that what this is all about, his unexpected death?"

"I can't say. Police procedure, you understand."

"Of course."

"How about their mental states. Did you notice any signs of diminished capacity, confusion, irritability, or anything like that?"

"Well, her memory was failing a bit, but then, that's only to be expected at their age. He would get a little gruff from time to time, but always apologized to her. She understood that it was a side-effect of his military service, and always forgave him."

"I think that's all for now. I understand that your sons are looking after their farm?"

"Yes, they're diligent and knowledgeable. If they come across anything they can't handle, I'm sure my husband will help, too."

He rose from his seat and thanked her, then departed.

When Nina came home, Ilda didn't tell her what had happened. She figured it would be best to wait until morning.

She stayed up another hour to pray, before climbing into bed. She didn't sleep at all that night, thinking, how did Billy die, and why do they suspect Josie? His death was sudden and unexpected, for sure, but they had assumed he'd had a heart attack or stroke. What could they have discovered that made them think it was murder, and why suspect Josie? Many scenarios played though her mind, in between prayers, until she finally gave up and rose before Albert did.

"What are you doing up so early?" he asked as he poured himself a cup of coffee. "Is it Josie and Billy?"

"Yes, a policeman came over after you went to bed last night. He asked some disturbing questions about their relationship, their health and their mental states. I can't imagine, for the life of me, what they could have found to make them suspect Josie of murdering Bill."

"I suppose we'll find out eventually. Try to get some rest after breakfast."

"I will. I told the policeman to come back around noon, if he wanted to talk to you."

"I suppose he thinks I might have a different perspective, being a man. If you want, you can keep breakfast simple and leave it on the stove for us."

"No, the boys will be up soon, and then Nina. They'll want to know what's going on. I'll consider going back to bed after breakfast, like you said."

He gave her a kiss and went out to do the morning chores. She went to the refrigerator and got out the bacon, eggs, butter and milk. The boys came running down the stairs and went straight out the front door.

She was carrying a platter of pancakes to the table half an hour later, when Nina came down in her nightgown and slippers. "Smells like you burned some," she, yawned. "Could you use some help?"

"Yes, I'd appreciate that. In fact, if you don't have any plans for this morning, I'm going to go back to bed, and let you take over the housework."

"I'd be happy to. Trouble sleeping last night?"

"I didn't get any. I was up all night thinking and praying about Josie's predicament."

"Predicament? Does it have something to do with her husband's death?" Nina asked, taking over at the stove. "What is it; financial, medical, legal?"

"Oh the law is *definitely* involved. She was arrested on suspicion of murder."

Nina nearly dropped the bowl of eggs on the floor. "What?!"

Ilda prepared and ate a short stack of pancakes, while she told Nina about the previous day's happenings. Then she snagged a piece of bacon, and went upstairs, where she fell into bed and slept until after lunch time.

She went downstairs, to find the house empty. She heard voices outside, and saw Nina, the boys and Josie's son on the porch. Albert and a different policeman were off by the barn, talking. She looked in the refrigerator for leftovers, and fixed herself a sandwich and half an apple. Before she had finished, Nina and Albert came back inside. The policeman talked briefly to the boys before he left.

While Ilda ate, and Nina went to the kitchen to wash up lunch dishes, Albert told her what Will and the policeman had told him.

"The preliminary autopsy seems to indicate poisoning as the cause of Billy's death. Since no one else was around there that day, they decided that Josie must have done it. I hope they change their minds, after all the interviews, and let her come home."

"It must have been an accident, if it *was* poison," Ilda surmised.

"That's what I told him. Did you get some sleep?"

"Yes, but I had some strange and disturbing dreams."

That evening, Josie was allowed to return home, as the judge had considered her a low flight risk, and based on her family's and neighbors' interviews.

On Sunday afternoon, the whole family was told about the neighborhood mystery.

"The coroner is claiming that Billy died of poisoning, but they aren't sure what kind of poison," Albert told them. "At first, they suspected his wife, Josie, but they let her come home on bail, while they research possible compounds, and plants that could have caused his symptoms."

"And check out Josie's background; looking for skeletons and such," Ilda added, shaking her head. "I can't imagine her having any."

"You might be surprised," Alice said. "You remember how Mattie and Linda started out, don't you? I'm certain a lot of people would be shocked if they knew their whole stories."

"Don't forget Sylvia. I heard she's engaged to be married, soon," Carsie said.

Guy spoke up next. "I wasn't exactly an angel, myself."

"Would you care to elaborate?" Carsie asked, as his eyebrow twitched mischievously.

"Uh, no."

"Oh, come on!" the children goaded. "We won't tell anyone!"

"Okay, I guess it doesn't matter anymore, anyway. It goes like this: I got roped into joining the Klu Klux Klan when I was in high school."

"I thought you were from Arizona," Grace said, looking at her husband with shock. "I didn't know the Klan was there."

"We moved to Mississippi for a couple of years when my father got a job promotion. He moved us back to Arizona when he found out what I was doing."

"How did he find out?" they all wanted to know.

"I fell off my friend's horse, in a victim's front yard, one night. I hit my head in the fall. The other Klan members rode off without me. The victim family picked me up, and turned me in to the police."

"Did you rat on your friends in the Klan?"

"Yes, but only the ringleaders. And then we moved back to Arizona and changed our last name."

All eyes were on Guy. There was dead silence in the room.

Then a smile started at the corners of his mouth. "It used to be Smith."

Alice got a strange quirky expression on her face. Carsie's eyebrow nearly leapt off his face. Albert punched him in the arm.

Grace stood up and faced him with her hands on her hips. "Oh, you are too good at lying," she scolded. "I don't know if I can ever trust you again!"

Leon and Ernie were confused, but Merle and Johnny caught on and tackled their father/uncle from behind. They started roughhousing, and the women had to put a stop to it. "This isn't a bunkhouse, boys," Alice chided. "We wouldn't want anyone to get hurt."

After dinner, the younger children went outside to play. Ginny, Ginger and Nina washed the dishes, and the rest of them adjourned to the living room to talk and pray.

They heard a car pull up out front, and Albert went to the door.

"Josie, Will, we were just about to have our usual Sunday afternoon prayer meeting, and you were at the top of the list. Come on in and join us."

Once they came in and sat down, Josie turned to Alice. "I'm wondering if you might be able to help with something."

"Name it, and it's yours, if I'm able," Alice replied.

"The police still aren't convinced that Billy wasn't poisoned, but they can't figure out what it was that killed him. I've wracked my brain, trying to think what it could have been, too. But we keep coming up empty. Ilda told me that you're an herbalist and a nurse. Maybe you can think of something that we haven't?"

"That's a tall order, but I'm willing to try. I suppose there's something in nature, that he came in contact with. Perhaps something that I've come across before, and the police haven't.

"Why don't I spend the night here, and come over to talk with you tomorrow? It's possible that we can figure it out, together."

Will spoke up next. "I think that she's just too nervous, with the police there, to think clearly."

"Wouldn't you be, if they arrested you for murder?" Josie asked her son.

Alice went over to Josie's house, right after breakfast, and spent the day with her, not grilling, like the police tend to do, but simply talking about Billy; what he liked to do, and his favorite foods. Then she had her relax, close her eyes and relive that fateful day, before he got sick.

"Billy was up with the chickens, as always, and had breakfast cooking when I got up. He warmed up some cornbread muffins that I'd made the day before, and was cooking ham and cheese omelets."

"Did he fix yours exactly the same as his?" Alice asked.

Josie's eyes popped open. "No, I like mushrooms and he doesn't... didn't."

"Close your eyes again and go back there. Then what?"

"I washed the dishes. We have a deal that whoever cooks, the other cleans up after. He went back outside, and I heard him playing with Sally; that's our dog. He came back in a little while later, and talked to his friend Cal on the phone for about half an hour."

"Did you hear what they were talking about?"

"Cal's wife passed away a few months ago and Billy has called him every Saturday since. Billy was laughing and telling him about Sally's antics. He'd been trying to get Cal to come visit us, but he's afraid of the train and can't drive this far."

"Then what?"

"It was getting warm, so I made up some sandwiches and lemonade. We played a game of cribbage while we ate." She opened her eyes again and looked at Alice. "Yes, they were identical."

She closed her eyes again and resumed, "He washed the dishes while I went back to my quilting. Then he went back outside and was gone for quite a while. I didn't worry, because he often goes for walks when the weather is nice. He came back in with some vegetables from the garden. He started washing them while I was making biscuits to go with the pork chops cooking on the stove.

"He never finished that meal." She started to cry. "He must have eaten something I didn't, but I can't remember what."

"Relax again, and think back to when he brought the vegetables in. Was there anything unusual; something that looked out of place?"

"Let me see; there were carrots, lettuce, some radishes, celery, and... something else... I don't remember."

She sat bolt upright at that point. "That must be it! He ate it and I didn't!"

"What did it look like?"

"I didn't notice it much, until after it was cooked. It was mostly white with some purple and red. It didn't smell or look very good to me, so I filled up on salad and potatoes."

"Was there any left over?"

"There wasn't very much; he ate it all."

"Do you think you'd recognize one if you saw it?" Alice had a hunch she knew what it was, and was hoping that she was right, so the police could close their investigation and Josie could bring this unpleasant chapter in her life to a close.

They went out to the garden together, where they probed and scrutinized every likely prospect. Finally, not finding what she was looking for, Alice took Josie by the hand, and they went over to Ilda's garden. She found and pulled up a turnip and brushed it off. "Did it look like this?"

"Well... sort of, but it was different, too. I think it had a pinkish line through it."

Alice grabbed Josie by the shoulders. She hadn't been this excited in quite a while. "I know what happened!" she nearly squealed. "I'm going to call the police right away and put an end to this whole mess!"

Josie was stunned. She stood there in the middle of the garden, with her mouth agape.

"Come on," Alice coaxed. "Let's go call the police!"

Alice rang the station and asked for the chief.

"He's not available right now. I'll put you through to the desk sergeant" the clerk said.

Alice asked him if he was familiar with the Worth murder case.

"Yes I am. Do you have some information that you think could help us?" he asked.

"Yes I do. If you'll send someone over to the Newman's farm on Morris lane, I'll give you the information that will solve this case!"

She hung up the phone and looked at Josie and Ilda, both looking stunned, but curious. "What are you talking about, Alice?"

"Why did you pull up that turnip? It's not ripe, yet."

"Water hemlock." she said, holding up the tuber. "He ate water hemlock, thinking it was a wild turnip."

"Why would he pull up a wild turnip, instead of growing them in the garden?" Ilda asked.

"Because you can't buy just a few seeds," Josie said, starting to cry. "He knew I didn't like them, and was being frugal."

"I suppose he thought he'd found a hidden treasure," Alice said, sadly.

When the policeman heard Alice's explanation, he asked if she could help him find some of the poisonous plants, to have them examined.

"How long until dinner?" Alice asked Ilda.

"About an hour. If you want to go now, I'll keep some warm for you."

"Josie, do you have any idea where he might have found the plant?"

"I don't know for sure, but he did like to go down to the creek sometimes, on warm days."

"That's good thinking," Alice replied. "Water hemlock grows best in wet areas. Let's go find some evidence, detective."

Alice knew where the creek was. Her grandsons had taken her there on crawfish hunts, years earlier. Within an hour of leaving, she found a specimen for the policeman to take for testing. Within a week, the case was closed, and Josie was absolved of all suspicion, in the case of Bill's death.

Alice and Albert led a party of volunteers out to the woods, to find and remove all the water hemlock they could find in the area, and then burned them.

Josie remained on the farm the rest of that summer, but once the weather started to get cold, Will had no trouble convincing her to move in with them and put the farm up for sale. She knew that Bill's dog Sally wouldn't be happy in the city, so asked if the Newmans would take her in. They accepted the assignment, and Sally became best buddies with their dog, taking over her duties when she died of old age a couple of years later.

Chapter Twenty-Nine

THE LAST WEDDING

It was eleven a.m. on Tuesday, April first, 1933. The hospital's neurological specialist, Doctor Edward Fisher, entered the examination room and was surprised to see Alice sitting there.

"Weren't you the head midwife here?" he said as he shook her hand. "My wife and the hospital staff speak very highly of you.

"My wife insisted on having our son at home, even though I had my doubts, and she said the experience was so much better than the ones she had with our daughters' births at the hospital. I wish I could have been there, but I was in the middle of an operation.

"I see that you were referred by Doctor Charles Brown. That's unusual. Most of my referrals come from GPs, not surgeons."

"Charles and his wife Mattie are good friends of mine. My usual payment for his services is fruit pies. Blueberry is his favorite."

Dr. Fisher smiled. "I know them well. They are fine people-honest, gracious and God-fearing.

"So, what brings you to me today?"

"The headaches I've been experiencing the last few years, which I had assumed to be migraines, have been getting more and more severe and frequent. If you can't help me, I'm going to have to retire. The pain never goes away completely anymore, and when it fires up, it's debilitating."

"What have you tried in the past to deal with it? Have you seen an herbalist, nutritionist or chiropractor?"

"I am an herbalist myself and have studied much about nutrition. I've tried eliminating all possible trigger foods, without much success. I've never had any back or neck pain, so never felt a need to try Chiropractic care. I've always been quite fit and never overweight. That's why Charles sent me to you. We think it may be a brain tumor."

He examined her and sent her for some tests and x-rays.

When she returned two days later, she could tell by his countenance that the news was not good.

"I hate to be the bearer of bad tidings," he said sadly, "but you and Charles were right in your assessment. It is a tumor, and it's inoperable-probably not cancer, though. There's no sign of it metastasizing."

"What's your prognosis?" She asked.

"It doesn't appear to be affecting your balance, memory or personality, yet. I expect that your vision will be affected more and more. You will probably experience some dizzy spells, and possibly fainting as time goes on. The pain may cause irritability.

"I'm going to give you a prescription for some narcotics for the pain, and one for Dramamine for the nausea. I'll leave the dates open, so you can get them when you need them without worrying about them expiring," he said as he wrote.

"Are you married?" he asked.

"I'm a widow, but my bachelor son lives with me and my daughters are close by, as well. We'll manage."

He tore the pages off the prescription pad and handed them to her. "It's a crying shame," he said as he put his hand on her shoulder. "I wish there was more I could do."

She stood and patted his hand "Thank you, doctor, for your honesty and compassion. But don't be too sad. I'm not afraid to die, and know I'll be going to a much better place than this when I do."

Alice kept this news to herself for a while, not wanting to rain on her family's parade until necessary. Her children and grandchildren had always planned something special for Mother's Day and Easter. Rebecca was due to come home from her missionary assignment in a couple of months, and Alice was certain that she and Carsie would be planning their nuptials soon after her return.

Alice made up her mind to enjoy this Easter season, and to make it memorable for her family as well. She stopped accepting new patients, and referred her newer ones to other midwives. When asked why she was doing this, she said that it was about time she slowed down a bit and enjoyed her great-grandchildren more.

Rebecca returned two weeks before Mother's Day, and Alice was at the Bridal Veil train station, with Ka-teen-ha, Ken and Carsie when her train arrived. They let Carsie go ahead of them on the platform.

Rebecca stepped off of the train into a bear hug and a long, passionate kiss. "You are a sight for sore eyes," Carsie said. "I thought you'd never get here. Promise you'll never leave me again."

"I promise."

After greetings were done, they collected her baggage and went home to Bridal Veil. Carsie and Alice went with them. Carsie and Rebecca spent the evening singing in the parlor and talking about their future plans.

Alice excused herself, and spent the whole night in bed with a headache. They went to services together the next morning before the Waldens returned home.

There were many phone calls, weekends in Bridal Veil, and letters going back and forth in the following weeks, as wedding plans were finalized.

As the June first date neared, Alice became more and more concerned about her health causing problems, so she had Tucker take her to see Ilda one afternoon in late May.

Tucker went out to the field to talk to Albert when Alice went inside.

"Mama, what are you doing here in mid-week?"

"I have something to tell you that I don't want everyone to hear all at once."

"It sounds serious. Come on in and sit down. I'll pour us some tea and be right back."

When Ilda returned with the tea and some cookies that she had left over from Mother's Day, she sat down next to Alice. She took a deep breath and braced herself. "Okay, I'm ready."

Alice stared into her cup as she swirled the tea bag. "You know I've been having migraine headaches the last few years?"

"Yes, have they been getting worse lately?"

"Yes, they have. Charles referred me to a Neurologist at the hospital and.... after taking some x-rays and other tests, he concluded that I have a brain tumor."

Ilda's stomach rose up to her chest and her brow furrowed more than Alice had ever seen before. "Can they operate to remove it?"

Alice looked back into her cup. "No. He said it's inoperable and that the symptoms will only get worse, and then within a year at most, I'll be leaving you."

The tears that had been brimming in Ilda's eyes started to flow freely at this point, as she held her mother. "What can I do to help?" she said after she regained her composure.

"I need you to keep this news to yourself until after the wedding, and help your sisters keep a close eye on me, to make certain I don't cause any disruption or distress to anyone else during the ceremony or the reception. You can tell Albert, but no one else, until after the wedding, all right?"

"I understand, Mama. You can depend on me. The children will be home from school, soon. Will you stay for dinner?"

"No, thank you. Tucker and I are going out for dinner. He's still clueless, even though he lives with me. I'll break the news to him tonight. He'll have to arrange to take over my place or find somewhere else to live after I'm gone.

"I told Grace when she was over to see me yesterday, and I'll stop by and tell Doley tomorrow or Thursday. Frank and Lafe will have to be told while they're here for the wedding next weekend.

"Carsie, Rebecca and the children will be the last to know. I don't want to spoil their wedding with this news."

"I understand, Mama. Now drink your tea before it gets cold, and have a snickerdoodle. Elsie May made them last week and they're very good. We need to eat them before they get stale. She made too many, considering that Albert and Cleo don't like them."

"How about if I take them for Tucker? You know he'll eat anything that doesn't bite back."

"Good idea! Now why didn't I think of that?"

Just then, the children came in the door and greeted their grandmother cheerfully.

"Can you stay for dinner, Grandma?" Elsie May asked.

"No. I was just in the neighborhood and stopped by to say hello. Tucker is taking me to dinner at my favorite restaurant tonight. I'll see you Saturday at the wedding.

"Cleo, would you please go tell your Uncle Tucker that I'm ready to leave?"

"All right. Nice to see you Gramma." He gave her a peck on the cheek and ran out the door.

Elsie May sat down next to Alice and gave her a hug, "Would you like to see the dress I made for the wedding?"

"Of course. Oh, you don't mind if I take the rest of your cookies do you? They're very good."

"Please do. I don't want to outgrow my dress before I wear it."

"You'd better make it quick; she's leaving soon," Ilda said.

As soon as Elsie May left the room, Ilda gave her mother a long hug, choking back tears. Then she stood and said, "I'll go get the cookies, and compose myself again."

Alice oohed and aahed over the fine handiwork and design of Elsie May's dress.

Then Tucker came in the door. They collected their spoils and hurried out the door before Ilda had a chance to lose her composure again.

Carsie and Rebecca's wedding was scheduled for four O'clock on Saturday, June first.

Lafe and his family arrived at the Newman's on Friday evening, after Albert and Cleo had gone to bed.

Guy drove to the train station on Saturday morning to pick up Frank and his family, then took them to his home, where they would be staying the night before returning to Seattle on Sunday.

Ken, Ka-teen-ha, Rebecca and her best friend, Elizabeth, came to Alice's home for lunch and their final preparations.

The Waldens' church was barely big enough for all the family and friends that wanted to come see the patriarch of the clan finally wed. He would most likely be the last of Alice's children to marry. Tucker was an odd duck and not expected to ever find love. He had not, in his entire life, shown much if any interest in the opposite sex, and vice-versa.

Carsie met Lafe, Rebecca, Elizabeth and Ken at the church at nine A.M. for a rehearsal. Doley, Ilda, Guy, Ginny and Ginger arrived at the church by ten O'clock, to start decorating and setting up for the ceremony and reception.

The wedding party returned to Alice's house for lunch. Shortly after that, Alice started to feel one of her headaches coming on. She pulled Ka-teen-ha aside to tell her about the doctor's diagnosis. "I wanted to wait until after the wedding, but I'll have to take some medication. I'll need someone to distract Carsie and Rebecca, so they won't notice that I'm not feeling well."

"Do your other children know?" Ka-teen-ha asked.

"Yes, I've told the girls, so they can cover for me at the church. They've not told their children, yet. Frank and Lafe will be told before they go home tomorrow. I need to lie down for a while. Make sure I'm up by two-thirty to get dressed."

Ka-teen-ha prayed with Alice before she left the room, and every quiet moment thereafter. When she came in to wake Alice at the prescribed time, her friend was feeling a little better.

"I took a small dose of medicine before lying down," she told her. "I'll put some more in my purse to take along, just in case. Would you help me get ready?"

"Of course. Rebecca is already dressed and getting her hair fixed up. Ken and Tucker went for a walk, while she and Elizabeth were getting dressed.

"I told them you were a little tired from all the wedding preparations and wanted to be fresh for tonight."

"Thank you, that was perfect, and true, too."

"This is a lovely gown," Ka-teen-ha remarked as she zipped up Alice's green brocade dress. "Did you make it yourself?"

"Yes, many years ago, when I was the Matron of Honor for a friend's wedding. I'm hoping she and her family will be able to make it to the ceremony today."

"Oh, what a lovely bride!" Alice exclaimed when she emerged from the bathroom a little later. "Carsie's eyebrow will hit the ceiling when he sees you in that dress!"

"Thank you. Keenie and Lizzy's mom made it for me."

"Mom helped me make my dress, too," Elizabeth added.

"You are both very lovely."

Kenneth came in the door and announced, "It's three O'clock, ladies; time to go!" Then Rebecca turned to face him, and he nearly swooned. "Oh, my!" he said in a husky whisper, as tears welled in his eyes. "You must be the most beautiful bride in the whole world!"

Rebecca started to cry, too. "Oh, Daddy!" she said as she threw her arms around his neck. "You're going to make me spoil my makeup."

"We wouldn't want that now, would we, especially if it ends up on my suit."

They all laughed and went out to the car, where Tucker was waiting.

When they got to the church, Ken went in first to make sure the groom didn't see his bride before the ceremony.

One classroom near the auditorium was designated for the groom, Lafe and Frank, who were the groomsmen, while another room at the rear of the church was set aside for the Bride and her attendants, Elizabeth and Ilda.

Faye's three-year old daughter, Harriett, was the flower girl, while nine-year-old John Jr. was the ring bearer.

At three-thirty sharp the church bell rang. The organist started playing softly as the guests started to arrive. Alice sat quietly at the back of the room, trying to avoid as much noise and stress as possible. She was glad that the only part she had to play in this whole affair, was the mother of the groom.

Ilda and Grace both checked on her from time to time. Then, as the auditorium was nearly full, and Alice had greeted Mattie, Charles, Teresa and her husband, and all of her relatives in attendance, Doley approached her and whispered, "We'll be starting in a few minutes. Do you need to use the restroom before we take our seats up front?"

"Yes, thank you. I think that would be a good idea. I need to take some medicine, too."

The ceremony was almost as beautiful as the bride. John Jr. took Harriett's hand and led her down the aisle, encouraging her to toss the rose petals as they proceeded, which made everyone smile. Following Lafe and Elizabeth, Kenneth walked his daughter down the aisle, then stepped up to officiate.

Rebecca and Carsie both sang their vows. They had been singing in church choirs all their lives, so nerves weren't too much of a problem for them.

The reception was held in the church basement. Tucker was given the job of ushering and counting the guests as they went down the stairs. They knew he needed something easy to do to keep him out of trouble. After he had finished his duties and fixed himself a plate of food, he wandered back upstairs. Lafe saw him go, and followed him.

Ilda noticed her mother sitting in the corner, nodding off, and went over to talk to her.

"Mama, are you all right? Don't you want something to eat?"

"I'm not particularly hungry. I had to take some medicine to get me through the ceremony. It's made me a little sleepy."

"What kind of medicine?" Frank had overheard their conversation.

"Should I tell him now?" Ilda asked Alice. She received a sad nod in answer. So she took her brother by the hand and went upstairs, where they met their brothers sitting together on the back pew.

"Sit down, Frank. I have something to tell you two before you go home, and this seems as good a time as any."

"I think I'll go get something to drink," Tucker said as he rose and sprinted down the stairs.

After Ilda told her brothers the sad news, and that Alice didn't want Carsie and Rebecca to know until after their honeymoon, they avoided their mother until they could be alone with her.

By the time the newlyweds returned from their trip to Yosemite the next weekend, the word had gotten around to everyone else in the family. The couple noticed a gloom pervading the atmosphere as they stepped off the train.

"You say you're happy to see us, but I can tell something's wrong," Carsie remarked. "Why isn't Mama here?"

"She's not feeling well today," Grace reported. "Why don't you come to our house for dinner tonight? You can start doing household duties tomorrow. The twins are making a big pot of venison stew from the leftover deer meat in the freezer."

"Yum! I haven't had venison stew for a couple of years," Carsie said.

Rebecca looked thoughtful. "I'm not sure if I've ever had it: though I have had venison jerky and steaks. They were mighty tasty."

So they went home with the Rowleys, giving Grace the opportunity to tell them of Alice's diagnosis.

"You two are the last to know of this," Grace told them. "She wanted to make your wedding day and honeymoon as perfect as possible."

"How long does she have?" Carsie wanted to know, once he recovered from the shock of Grace's announcement.

"The doctor isn't sure, of course, but thinks no more than a year."

Carsie sat still a minute, trying to assimilate this dreadful information. Rebecca held him, and no one spoke for several minutes.

When Carsie sighed and sat up, Rebecca broke the silence. "Do Keenie and Daddy know?"

"Yes; she told her just before the wedding."

"I was so happy and wrapped up in preparations, that I never noticed any signs that she might be ill," Carsie admitted, sadly. "She has always been so strong and healthy; the anchor of our family."

"You probably don't feel much like eating cherry pie right now. Should I wrap some up for you, for later?" Grace asked.

"Thank you, that would be nice," Rebecca answered. "We may just have it for breakfast tomorrow before we charge into married life."

Grace smiled at the thought of pie for breakfast, then asked Guy, "Didn't you go out for doughnuts on *our* first morning together?"

"Yes I did, and have almost every Sunday morning since."

"And that's why I've gotten so wide around the hips and you've gotten that tummy," she teased him.

"*I* think it's your good cooking and the girl's pie-making skills," he countered.

"I think we'll go on home now," Carsie said. "I trust you didn't use up all the gas in my car while we were gone."

"Couldn't," Guy replied. "You had the keys with you."

"Uh, oh. Where are my keys? I forgot all about them!" He started patting his pockets, when Rebecca pulled them out of her purse and dangled them in front of him.

"You left them on the night-stand this morning, and I picked them up on the way out."

"Whew, what a relief! What would I do without you?"

"You'd probably forget your pants," she said, as she gave him a kiss.

Merle was coming into the room, just then. "Eeuw, mush!"

323

They all chuckled, and the newlyweds were on their way with the pie that Ginger and Ginny had cut and wrapped up for them. They hardly spoke the whole way home. They were both sad about the hand that Alice had been dealt.

Carsie had never thought about losing his mother. In fact, he had recently told someone that she would probably live to be a very old lady. He wondered if their family could hold together without her. She was not only their anchor, but possibly their glue, as well. Frank and Lafe had already moved away, so that they seldom saw them anymore. Would he or his brothers-in-law get transferred or find better jobs elsewhere, breaking the family up even more?

Carsie's co-workers had expected him to be in a good mood when he returned, but he was very somber instead. He was efficient and quiet, so they didn't ask what the problem was, wondering if perhaps the wedding had been cancelled.

Chapter Thirty

THE LAST HURRAH

On Saturday, July seventeenth, 1933, Doley, John and their children packed a picnic basket and jumped into the car. On a whim, they stopped by to ask Alice if she wanted to go to Blue Lake with them for the afternoon. She was feeling particularly well that day and decided to go with them.

She put on the skirt that Ka-teen-ha's grandmother had willed her, grabbed her hat, stuffed her prescriptions in her pocket, and off they went. They hadn't gone very far out of town, when they stopped to buy some sodas. Alice stretched her legs and breathed in the fresh air at the edge of the store's parking lot, when she spied a hillside nearby with a large patch of wild blueberries bushes. They appeared to be heavily loaded with ripe berries. She thought to herself, I should pick some of those, and make Charles and myself some blueberry pies. She could almost taste it, and decided to do just that.

When everyone reassembled at the car, she asked, "Would you be terribly offended if I bowed out of your picnic?"

"Are you sick? Do you want us to take you home?"

"No, no, nothing like that. I just got a hankering for blueberry pie when I saw that hillside there brimming with wild berries. I haven't made Charles a pie since last year, and thought that it might be the last chance I have to do it. I miss living in the woods and think I'd like to spend some time here, alone with God, enjoying his creation."

So, against their better judgement, they left her there with a soda and the agreement that they would pick her up in about four hours. Then they went on to the lake, and had a nice swim while they were there.

After they left, Alice picked a few dozen berries and ate them. She pulled up some long blades of grass. Then she started looking for basket materials in the nearby woods. She found some tender willow shoots, and wove them into a purse-shaped basket with a loop handle, binding them together with the grass. When the basket was done, she went deeper into the woods and pulled some moss from a fallen log, to line the basket, so the berries wouldn't fall through.

On the edge of the meadow, she had spied some wild sweet potato greens to her left. She found a pointed rock and dug a couple of them up. She remembered seeing a small waterfall just about two hundred feet before they had pulled off the road. So she back-tracked to find it, for food-washing purposes. She took a long drink of cool, fresh water. Oh, that brings back memories, she thought to herself. "This tastes so much better than city water."

When the potatoes were clean, she returned to the meadow to fill her basket, saving the potatoes and the soda for later. By the time her basket was full and she had eaten a few dozen more berries, she was in need of a rest in the shade. She returned to the edge of the woods, where she had left the rest of her lunch, sat down on a large rock and waited for her ride while she ate.

When the Bauers returned to where the agreed meeting place, Alice was nowhere in sight. Everyone started anxiously scanning the area. A few minutes later, Audie spied her grandma emerging from the woods behind them, loping along like a young girl, her skirt flying, and carrying a basket of some kind. When she got closer, they could see that her hair and clothes were all disheveled, and her face and hands were stained with blueberry juice. She had an angelic smile on her face. She showed them the basket she had made, filled with enough blueberries for at least two pies.

"Did you have a good time at the lake?" she asked.

"Yes, and it looks like you had a good time, too. Do you want a sandwich? We have one left over."

"No, thank you. I filled up on berries and wild sweet potatoes. Oh, what a glorious day!"

By the time they dropped her off at home, she was starting to get a headache. She washed her face and hands, and took some medicine. She rinsed the berries, while waiting for the medicine to take effect. Then she undressed and lay down for a nap.

She awoke just in time to see a beautiful sunset. She was feeling better, but not as good as she had earlier. She fixed and ate a light dinner before tackling the pies. Once they were done, she left them to cool overnight and went back to bed.

She felt a little dizzy in the morning and her vision was off. She couldn't quite think straight as to what might be different about it; just that it wasn't normal. She couldn't decide what to fix for breakfast, or even if she felt up to it, so she cut a piece of pie and washed it down with a glass of milk.

After calling Mattie, to arrange for her to pick up the other pie, she felt a little better. She brewed a pot of coffee and fried up some bacon.

Doley called to ask if she was feeling all right, after such a busy day the day before, and she told her, "It did drain me a bit, but it was worth it. I made two pies last night, and had a piece for breakfast."

"Pie for breakfast?"

"And why not? I might as well do whatever makes me happy in the time I have left. Don't you agree?"

"Of course. Why not? Enjoy yourself while you can."

On Thursday, Grace stopped by to check on her, and ask if she wanted to go out for lunch. "It's such a beautiful day. I thought you might like to get out of the house, if you're up to it, of course."

"I'm not one hundred percent, but then I probably will never see that again. I know of a quaint little cafe with the best clam chowder and cucumber sandwiches. We can sit outside and enjoy their view of Mt. Hood."

"Sounds lovely. Don't forget your hat. It looks like you got quite a bit of sun the other day."

"I'm not too worried about sunburn," Alice said as she picked up her purse.

"I know, but it could help keep you from getting overheated."

They had just finished their chowder, and had started on the sandwiches, talking about "the good old days", when Alice's vision started to blur, and her headache came back with a vengeance. She winced, squinted her eyes to try to keep out the sunshine, which seemed so much brighter all of a sudden. When she reached for her purse, to get her pills out, she dropped it, spilling the contents on the ground. She bent over to pick it up, and nearly fell off her chair. Her stomach started to churn, and the world started to spin.

"Mama, are you all right? Here, let me get that for you."

Grace scooped up the contents of Alice's bag and handed her the pill bottles. "Do you need these?

"Yes."

When Alice tried to open the first bottle, her hands started to shake, and wouldn't grip properly. "Would you open these for me, please?"

Alice took the pills that Grace took out for her, with one hand, while hanging onto the chair with the other, to make sure that she wouldn't fall.

Grace crouched down beside her mother, while Alice sat, with her eyes closed, waiting for the medicines to start working. When Alice opened her eyes again a few minutes later, Grace said, "I think I should take you home, now."

"I agree. Will you wrap up my sandwich, for later?"

She hadn't said anything when they had sat down and looked toward the mountain to enjoy the view. She had been disappointed, but not too surprised, that she couldn't distinguish between the mountain and the wispy, high clouds. Grace was enjoying it so much that Alice hadn't wanted to spoil it for her, so she pretended to enjoy it, too.

Grace wrapped their sandwiches up in their napkins and put them in their purses. Then she helped her mother to the car, took her home, put her to bed and stayed with her. She called Dr. Fisher's office and left a message for him to call her back as soon as possible. Then she called Doley and Ilda, to arrange a schedule for the three of them to stay with Alice, when Tucker was at work. As soon as she knew they were home from school, she called home to let Merle and the twins know where she was.

When Tucker came home from work, she told him what had happened, and to be watchful of their mother. "The rest of us will take turns staying with her while you're at work. Have you figured out if you can afford to stay here, or started searching for another place to live?"

"No, well, yes, Ma and I added up my finances and figured out that I can afford to stay here, but just barely. I haven't looked for another place, yet. I've mentioned it to my boss and a couple of co-workers, but that's all."

"I think you should start looking harder. I just got off the phone with her doctor, and he thinks Mama's going to start going downhill fast. She was really sick today, and the pain pills didn't help that much. I could tell that her vision and balance were off, and the meds didn't help with that, either. He said that she may bounce back some, but probably not very much or for very long. You need to be prepared when her time comes."

The next time the family got together, Alice asked to spend as much time as possible out in nature with the time she had left, "As long as it doesn't inconvenience anyone too much," she said.

They all agreed that they were happy to do anything she asked. "Don't worry about putting us out, Mama. We all want your last days to be as pleasant as possible."

Alice's vision grew narrower each week, and she grew even thinner than normal, due to the narcotics and the nausea that accompanied the dizziness.

Though upbeat most of the time, she did catch herself snapping at her helpers once in a while when she was uncomfortable. She started needing someone or something to steady her when she walked, and fainted during a church service one Sunday in early October. At this point she decided it was time to stay out of the public.

By November, she needed more care than Tucker could handle at night, so he moved back in with the Newmans. All their chicks, except Cleo, had already flown the nest. Mattie and Teresa joined the ranks of Alice's caregivers, so there were enough of them to stay with her twenty-four hours a day.

Her children, grandchildren and great-grandchildren started visiting her more often at this point, knowing that they wouldn't have much more time with her and wanting to keep her from getting depressed.

"Don't worry about that," she told them. "I have Jesus to keep me company when you're not here. I sense his presence more strongly now than ever before. He's waiting to take me home when the time is right."

She *was* concerned about who would stay with her for Thanksgiving. "I don't want anyone to miss out because of me," she told Carsie and Rebecca when they came to visit in mid-month.

Carsie's eyebrow lifted slightly. "Don't you worry about it. We have a plan."

Alice also had a plan that she was keeping to herself for now. She knew what she wanted but was having some difficulty thinking clearly and writing it down. Her goal was to have her last wishes written out by Thanksgiving. She had a feeling that she wouldn't last until Christmas.

When Thanksgiving arrived, she was much too sick and weak to go out, but the surprise that the family had arranged for her made up for it.

When she awoke that morning, Rebecca was on duty. She had only been there a couple of times since Alice became house-bound, and then with Carsie on a Saturday or Sunday.

"I have a surprise for you," she announced once Alice was medicated and awake as much as could be expected with the narcotics on board.

"Good morning, Alice," Ka-teen-ha said, as she came in with the breakfast tray.

"What a wonderful surprise! I must be a sight," Alice said as she combed her fingers through her hair and sat up for Rebecca to put the pillows behind her.

"Yes, you are," her friend replied. "A sight for sore eyes." She gave Alice a hug, and a kiss on the cheek. "I've missed you so much, and thought it was about time I came for a visit."

"We invited Daddy and Keenie to come here for Thanksgiving," Rebecca reported.

"And we're having it here, with you," Ka-teen-ha added.

Alice started to object, but Ka-teen-ha told her, "We don't have any other family in Oregon, and wanted to spend it with our daughter, new son-in-law and our dearest friend."

"What about your church family,"

"We celebrated with them on Sunday, so we're all yours, today."

"You aren't going to fix a regular turkey feast, are you?" Alice asked. "My appetite isn't what it used to be, and my kitchen is awfully small."

"We fixed most of it ahead-of-time and brought it with us. Don't you worry about us. We just want to accommodate you as much as possible."

Alice was awake and able to visit with her guests for about two hours before dinner time. She only managed to eat a little mashed potatoes and gravy and a small slice of pie before she needed to lie back down.

Mattie showed up to relieve Rebecca, while she and Ka-teen-ha were settling her into bed.

"Good night, Alice. I hope you have a wonderful dream about your forever home," Ka-teen-ha said as she kissed her friend for the last time.

By December tenth, Alice was completely bedbound and in so much pain that she was on massive doses of Morphine and Dramamine twenty-four hours a day. She was only half awake for about an hour a day, and only able to eat a small amount of mashed banana or toast occasionally.

At four a.m. on Tuesday, December seventeenth, Ilda was with her when Alice called out.

"Mama, what's is it?" Ilda asked.

Alice had the most peaceful look on her face that Ilda had ever seen. She came close to her mother so she could hear her.

"Jesus is here... to take me home... Sister... Tell them that... I love them... and that... I'll see them... on the other side." She squeezed her daughter's hand and took her last breath.

Her body was cremated and her ashes put in an urn. She had requested, in the document that she had written and entrusted to Ken on Thanksgiving, that if the weather permitted, her memorial service be conducted in the forest she loved. She had further instructed that no one should, by any means, dress in mourning clothes, and the hymns sung at the wake be cheerful and uplifting.

Ken led the congregation to a forest clearing off of a trail on the east side of Bridal Veil. It was a quiet, peaceful day, snowing lightly, with no wind.

Carsie played "In the Garden" on his violin, then Ken stepped up onto a milk crate and addressed the crowd.

"Let us pray," he said, and bowed his head.

"Lord, we are gathered here to bid farewell to our loved one, friend and champion, Mary Alice Beebe Walden. We will miss her greatly, but celebrate her homecoming and the end of her suffering. We know she is with you, and that there is a celebration for her in your presence. We want to thank you for lending her to us, and for the work you did through her on this earth, amen.

"Alice Walden, as most of us knew her, was born in a sod house somewhere in northern Missouri or southern Illino to a Gypsy girl named Ercyline and a backslidden Christian named Ernest.

"The little family moved frequently because of Ernest's wayward ways, but when he was stricken with a serious and prolonged ailment, his wealthy uncle took them in.

"Under his uncle's influence, Ernest returned to the righteous path from which he had strayed. Ercyline had become a believer during their travels, and had a hand in his revival as well.

"Mary Alice grew up in a home of worship and learning; proving to be an excellent student, eagerly soaking in every field of learning she could. When her formal education came to a close, she met a handsome gentleman named Frank, and they fell in love at first sight. This young man turned out to be an unbeliever, though. Alice knew that her parents and her Lord would not want her to marry Frank Walden as he was.

"They were both broken-hearted, and separated for a brief time, during which he became a Christian. Then they married and came to Oregon to start a new life together.

"They lived and worked in several logging camps while raising seven children. Frank passed away in 1906, leaving Alice to depend solely on God and the strength he gave her to finish raising their children.

"Obviously, they were a good team, as evidenced by all the children, grandchildren and great-grandchildren present today. Most if not all of them are following in their parents' footsteps as disciples of Jesus, and by helping the helpless, as their parents did.

"Just out of curiosity; how many of you would say that you owe your life, a loved one's life or your well-being to Alice's service to God and love for people?"

Almost everyone in the assembly raised their hands.

"Wow! I was going to ask if any of you care to elaborate," Ken remarked, "but I think we'd be here 'till we froze to death. How about one or two sentences from each one?"

People lined up to mount the box, with comments such as, "My wife was at death's door when Alice showed up and pulled her through."

"I'm convinced that my baby wouldn't be alive if Mrs. Walden hadn't been my midwife."

Ka-teen-ha stepped up. "I was badly injured in a train accident when Alice came to my aid, and then a few years later she took me in and helped me recover from the scarring so I could walk normally, without pain."

"She saved half this town, myself included, by taking charge during a flu epidemic many years ago." Several heads nodded in remembrance of that time.

The temperature was dropping, a breeze came up, and the snow was falling more heavily. Ken asked Carsie and Lafe to close the service with their mother's favorite hymn, "How Great Thou Art", the spreading of her ashes, and a prayer.

Carsie mounted the box and pulled out his violin, while Lafe held an umbrella over him. He played it with vigor while the crowd sang out, filling the woods with the most beautiful sound ever heard by the forest creatures.

Each of Alice's children took a small handful of her ashes and spread them to the wind.

Lafe said the closing prayer, and they all trekked back to town.

Everyone in Bridal Veil, West Linn and Oregon city, it seemed, had gathered in the high school gymnasium for the reception, because it was the only building in town large enough to accommodate that many people.

That Sunday, there was another memorial service at the Walden's home church in Portland for those who couldn't make it to Bridal Veil.

Postscript

Mary Alice Beebe Walden was survived at her death by all seven of her children, nineteen grandchildren and five great-grandchildren.

Many children born with her assistance, or who's family members she had rescued from death or calamity, were named after her.

Carson (Carsie) Walden and Rebecca had no children of their own, but became Foster parents. He died in 1972, leaving his widow and no heirs.

Ilda Ercyline Walden Newman was widowed in 1952 and died in 1978 at the age of 90. At that time, she had six children, ten grandchildren, twenty-two great-grandchildren and six great-great grandchildren.

Henry Cody (Tucker) Walden, stayed on the Newman farm after Alice died. He never married, and died in 1964 from injuries he received in a farming accident.

Grace Leah Walden Rowley died of cancer in1969, leaving Guy, five children, three step children, fifteen grandchildren and four great-grandchildren. She was preceded in death by one daughter, Ercyline Rose, who died at age three.

Frank Walden Jr. died in 1978. He was survived by his son, but preceded by his wife Mary and daughter, Dolores. He had no surviving grandchildren.

Ernest Lafayette (Lafe) Walden and Nettie had another son in 1941, whom they named Carson. Lafe died in 1992. He was survived at that time by his wife, all three children, eight grandchildren and seven great-grandchildren.

Dolores Walden Bauer died in 1985. She was preceded in death by John Sr. and their son, Carson (Bud). She was survived by John Jr. and Ilda Bauer Weatherford, eight grandchildren and ten great-grandchildren.

Ilda Bauer Weatherford, the primary author of the first Mary Alice novel, died in January, 2003. She was preceded in death by both of her parents, her brother, Carson (Bud), husband, Francis (Frank), and son, Frank (Frosty). She is survived (at the time of this book's release) by 6 grandchildren, 7 great-grandchildren, her daughter, Carol O'Neal, and youngest daughter, Cora Brantner, who co-authored the first book and wrote this sequel in her honor.

Printed in the United States
By Bookmasters